THE CANADIANA COOKBOOK

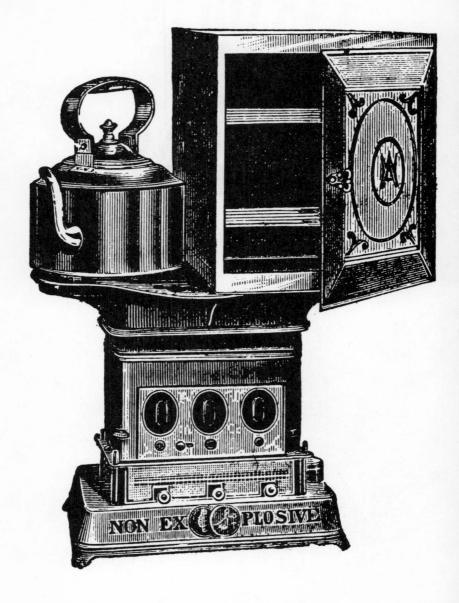

THE CANADIANA COOKBOOK

*A Complete Heritage
of Canadian Cooking*

By
Mme. Jehane Benoit

PAGURIAN PRESS LIMITED

TORONTO

CONTENTS

CONTENTS (Continued)

FOREWORD

This new cookbook is based on an exhaustive search for traditional Canadian recipes through material accumulated over the years, much of it never published before. The result is a unique and extraordinarily comprehensive cookbook which reveals the most appealing features of traditional Canadian cooking.

The success of Canadian cuisine springs from the intermingling of different cultures, different geography, and the use of simple ingredients cooked simply, but with care and imagination. This book will show you just how much can be done with choice, fresh ingredients from your local countryside, the Canadian way. It will unfold before you a rich variety of authentic traditional Canadian recipes conceived in the pioneer farms and towns of early Canada, then developed, refined and passed down through the generations from mother to daughter, and finally assembled in *The Canadiana Cookbook* for you to try and to savour.

You will find that many of the same cooking ingredients used in the pioneer days of Canada are still available to you today: aged Oka cheese and rich maple syrup from Quebec; superb salmon from B.C. and the Gaspé; delectable bass, pickerel and white fish from lakes in Ontario; millet in the West; the finest of venison and game birds in all parts of Canada; succulent apples from the orchards of Quebec and the Okanagan and Annapolis Valleys; fiddleheads in the Maritimes; and other fine ingredients.

More than simply a recipe book *The Canadiana Cookbook* also sheds more light on a basic aspect of life in the pioneer days of Canada, for what is a more basic characteristic of a people than the food they eat? When you have tried some of the Canadian specialties presented in this book, you will truly appreciate why these recipes have survived for generations and why so many Canadians today are enjoying a rediscovery of traditional Canadian cooking.

Christopher Ondaatje

PUBLISHER

QUEBEC

We cannot say that Québec's cooking is basically French. Because of two founding countries, Québec traditional foods are sometimes very French, sometimes very English, or a mixture of both. The French influence is felt more strongly in the method used to prepare and flavor foods than in the actual ingredients. That is what gives it its particular charm.

There is no doubt the English influence has been stronger, and still is. Foods such as beans, peas, salt pork, molasses, spices, puddings, cakes and pies are of English origin. This is easily explained. Jacques Cartier and his men were mostly from La Bretagne (Brittany) which was never quite as French as the rest of France, because of its proximity to England, and because its inhabitants were seamen and fishermen who were in constant contact with the English.

In Québec, as anywhere else, good food means good materials, lovingly prepared by someone who cares for the people who will eat it.

In Québec women do care. It is part of our French heritage.

FROM THE BLACK IRON KETTLE

The Pot-au-feu was the great "doings" and "fixings" of the traditional Québec table — a large or small black cast-iron pot with a good cover was part of everyone's heirloom, used for the long, slow simmering of soup or stew, or even special pies for festive fare. Meat simmered in liquid with lots of fragrant root vegetables was the true pot-au-feu. It was served with large slices of oven homemade bread, toasted on the wood stove. A slice of bread was placed in the bottom of a large deep soup plate, then bouillon from the "pot-au-feu" was poured on top until it was all soaked in by the bread; the bread topped with pieces of meat and vegetables, the whole covered with finely chopped parsley.

Although no longer part of the bride's dowry, it is still used to simmer many a good old fashioned dish.

SOUPE AUX QUATORZE AFFAIRES

The true pea soup, slowly simmered to perfect goodness, was so named because fourteen ingredients had to be used to make it perfect. Part of these ingredients were the famous "herbes salées" which some still make. Freezing improves the robust pleasant texture and flavor of this soup.

1 lb. salt pork, lean and fat	⅛ teaspoon thyme*
1 tablespoon dry mustard	¼ cup fresh parsley, minced*
1 lb. dried peas	1 clove garlic, minced
8 cups cold water	1 can hominy corn
1 large onion, sliced thin	1 cup dried bread chips
½ teaspoon savory*	1 tablespoon coarse salt*
¼ teaspoon wild or dried mint*	1 tablespoon butter

Rub the salt pork with the dry mustard. Cover and refrigerate for 12 hours. Meanwhile sort, wash, then soak the peas in the cold water for 12 hours.

Place in a soup kettle — the peas and their water, the pork, onion, savory, mint, thyme, parsley and garlic. Bring to a boil, cover and simmer from 3 to 4 hours, or until the peas are tender and the soup appears to be creamy. Add the hominy and simmer for 15 minutes. Add the bread chips, salt and the butter. Taste for seasoning and serve.

*These five ingredients may be replaced with ¼-cup salted herbs.

QUEBEC "POT-AU-FEU"

Hot, the meat is served surrounded with pot-au-feu vegetables and boiled potatoes sprinkled with chervil or parsley.

Cold, the boiled beef is delicious, sliced very thinly and sprinkled with French dressing, garnished with chopped parsley and chopped small onions.

3 lbs. flat beef ribs
3 quarts cold water
1 tablespoon coarse salt
3 whole carrots, peeled
1 small turnip, peeled and halved
3 onions, peeled, a clove stuck in each

3 onions without cloves
1 medium parsnip, peeled and halved
2 celery stalks, cut in four
1 clove garlic, finely chopped
3 branches chervil, if possible, or parsley

Place the meat in the bottom of the soup kettle. Add water and coarse salt. Place the uncovered kettle over medium heat. Bring slowly to a boil. This is important for the flavor and the final clarity of the pot-au-feu. The meat, slowly penetrated with heat, lets the scum escape (this may take up to 30 minutes). Remove the first scum with a skimmer. When the water reaches a rapid boil add ½ cup cold water, which will slow down the boiling and allow the balance of the scum to reach the top where it must be removed.

Add the remaining ingredients. Bring to a boil once again. Cover. Simmer over low heat until the meat is tender, from 2 to 3 hours.

When cooked, remove the meat if it is to be served hot. To serve cold, let it cool in the bouillon, drain and place the meat on a platter. Cover with waxed paper and refrigerate.

COUNTRY VEGETABLE SOUP

When clean crisp air and snow are all around us, nothing is better

11

than this bubbly hot soup, one of my great favorites. The combination of savory, marjoram, dill or anise used as flavoring bouquet I learned many years ago from a German Canadian lady who was a wonderful cook.

1½-2 lbs. beef brisket or shoulder
1 meatless beef bone or roast beef bone
2 cups carrots, diced
½ cup parsnip, diced
3 large onions, sliced very fine
1 cup celery and leaves, chopped fine
1 large leek, sliced thin (optional)

1 teaspoon savory
½ teaspoon marjoram
¼ teaspoon anise or dill seeds
1 teaspoon dry mustard
½ teaspoon peppercorns
2 tablespoons coarse salt
1 tablespoon sugar
1 can (20 oz.) tomatoes
3 quarts water
½ cup whole barley or rice

Place all the ingredients in a soup kettle. Bring to a boil. Cover and simmer over low heat for 4 hours. Stir 2 or 3 times during the first hour of cooking. The beef is served as the pot-au-feu beef.

GREEN TOMATO SOUP

I have never seen this soup served anywhere in Canada except in Québec. The following is a recipe from my family.

3 cups green tomatoes, unpeeled and chopped fine
1 onion, chopped
¼ teaspoon cinnamon
⅛ teaspoon ground cloves
1 teaspoon sugar

¼ teaspoon pepper
2 cups water
¼ teaspoon soda
3 tablespoons butter
3 tablespoons all-purpose flour
4 cups milk

Place in a saucepan — the tomatoes, onion, cinnamon, ground cloves, sugar, pepper and water. Bring to a boil and boil for 30 minutes. Add the soda.

Melt the butter, add the flour. Mix and add the milk. Cook until creamy, stirring constantly. Add the green tomatoes to the cream. Mix thoroughly. Salt to taste and serve.

VEAU DANS LE CHAUDRON
(Veal Pot Roast)

"Veau dans le chaudron" is an old favorite of French Canada. No matter which cut of veal is used, it is always tender and juicy.

3 tablespoons bacon fat or salad oil
2 cloves of garlic, cut in two
3 or 4-lb. rolled shoulder of veal or half leg of veal
1 teaspoon salt

¼ teaspoon pepper
¼ teaspoon thyme OR
½ teaspoon savory
1 bay leaf
6 to 8 medium potatoes
6 to 8 medium onions

Melt or heat the bacon fat or oil in a cast-iron saucepan. Stuff the 2 cloves of garlic, cut in two, into incisions made in the veal. Place the meat in the hot fat and brown on all sides over medium heat. Don't rush this as the color and flavor of the finished gravy will depend on how well the meat has been browned. Season with salt and pepper. Add the thyme or savory and the bay leaf. Place the potatoes and onions, whole, around the meat. Don't add any liquid. Cover tightly and cook over medium heat until the meat is tender, about 2 hours. The potatoes and onions will not break as there is no liquid added. The veal will make its own gravy. When cooked, remove meat from pan to a heated platter. Place the pan over high heat and stir gently, so as not to break the vegetables. When they are well coated with gravy, boil another minute or so until the gravy has a nice consistency. This is a complete meal.

MEAT LOAF COUREURS DES BOIS

This is a popular dish with Quebec hunters and great to serve after skiing or skating. Traditionally it was cooked in a cast-iron frying pan.

2 lb. ground beef chuck	½ teaspoon pepper
1 onion, finely chopped	6 link sausages
2 raw potatoes, peeled and grated	¼ cup prepared mustard
2 eggs	1 teaspoon ground ginger
1 teaspoon salt	2 cans baked beans

Blend thoroughly together the ground beef, chopped onion, peeled and grated raw potatoes, eggs, salt and pepper. Put the mixture on a large sheet of waxed paper and spread it to form a rectangle the size of the baking pan you'll use. Place 2 rows (about 6) link sausages next to each other down the middle of the rectangle. Roll the meat mixture to enclose the sausages. Shape into a neat roll, lift with the waxed paper and slide it into your baking pan. Mix the prepared mustard and the ground ginger and spread over the meat roll. Bake 45 minutes in a 350°F. oven. Add the baked beans and bake another 30 minutes. Serve hot or cold, including the beans.

SAUCISSES AUX POMMES
(Fried Sausages and Apples)

Here is a longtime supper favorite in my family. The black iron pan is a must. Serve with baked potatoes or a cabbage salad.

1 lb. link sausages	Milk and all purpose flour
4 to 6 small, unpeeled apples	Cinnamon and brown sugar

Pan fry the sausages. Use a cast iron frying pan if you have one. When done, remove to a hot platter and keep warm. Remove none of the fat left in the pan. Heat.

Core the apples and slice into rings about ½-inch thick. Dip each ring in milk, roll in all purpose flour and place in the hot sausage fat. Sprinkle with cinnamon and brown sugar. Cook over low-medium heat turning a few times to brown evenly. Serve immediately.

PERFECT PAN-FRIED ONIONS

The tasty country garnish for liver or minced steak. Again the cast iron pan works wonders.

3 large onions	**3 tablespoons butter**
2 tablespoons cold water	**Salt, pepper and sage**

Slice the onions about ¾-inch thick and peel. Put the cold water, butter and then the onions in a frying pan. Sprinkle with salt, pepper and sage. Cook over medium heat, covered, for the first 5 minutes, then uncover and cook golden brown over a slightly higher heat. Turn with a broad spatula, but not too often, to keep rings whole.

POULE-AU-POT
(Chicken Pot Pie)

It is impossible to talk of pie and omit the perennial favorite, Chicken Pot Pie. In the summer, I replace the parsley in the topping with fresh basil, tarragon or sage.

4-5 lb. boiling chicken	**3 whole cloves**
3 tablespoons butter	**1 garlic clove, whole**
6 cups water, boiling	**1 bay leaf**
1 carrot, sliced	**2 teaspoons salt**
1 onion, sliced	**¼ teaspoon pepper**
¼ cup celery leaves, chopped	**4 medium potatoes, uncooked**

Cut the chicken into individual pieces and brown lightly in the butter. Add the boiling water, carrot, onion, celery leaves, cloves, garlic, bay leaf, salt and pepper. Bring to a boil, cover, then simmer over low heat until the chicken is tender.

Place the cooked pieces of chicken in a casserole and top with the potatoes, sliced paper-thin. Make a gravy with 3 cups of the consommé left after the chicken has been cooked, 3 tablespoons of the fat from the top of the consommé and 4 tablespoons of flour. Salt and pepper to taste and pour over the potatoes and chicken.

Then top the chicken, potatoes and gravy with a parsley pinwheel, which is prepared in the following manner.

2 cups all-purpose flour	**⅓ cup shortening**
1 teaspoon salt	**½ cup milk (approximately)**
3 teaspoons baking powder	**½ cup fresh parsley, minced**

Stir together the flour, salt and baking powder. Cut in the shortening with 2 knives, until the particles are the size of peas. Add the milk gradually. Toss lightly with a fork until all the flour has been dampened, then knead quickly into a round ball. Roll on floured board into an oblong shape ⅛-inch thick.

Butter top of dough and sprinkle with the minced parsley. Roll the same way you would a jelly roll. Cut in 1½- to 2-inch lengths. Place cut side on top of casserole in an attractive design. Bake at 425°F. for 30-40 minutes, or until top is golden brown.

LE BOUILLI DU QUEBEC
(Québec Boiled Chicken Dinner)

With the first breezes of summer come tender vegetables, tantalizingly fresh, and boiling fowl at the peak of perfection. It is then that French Canadians cannot resist serving and eating their super-delicious "Bouilli".

I started eating what was called in my family the "Bouilli d'Eté" as a very young child. I remember clearly my grandfather keeping an eagle eye on the young wax beans growing on the vines which meant that the first carrots and spring onions, along with the cackling hens, were ready to be sacrificed for the pleasures of our stomach . . . Grandpère would then announce to the women of the household that the time was ripe for a weekly "Bouilli". Here is the recipe which I hope will give you as much pleasure as it always gives me.

4-5 lbs. stewing chicken	½ teaspoon savory
½ teaspoon nutmeg	2 onions, minced
3 teaspoons lemon juice	½ cup celery leaves
Salt and pepper	1 small green cabbage, cut in four
½ teaspoon thyme	12 carrots scraped
2 lbs. salt pork, lean and fat	12 small onions, whole
3 quarts hot water	2 lbs. yellow or green beans
1 teaspoon coarse salt	12 new potatoes, scraped
Sauce:	⅓ cup parsley, minced
½ cup butter	½ cup chives

Remove the excess fat around the cavity. Cut the chicken in small pieces and melt in a saucepan, over low heat. Rub it outside with the nutmeg and lemon juice. Sprinkle inside with salt and pepper and thyme.

Brown the chicken over medium heat. Add the salt pork, water, coarse salt, savory, minced onions, celery leaves. Bring to a boil. Cover and simmer for approximately 2 hours or until the chicken is almost done.

Then add the quartered cabbage, whole carrots, small round onions, yellow or green beans tied up with coarse thread in small bundles, and the new potatoes.

Return to a boil, cover and cook 30 minutes or until all is tender.

To serve, place the chicken and salt pork in the middle of a warm platter, surround with the vegetables, top with the butter warmed with the parsley and chives.

OLD-FASHIONED MILK FRIED CHICKEN

This recipe was given to me by an Eastern Townships farmer's wife. She said it was one of her "heirloom recipes".

2½-3 lb. frying chicken	2 tablespoons fat (any kind)
¼ cup flour	Generous pinch of turmeric
1½ teaspoons salt	3 tablespoons flour
¼ teaspoon pepper	2½ cups milk
¼ teaspoon sage	

Cut chicken into serving pieces. Mix the ¼ cup flour with the seasonings, then dredge chicken thoroughly. Melt the fat (she likes to use melted chicken fat) and brown chicken over medium heat. Place pieces in a baking dish.

To fat remaining in pan, add the 3 tablespoons flour and stir until blended. Add milk, cook until creamy and smooth, then pour over the chicken.

Cover and bake at 350°F. for 45-60 minutes, or until chicken is tender.

GALANTINE DE PORC
(Moulded Pork)

This is one of the best ways to eat pork in the summer. The fat and the jelly around the meat are also eaten. Spread it on bread — it is Quebec's famous "graisse de rôt".

4-5 lb. pork shoulder,	**¼ teaspoon ground cloves**
with rind if possible	**½ teaspoon savory**
2 lbs. pork hock	**1 cup hot water**
2 large onions, minced	**½ cup green or black tea**
Garlic to taste	**or cold water**
1 tablespoon coarse salt	

Place the meat, fat on top, in a cast iron or enamelled cast iron saucepan with a good cover. Cut the hock in 3 pieces and place around the meat. Add remaining ingredients, except the last two. Do not cover saucepan. Bake at 325°F. for 2½ hours, without basting or opening the oven door. Then add the hot water and bake another hour, this time with the cover on.

Remove from oven and separate the meat from the juice. Bone the meat, then break it up with two forks. Don't tear it apart too much. Cut the skin from the hock into small pieces and place it in your mould.

Reheat the saucepan and bring the contents to a boil. Add the tea or cold water. Scrape the bottom and sides of the saucepan. Put the gravy through a sieve and pour over the meat. Cool, cover and refrigerate. Unmould when ready to serve.

FRENCH ETOUFFÉE

Salt pork, bouquet garni and garlic are the flavors, thinly sliced carrots and fresh mushrooms are the garnish. The result is a thoroughly delectable dish, always served with mashed potatoes and a bottle of red wine.

4 lbs. rump, chuck or	**1 teaspoon salt**
round beef	**6-7 small carrots, thinly sliced**
¼ lb. fat salt pork	**½ lb. fresh mushrooms, sliced**
1-2 garlic cloves, minced	**6-8 small white onions**
Bouquet garni*	**3 tablespoons red wine or water**

Dice the salt pork and fry it in a heavy metal casserole until the fat melts and the pork is crisp and deep brown. Over low heat, brown the beef on all sides. Top with garlic, bouquet garni, salt and pepper. Surround with the carrots, mushrooms, and onions, then add the wine or water.

Cover tightly and cook 2 hours over very low heat, or until the meat is tender. Remove bouquet garni and excess fat from gravy when the meat is cooked.

*Bouquet garni: Tie a few celery leaves, a few sprigs of fresh parsley, 1 bay leaf and a leek, or half an onion, together with a string.

MAMAN'S CREAMY CHICKEN

In my family, this delicious creamed chicken was served the first Monday of every month. I still don't know why, but I do remember how eagerly we waited for that day. It was served with a large basket of hot biscuits and a salad of cabbage and apples.

1 **boiling chicken***	1 **parsley sprig**
1 **small onion**	¼ **teaspoon mace**
2 **cloves**	**Salt and pepper, to taste**
1 **bay leaf**	3 **tablespoons soft butter**
3 **cups milk (not homogenized)**	3 **tablespoons all purpose flour**
1 **celery stalk and leaves, diced**	

Stick the cloves in the onion and place inside the chicken. Tie the legs loosely. Put it in an iron pot or deep casserole with the bay leaf on top. Add the milk, celery, parsley, mace, salt and pepper. Cover and bake at 275°F. for 2-3 hours, depending on the chicken.

When the bird is tender, remove it from the dish and cut it into pieces. Make a ball of the soft butter and flour, add to the hot milk and stir well until creamy. Taste for seasoning and pour it over the chicken.

*Any type of chicken can be used. Try it sometime with a small 6-8 lb. turkey. Only the baking time will vary. If you prefer, cut the chicken before cooking and put the onion in the milk.

APPLE PORK CHOPS

The apples keep the chops moist and tender. I sometimes use 6 to 7 apples, then use 1 tablespoon sugar. Serve very hot.

6 **pork chops**	3 **unpeeled apples, with cores**
Pork chop fat	1 **teaspoon sugar**
2 **teaspoons butter**	**Cinnamon or ground cloves**
Salt and pepper, to taste	

Cook the chops using melted fat trimmed from the meat and 1 teaspoon of the butter. Season to taste and set on a hot platter. Keep warm.

Slice the apples ½-inch thick and add to the pan with the other 1 teaspoon of butter, the sugar and a few pinches of cinnamon or cloves. Cook over medium heat for about 10 minutes, turning once or twice, until some of the apples are browned. Arrange them around the chops and serve.

RÔTI "GRAISSE DE RÔT"
(Québec Roasted Pork)

This is one of the authentic Québec daubes. The famous "graisse de rôti", which is served cold on toasted bread, is made from the meat drippings. It is at its best cooked in an iron kettle.

4-5 lb. loin of pork	**Salt and pepper, to taste**
2 garlic cloves	**1 pork rind or pig's foot**
1 teaspoon dry mustard	**1 cup water**
1 teaspoon savory	

Make 4 incisions in the loin and place one half a garlic clove in each incision. Rub the meat all over with the dry mustard, letting most of it adhere to the fat. Then sprinkle with the savory, again letting most of it adhere to the fat.

Place the loin in the pan, then add salt and pepper to taste. Cut the pork rind or pig's foot in several pieces and place them all around the meat. Add the water.

There are two ways you can now cook the roast:

1. Place the pan over high heat and bring the whole to a boil. Cover and simmer over low heat for 2 hours, then uncover and cook over high heat until the liquid evaporates. Brown the fat part of the roast, then set the meat on a warm platter.

2. Roast uncovered at 325°F. for 45 minutes per pound. When done, remove the meat to a warmed platter and place the pan over direct heat to make the gravy.

To make the gravy, in both methods, add one cup of water to the residue, then simmer for 10 minutes, stirring and scraping the bottom of the pot all the time.

If you wish to have the graisse de rôti instead of gravy, pass the pan juices through a fine sieve, after scraping all the residue from the bottom of the pot. Refrigerate overnight.

PICKLED ONIONS WITH A FRENCH TOUCH

If onions are stored in sterilized sealed jars they will keep for months. (I have never managed to keep mine because they are eaten all too quickly.) Although there is quite a bit of wine in them, they do not have that strong wine taste. They make a truly superb relish with barbecued steak.

4 cups small white pickling onions	1 dry chili pepper
3 cups Canadian white wine, sweet or dry	1 bay leaf
	3 whole cloves
½ cup cider vinegar	½ teaspoon thyme
1 tablespoon tomato paste	½ cup white or golden seedless raisins
3 tablespoons salad oil	
3 tablespoons sugar	

Heat oven to 325°F. Place the unpeeled onions on a baking sheet and bake 10 minutes. (This is not absolutely necessary, but it will enable you to peel them without a tear.) Peel and scrape onions but do not cut off all the root — otherwise they will break up during the cooking. Place remaining ingredients in a non-aluminum saucepan — you can tie the chili pepper, bay leaf, cloves and thyme in cheesecloth if you don't want them left in with the cooked onions.

Simmer uncovered over low heat until onions are tender and sauce is thick and a golden red color. If onions are done before sauce is of proper consistency, remove them with a perforated spoon and continue cooking the sauce. Pour into jars and seal. Yield: 2 pint jars.

RASPBERRY VINEGAR

Some of us may have once had this old-fashioned drink, and have forgotten it. Remember it when the raspberry season is on.

6 quarts raspberries	Sugar
1 quart cider vinegar	

Mash 2 quarts of the raspberries in a large glass or earthenware bowl or jar — don't use metal. Pour the vinegar on top, cover and let stand overnight.

Wet a jelly bag by dipping it in white vinegar. Place it over a bowl and pour in the raspberry vinegar. Hang the bag, letting the juice strain thoroughly, over 2 more quarts of the raspberries. Cover and let stand 24 hours.

Repeat the straining over the remaining 2 quarts of berries. Cover and let stand overnight.

Strain the whole through the wet jelly bag until all the juice is extracted. Measure the juice by cups and add an equal amount of sugar. Bring to a fast rolling boil while stirring, and boil for 3 minutes.

Pour into bottles, cover and store in a cool, dark place — it will keep from one season to the next. To serve, use ¼ cup of raspberry vinegar to ¾ cup of water or soda poured over ice cubes.

MONIQUE'S DOUGHNUTS

Monique is my daughter, and I think she makes the very best doughnuts there are. Her secret is as little flour as possible and the dough is refrigerated until it is very cold and hard.

3 cups all-purpose flour
3½ teaspoons baking powder
1 teaspoon salt
1 teaspoon nutmeg
½ teaspoon cinnamon
½ teaspoon ginger
3 eggs

1 teaspoon vanilla
¾ cup sugar
3 tablespoons soft butter
¾ cup milk
1 cup all-purpose flour
Oil or shortening
Icing sugar

Sift together flour, baking powder, salt, nutmeg, cinnamon and ginger. Beat eggs. Add vanilla and sugar. Beat until light, then add soft butter. (When butter is beaten in, mixture may look curdled.) Add milk and sifted dry ingredients alternately to creamed mixture. Mix into a very soft dough.

Spread 1 cup of flour on a table. Turn dough on top and knead lightly for 1 minute incorporating just what flour is needed, so dough won't stick. Wrap and refrigerate for 1 or 2 hours.

Cut dough in four and roll each piece on a lightly floured board. Cut with a floured doughnut cutter. Heat some deep fat — oil or shortening — to 375°F. Lift each doughnut with a wide spatula, carefully ease it into the hot fat. Put as many in as can be turned easily.

Fry about 3 minutes, turning only once, until browned on both sides. Lift from fat with a long fork passed through the hole — be careful not to pierce doughnut. Drain on absorbent paper. When all doughnuts are cooked, deep fry small round pieces cut from centres.

Cool and roll in icing sugar.

POMMES CARAMEL
(Caramel Apples)

Make these with the first fresh apples. In Québec we use the first ripe Melbas. Served hot or cold, they are superb on ice cream.

⅓ cup margarine or butter
1 cup white or brown sugar

1 teaspoon vanilla
6 apples

Melt the margarine or butter in a frying pan and add sugar. Stir until sugar is dissolved or softened and everything is well blended, then add vanilla.

Core unpeeled apples, cut them into quarters and add to hot sugar. Simmer uncovered over medium heat, basting often with the syrup, for 15-20 minutes.

NORTHERN QUÉBEC AND BIG APPETITES

Northern Québec is rich in natural beauty and bounty. It offers game, fish and wild fruit in abundance.

In the beautiful Lake St. John district they say that "If we are to assure that the things we cherish shall stay tomorrow and for posterity, we must cultivate the principles of intelligent preservation. We must labor in unison to this end."

LAKE ST. JOHN GOURGANE SOUP

The Lake St. John district is renowned for three special foods. One, the Gourgane (Vicia Faba), a large broad bean used fresh in the summer, dried in the winter. Two, the Ouananiche, a fresh water salmon, smaller than the Atlantic type, which feeds only on white fish and smelts and whose meat is very delicate. Three, the blueberries which are known as the "Perles bleues du Saguenay" (blue pearls of the Saguenay). They are exceptionally large and very, very good.

1 lb. fresh broad beans or gourganes	½ teaspoon savory
4 cups boiling water	2 large onions, chopped
1 teaspoon coarse salt	½ lb. fat salt pork
½ teaspoon sugar	1 tablespoon cider vinegar
	1 tablespoon butter

Shell the fresh broad beans and remove a thin peel from each bean (unless they are very young). Bring the water to a boil, add the beans, salt, sugar and savory. Cover and simmer from 1 to 1½ hours or until the beans are tender.

Dice the salt pork, fry until golden and crisp. Add the onions and brown. Pour into the soup and continue cooking for another hour. When ready to serve, add the cider vinegar and butter.

PARSNIP SOUP

My mother always cut the unpeeled parsnip in 3 pieces, placed them in a saucepan and poured boiling water over them. She boiled them for 20 minutes, then drained, peeled and sliced them. The parsnip stayed creamy white with a most delicate flavor.

3 cups parsnips	1 cup cream
1 cup potatoes	2 cups milk
2 large onions	3 tablespoons butter
5 tablespoons butter	¼ teaspoon savory
Boiling water	¼ teaspoon pepper

Peel and slice the parsnips and potatoes. Peel the onions and slice thinly. Melt the butter. Add the onions. Cover and simmer for 10 minutes over low heat.

Add the prepared vegetables. Pour enough boiling water over them to cover completely. Salt. Cover and cook over medium heat until the vegetables are tender (from 20 to 30 minutes). Add the milk, cream, butter, savory, pepper. Heat without boiling, and serve.

21

FRESH COD SOUP

Gaspé has many interesting ways of using cod—fresh or salted. The following soup is a sort of chowder.

3 slices salt pork	2 cups hot milk
2 lbs. fresh cod	1 teaspoon salt
1 large onion, sliced thin	¼ teaspoon savory
2 cups sliced potatoes	2 tablespoons butter
1½ cups hot water	

Cut the salt pork into 1½ inch squares. Brown it over medium heat in a large saucepan. Cut the cod fillets or slice them into one inch pieces.

Make alternate layers of potatoes, onions and fish in the pan. Add the hot water. Cover. Bring to a boil and simmer from 10 to 15 minutes or until the potatoes are tender. Add the milk, salt, savory and butter. Do not mix, but keep everything warm until ready to serve.

CIPAILLE

1 small 6 to 8-lb. turkey or a 5-6-lb. chicken	½ cup parsley, minced
	1 teaspon savory
1 partridge or 1 wild or domestic duck	1 tablespoon salt
	½ teaspoon pepper
1 pork fillet	¼ teaspoon cinnamon
1 cup flour, salted and peppered	2 cups bread crumbs or 2 cups cooked potatoes, grated
¼ cup celery leaves minced	Pie dough
10 slices salt pork fat, melted	
4 onions, minced	

Cut the turkey or chicken, partridge or duck (do not include the back of a domestic duck) into individual pieces. Put the pork fillet through a meat chopper. Bone the birds when possible, as it makes serving far easier.

Roll the poultry pieces in the seasoned flour and brown in the melted salt pork. Place the pieces in a dish as they brown. Brown the onions, parsley and savory in the remaining fat. Remove. Then add the pork fillet, celery leaves, salt, pepper and cinnamon, and brown.

Roll the pie dough ½-inch thick. Line a 4- to 5-inch high baking dish with the dough. Garnish with the fillet mixture. Sprinkle with some bread crumbs. Add a few slices of the browned salt pork and a few spoonfuls of the onion mixture, parsley and savory. Pour a cup of consommé over it all. Then cover with a layer of dough rolled very thin which takes on the shape of the dish. Then add a layer of turkey or chicken pieces, breadcrumbs or grated potatoes, salt pork slices and a few spoonfuls of onions; add a third layer of dough. Over this is placed duck or partridge pieces and the same ingredients as over the turkey or chicken. Top everything with dough rolled one-half inch thick. Bake in a 300°F. oven for 4 hours.

Cipaille may be eaten cold or hot.

It also freezes very well.

LAKE ST. JOHN HARE CIPAILLE

1 or 2 hares (or rabbits)	1 tablespoon coarse salt
3 pork fillets, whole	4 small carrots peeled
2 chickens 4-5 lbs. each	2 leeks cleaned
3 lbs. minced beef	2 parsnips, peeled
3-4 lbs. veal	10 sprigs parsley, washed
2 partridges (if possible)*	3 bay leaves
½ cup lard or roast pork fat	4 cloves
2 quarts water	2 cinnamon sticks
6 large onions, sliced	Celery leaves
1 teaspoon thyme	

Clean and cut the hares or rabbits into individual pieces. Rub the pork fillet with a clove of garlic. Cut it in two. Cut the chickens into individual pieces and rub each piece with a whole nutmeg.

Season the minced beef with salt and pepper and make into balls. Make incisions in the veal and stuff with 2 cloves of garlic.

Clean the partridges and tie them.

Melt the fat in a cast-iron saucepan. When the fat is hot, brown each kind of meat separately, over high heat. Remove one meat when done and add the other.

Add the onions to the remainder of the fat and soften them, stirring most of the time. Pour over the meats, dividing them as evenly as possible.

Tie together into a bouquet garni, the carrots, leeks, parsley, celery leaves. Stick the cloves into the parsnips, and place the bay leaves and cinnamon sticks in the middle of the bundle.

Bring water to a boil in the saucepan used for browning. Add the thyme and coarse salt. When water boils, put the bouquet garni in the middle of the saucepan, place the veal and hares around. On top of the hares place the fillets, on top of the veal, the chicken and finish with the partridge. Bring to a boil. Cover and simmer over low heat, but do not allow to boil, 1 to 1½ hours or until the meats are cooked.

Brown the minced beef balls, cover and refrigerate until ready to prepare the cipaille.

Place the cooked meats in a large bowl and pour the broth on top. Add the bouquet garni. Cover and refrigerate 24 hours.

To finish the cipaille, remove with care the fat accumulated on top of the chilled meats. Throw out the bouquet garni. Start placing the meats in a large cast-iron saucepan or a casserole. They may be placed in layers or mixed together. The veal may be cut in cubes and the partridges split in four. Over the first layer of meat, pour ¾ cup cooking broth. Set the remainder aside for the cream sauce. (If the cooled broth is jelled, wam it up.)

Cover this layer of meat with a large round circle of dough (according to recipe which follows). Continue in this manner until there are 5 layers of meat and 6 of dough, finishing with one of dough. Make

*Partridges or other small birds may be omitted and replaced with pigeons.

a few incisions on the last layer of dough. Bake in a 375°F. oven, 1 to 1½ hours, or until the top dough is very well browned .

Make a cream sauce, with the remaining broth, butter and flour. When ready to serve the sauce with the cipaille, add ¼ cup rich cream and chives to taste.

Sift and measure 3 cups all-purpose flour with ¾ teaspoon baking powder and 1½ teaspoons salt.

In a large bowl, place ¼ cup butter, pour ½ cup boiling water. Stir quickly until the butter is creamed, add the lightly beaten egg. Fold in the sifted flour. Mix together. It is sometimes necessary to add a little flour, but this dough is rather light. It must be covered and refrigerated 6 to 8 hours or until it is firm enough to be rolled.

TOURTIÈRE

A hundred years ago, the tourtière was a must on every Christmas table. It can also be served in small tartlets as an apéritif. You can find almost as many Québec tourtière recipes as there are cooks, since each one has her own ways and variations. This one is "my way" and is three generations old.

1 lb. pork, minced	¼ teaspoon ground cloves
1 small onion, chopped	½ cup water
1 small garlic clove, minced	¼-½ cup breadcrumbs
½ teaspoon salt	Pastry of your choice
¼ teaspoon celery salt	

Place all the ingredients except the breadcrumbs in a saucepan. Bring to a boil and cook uncovered for 20 minutes over medium heat. Remove from heat and add a few spoonfuls of breadcrumbs. Let stand for 10 minutes. If the fat is sufficiently absorbed by the breadcrumbs, do not add more. If not, continue in the same manner.

Cool and pour into a pastry-lined pie pan. Cover with crust. Bake at 400°F. until golden brown. Serve hot. A cooked tourtière can be frozen 4-5 months. It does not have to be thawed out before reheating.

SPECIAL DOUGH FOR TOURTIÈRES

A very old recipe, that makes a melt-in-the-mouth crust. Use for all meat pies and "tourte".

4½-5 cups all-purpose flour	1 cup hot water
4 teaspoons baking powder	4 teaspoons lemon juice
2 teaspoons salt	or vinegar
1 lb. pure lard	1 egg, well beaten

Combine flour, baking powder and salt in a large mixing bowl. Measure 1⅓ cups of the lard and cut into the flour until it is mealy. Completely dissolve the remaining lard in the hot water. Add the lemon juice and egg. Mix these liquids into the flour mixture until dough leaves sides of the bowl. Turn on lightly floured board and knead about 1 minute or until all the flour is blended. Wrap in waxed paper, refrigerate 1 to 12 hours. Very easy to roll.

TOURTE DE NOEL

The pastry for the tourte is very special, and different from the tourtière type. It is rich, flaky, light and always flavored with savory. In the old days, wild savory was gathered in the autumn and hung on the kitchen rafters to dry until Christmas. The tourte is quite different from the tourtière.

2-3 lbs. very lean pork, finely diced	1 tablespoon savory
4 small onions, chopped	1 tablespoon salt
4 cooked potatoes, diced	½ teaspoon pepper
1½-2 teaspoons sage	2 tablespoons butter
	3 tablespoons flour

Place the meat and onion in saucepan, with just enough water to barely cover the meat. Cover and simmer 1 hour. Add the cooked potatoes, sage, savory, salt and pepper. Simmer together 20 minutes.

Make a ball of the butter and flour. Add to meat juice and cook until sauce is creamy. Taste for seasoning, then cool. Pour into pastry-lined baking dish and cover with a top crust (recipe follows). Bake at 400°F. until golden brown. This tourte also freezes well.

Pastry:

4 tablespoons butter	½ teaspoon savory
4 tablespoons lard	2 cups all-purpose flour
1 egg, well beaten	6-8 tablespoons ice water
¼ teaspoon salt	

Cream together the butter and the lard. Stir in the eggs, salt and sage. Mix well and work in the flour with your hands. Sprinkle half the water on top and blend; then add the rest of the water, enough to make the dough cling together. Do not overwork the pastry nor make it too wet. Roll out as thinly as possible on a floured board and line the bottom and sides of a round baking dish. Refrigerate until ready to use.

ROASTED SADDLE OF LAMB NOIRMOUTON

A jovial Scots friend of my father used to say that a roast saddle of lamb standing proudly on the Christmas table was "hospitality sitting with gladness". A perfect saddle is prepared with the uncut loins and shortened flank of a young lamb. (It may be wise to order it in advance from your butcher.)

1 saddle of lamb	¼ teaspoon basil
¼ cup olive oil or salad oil	2 cups lamb bone stock*
1 teaspoon dry mustard	2 tablespoons butter
1 teaspoon salt	1 teaspoon curry powder
½ teaspoon pepper, freshly ground	2 tablespoons all-purpose flour
½ teaspoon rosemary	

*Lamb bone stock: ask your butcher to give you the saddle trimmings. Boil them with 4 cups water, a stick of celery, small onion halved, bay leaf, salt and pepper. Cover and simmer for 3 hours, then strain. When prepared in advance, as it should be, refrigerate and pour cold over the hot fat.

25

Stir together the oil, dry mustard, salt, pepper, rosemary and basil. Place the saddle of lamb in a dripping pan and spread mixture on top. Roast at 400°F. for 10-15 minutes to the pound.

When done a deep, golden brown, with a lovely fragrance, remove from pan, cover with wax paper and set aside in a warm place, or on an electric tray. The saddle comes to its point of perfection after 20 minutes. Add the lamb bone stock to the drippings and stir all the crusty bits from sides and bottom of pan into the stock. Make a ball of the butter, curry and flour. Add to boiling stock in the dripping pan and stir quickly over low heat until creamy and smooth.

In Scotland, the Christmas saddle of lamb is brought to the table on a large silver platter, surrounded by blue flame. Hot whisky can be poured on top and lit just before the meal is served. My grandfather was shown how to do this by his many Scottish friends.

BEAN POT BOILED BEEF
(Boeuf en pot)

3-4 lbs. beef shoulder	1 tablespoon salt
3 onions, thinly sliced	½ teaspoon pepper
2 carrots, cut in three	1 tablespoon honey
1 bay leaf	Cold water to cover
1 teaspoon savory	

Place all the ingredients in a bean pot or a baking dish with a good cover. Cover and cook 4 hours in a 300°F. oven.

The bouillon is delicious and the fat is very good for frying. The meat may be served as is, or with vegetables, hot or cold. If served cold let the meat cool in its juice without removing the lid. Place in the refrigerator when cooled. Remove the fat from the top when ready to serve.

RAGOUT DE BOULETTES

1 lb. fresh lean pork	¼ teaspoon dry mustard
½ lb. minced beef	2 slices bread, diced
¼ lb. salt pork	½ cup milk
1 small onion, minced	Salt and pepper
2 tablespoons parsley	3 tablespoons fat
¼ teaspoon ginger	3 cups water
¼ teaspoon cinnamon	4 tablespoons browned flour
¼ teaspoon ground cloves	½ cup water

Put through the meat chopper 3 times, the fresh pork, minced beef and salt pork. Add the onion, parsley, ginger, cinnamon, cloves and dry mustard. Add the bread, soaked in the milk and blended into a paste. Add salt and pepper. Make into balls.

Fry the meat balls in fat. Pour 3 cups water over the meat balls. Cover and simmer for 30 minutes.

Shake the flour and ½ cup of milk together in a jar. Pour into the broth and continue cooking, stirring until it thickens to a good consistency.

RAGOUT DE PATTES

2-3 lbs. pork hocks, cut in pieces
1 teaspoon coarse salt
¼ teaspoon pepper
½ teaspoon cinnamon
¼ teaspoon ground cloves
⅛ teaspoon nutmeg

2 tablespoons fat
4-6 cups lukewarm water
1 cup onions, sliced thin
4 tablespoons browned flour
½ cup water

Roll the hocks in a mixture of salt, cinnamon, cloves and nutmeg.

Melt the fat in a heavy saucepan. Brown the hocks until dark brown in color (there lies the secret for successful ragoût). When the meat is well browned, add the onions and stir until light brown. Add the tepid water. Cover and simmer until the meat is tender, approximately 2 hours.

Shake the flour and one-half cup of water together in a glass jar. Pour into the broth and cook, stirring, until thick.

HEAD CHEESE

The jelly of head cheese will always be clearer if the head is wrapped in a cloth and sewed in well, for cooking. It is then easier, when done, to remove the meat from the bones. Do not use more than 3 quarts of water for each head. Part of the water may be replaced by apple juice (as in Normandy) or white wine (as in Poitou), or by chicken or beef consommé (as in Brittany). Head cheese will keep for 2 to 3 weeks as long as it is not stored in metal molds and is well wrapped. It freezes for 2-3 months, but the jelly loses some of its clarity although the flavor remains the same.

½ or 1 small pig's head or
  ½ a large one or
  4-6 pig's feet
6 cloves
2 sticks or 1 tablespoon cinnamon

2 tablespoons salt
2 large onions chopped
1 large carrot, grated
2 quarts hot water

Wrap the head in a cloth. Place in a saucepan with the remaining ingredients. Bring to a boil. Cover and simmer over low heat for 3½ to 4 hours.

Unwrap the head, chop the meat from the bones and put into the hot broth. Boil quickly for 10 minutes.

Pour into molds and refrigerate until jelled.

QUEBEC CRETONS

4 lbs. leaf lard
  Salt, pepper
1 pinch ground cloves

A little cinnamon
1 small piece garlic, crushed
2-4 tablespoons fat

Remove the skin from the leaf lard. Cut the lard in small pieces and melt it in an enamelled cast-iron saucepan, over low heat, until the residues are crisp and well browned. Remove from heat and let stand until tepid.

Strain the liquid and turn the browned lardons into a bowl, add the salt, pepper, cloves, cinnamon and garlic. Mix together and crush the lardons with a wooden spoon or mallet. Empty into a small bowl and add the fat. Keep refrigerated.

QUEBEC CREPE AU LARD

5-10 slices salt pork, more fat than lean	**5 tablespoons all-purpose flour**
Cold water	**½ teaspoon salt**
4 eggs	**¼ teaspoon pepper**
	2 cups milk

Place the sliced salt pork in a cast-iron or enamelled cast-iron frying pan. Cover with cold water. Bring to a boil over medium heat. Simmer for 2 minutes. Drain.

Replace the frying pan over medium heat and cook the salt pork slices until well browned on both sides and until the fat is melted. Do not remove any of it.

To prepare the pancake (crêpe), break the eggs in a bowl, add the flour, salt and pepper. Mix together until the batter is smooth, preferably with an electric beater.

Add the milk. Mix and pour over the hot grilled salt pork slices and fat. Let cook for 10 minutes over medium heat without disturbing. Lift the side of the pancake gently, here and there, tilting the frying pan for the uncooked part to run under. After working a few moments in this manner, lower the heat substantially. Cover the pan and let cook for 5 minutes. This pancake is easily removed from the frying pan.

CHEVREUIL DES GUIDES

This dish is very popular among hunters and their guides.

2 lbs. deer	**2 carrots, diced**
3 cups dried beans	**4 large onions, thinly sliced**
1 quart pale ale	**1 teaspoon savory**
1 bay leaf	**1 cup molasses**
½ lb. salt pork	**Salt and pepper**

Sort the beans and soak in cold water for 12 hours.

Drain, setting the water aside and place in a bean pot, then add the beer, 3 cups of the water used for soaking the beans, bay leaf, salt pork cut in 1-inch cubes, carrots, onions, savory, molasses, salt and pepper to taste. Cover and bake in a 300°F. oven for 5 hours. Should more water be required, add the bean soaking water.

When the beans are tender, but not completely cooked, add the deer meat cut in 1-inch cubes and cook covered, for another 2 hours.

Partridge may be prepared in this way: tie and put it in the middle of the beans, after 6 hours of cooking. Cook another hour instead of two.

QUEBEC FRICASSÉE

Although this recipe seems very plain, I consider fricassée a delicious family dish, when well prepared. The following are a few suggestions to help you succeed: when fricassée can be made with chicken or turkey fat, it is the best. If possible use left-over gravy, taking the top fat, and adding to the fricassée gravy the brown bottom jelly. The meat must always be diced finely. Preferably, winter potatoes should be used as the starch they contain helps to thicken the gravy. To give this dish a truly French-Canadian flavor, you must not forget the savory.

½ cup meat fat or left-over gravy fat
2-3 cups cooked meat, diced
2 cups onions, chopped
4 cups raw potatoes, diced
1 teaspoon savory
Salt and pepper

Melt the fat, add the diced meat and onions. Fry for a few minutes. Add the raw potatoes, season and flavor. Cover with water, cook over medium heat, 30 to 40 minutes, preferably covered, until a creamy texture is obtained.

PÂTE CHINOIS
(Shepherd's Pie)

1 - 2 cups cooked left-over beef, chopped, or 1 lb. minced beef
3 tablespoons meat fat
2 large onions, minced
½ teaspoon savory
Salt and pepper to taste
1 can creamed corn
4 cups mashed potatoes

Melt the fat and brown the onion over high heat. Add the cooked or raw meat, savory, salt and pepper. Stir over medium heat 3-4 minutes.

Place in a baking dish. Pour the corn over the meat and top with potatoes mashed with milk. If you like, a small piece of butter may be added. Smooth top with a knife, making pretty designs and dot with butter. Bake in a 375°F. oven for 20 minutes.

THE PERFECT WAY TO BOIL A PIECE OF SALMON

The secret of moist, flavorful, tender boiled salmon is temperature control. If you wish to serve the salmon cold it should be cooled and refrigerated in its court-bouillon.

To prepare court-bouillon, be sure you have about 4 times as much water as the fish to be cooked — 10 cups for a 3 to 5 lb. piece of fish. Add salt at the rate of 1 teaspoon per 5 cups of water and ¼ cup fresh lemon juice or white wine. A bay leaf and a pinch of rosemary add to the flavor.

Bring the court-bouillon to a full boil. Add the salmon as is or wrap in cheesecloth. The cloth makes it easier to remove in one piece after it has cooked. After adding the fish do not let the water boil. Cover and simmer gently 10 minutes for each pound of fish. If you wish to serve the salmon cold, put it in a deep bowl without removing the cheese-cloth. Cover with some of the court-bouillon and refrigerate 12 to 24 hours.

Serve it cold with pressed cucumbers, or hot, with a white sauce garnished with eggs or parsley or chives.

HOW TO POACH A WHOLE SALMON

Served hot with an egg sauce, or served cold with sour cream cucumber sauce, both ways are perfect and are great favorites of mine.

5 - 10 lb. fresh salmon	**12 peppercorns**
3 quarts water	**2 tablespoons salt**
Juice of 1 lemon	**6 - 10 parsley stems**
2 carrots, sliced	**1 bay leaf**
2 onions, sliced	

Place water and all the ingredients except the salmon in a large pot or saucepan large enough to hold the fish. A dripping pan covered with foil paper is best for a large fish.

Boil the water miture for 30 minutes. Wrap cleaned salmon in a piece of cheesecloth. Remove pan from heat and place fish in water. Cover and cook over medium heat 20 minutes for each inch of thickness — measuring in the thickest part of the fish.

When done, take fish from the pan by inserting two large forks, one at each end of the fish, in the cheesecloth. Place on a hot platter. Remove cloth by slowly pulling from under the fish, or turning fish over by holding the cloth — the second way is more difficult to handle.

To serve it hot, garnish with parsley, sprinkle top with a little curry powder and spread a little egg sauce all along the back. Serve the rest of the sauce separately.

To serve it cold: place fish on a platter. Dip cheesecloth in fish broth until soaking. Spread all over the fish, so it will be well covered. Pour a few spoonfuls of broth on top. Refrigerate until ready to serve. Remove the cloth carefully. Spread the fish with mayonnaise and decorate with capers. Serve with a large bowl of this delicious sauce:

To a pint of sour cream, add 3 green onions, minced, or ¼ cup minced chives, 1 large cucumber, peeled and finely diced, salt and pepper to taste and 2 tablespoons lemon juice. Blend well.

QUEBEC POACHED SALMON

Use salmon steak for this colorful and tasty dish. It is then as easy to make for 2 as for 10. It is served with the classic "sauce verte".

4 - 6 salmon steaks	**1 tablespoon salt**
1 tablespoon salad oil	**1 small onion, quartered**
Juice of 1 lemon	**3 - 6 sprigs parsley**
Peel of ½ lemon, grated	**6 peppercorns, crushed with back of spoon**

Spread the oil in a frying pan or in a flat baking dish. Place the salmon slices next to one another, but not overlapping. Add the lemon juice and peel, peppercorns, salt, onion and just enough hot water to just cover the fish. Cover and poach on top of the stove (if in frying pan) over low heat, for 10-20 minutes: or in a 325°F. oven (in baking dish) for same length of time, or until the salmon flakes.

Allow the fish to cool in the liquid. Drain well and remove the skin.

Arrange on a serving platter, then completely cover the fish with the following sauce. Serve with a cucumber salad.

Sauce Verte

If you have a blender, this sauce will be ready in minutes. If not, ingredients will have to be chopped very finely.

½ **cup green onion tops or chives**	½ **cup spinach, uncooked**
½ **cup green pepper**	2 **tablespoons lemon juice**
¼ **cup parsley**	1 **cup mayonnaise**

Chop the vegetables coarsely and place in blender with lemon juice. Cover and blend until it turns into a sort of mush with small bits of this and that in it. Add to the mayonnaise and blend.

If you don't have a blender, chop the ingredients very finely and blend them into the mayonnaise with the lemon juice, crushing them in order to give as much color as possible to the sauce.

QUEBEC MARINATED SALMON

A marinated salmon is always ready to serve and keeps 15 to 20 days under refrigeration. Cucumbers and green salads are good accompaniments, or you can try this one with hot boiled potatoes rolled in parsley.

10 - 12 any small fish or	1 **tablespoon salt**
4 - 5 lbs. fresh salmon	3 **whole cloves**
½ **cup cider vinegar**	¼ **teaspoon thyme**
2 **cups white wine**	6 **peppercorns**
1 **large onion, thinly sliced**	½ **teaspoon celery salt**
1 **carrot, thinly sliced**	

Place all the ingredients except the fish in a saucepan. Bring to a boil, then simmer uncovered for 20 minutes.

Clean the fish (if using salmon, slice it or leave whole) and place in the hot liquid. Simmer uncovered — be sure not to boil it — for 20 minutes.

Remove the fish to a dish and pour the cooking liquid on top. Cover and refrigerate until cold, then serve in its juice.

PRESSED CUCUMBERS

Serve with hot or cold boiled Gaspé salmon.

2 or 3 medium cucumbers	**Pepper**
Salt	**Lemon juice**

Score the cucumbers lengthwise with the tines of a fork. Remove the ends and slice thin. Put the slices in a bowl and cover completely with ice cubes. Refrigerate 2 or 3 hours. To serve, drain well and spread the slices on a clean cloth. Twist the cloth tightly to extract all the water from the cucumbers. Arrange in a vegetable dish. Add salt and pepper, and sprinkle with a spoonful of lemon juice.

MASHED TURNIP PETITS POIS

This combination will be liked even by those who never eat turnips. However, the turnip must not be overcooked.

1 large turnip	½ teaspoon pepper, freshly ground
½ teaspoon monosodium glutamate	Juice of 1 lemon
1 teaspoon sugar	2 cans or packages of frozen French green peas
3 - 4 teaspoons butter	Salt to taste

Don't peel the turnip until you're ready to cook it. Remove the peel thickly enough to eliminate the color line that is clearly seen between the turnip and the rind: this is where the bitterness is. Slice the turnip and scald with just enough water to generously cover it. Then add the m.s.g. and sugar.

Boil rapidly, uncovered, for 20 minutes. Prolonged cooking darkens the color of the turnip and gives it a strong flavor. Drain and wash, add the butter, pepper and lemon juice. Mash and beat well and fold in green peas, making sure they have been well drained. Salt to taste and serve.

PICKLED BEETS

There is nothing better served with western hash or Québec Fricassée. When a jar is empty, I use the vinegar to pickle hard-boiled eggs.

8 cups cooked beets	1 teaspoon salt
2 cups white vinegar	16 whole cloves
½ cup sugar	1 bay leaf

Boil together for 10 minutes the vinegar, sugar, salt, cloves and bay leaf.

Beets should be left whole if they are small. If large, slice or cut them with ridged cutter for a fancy appearance, or dice coarsely. Add prepared cooked beets to the hot syrup. Bring to a boil and seal in hot jars. Yield: 2 quarts.

RED DEVIL EGGS

This colorful variation of pickled eggs, served with potato salad, celery, carrot slices or sliced cold ham is one of my favorite quick lunches.

12 eggs	2 bay leaves
Juice of pickled beets	1 garlic clove (optional)

Place the eggs in cold water and let come to a boil, uncovered. Turn heat down and simmer (do not boil) 15 minutes. Remove from heat and pour off boiling water. When eggs have cooled, peel them and put them in the beet juice with a bay leaf and garlic. Cover and marinate, three to four days, in the refrigerator.

QUEBEC BANANA TRIFLE

This is a variation of the traditional English trifle and is a favorite on many Québec dinner tables.

A sponge cake	¼ teaspoon almond essence or
4 bananas	3 tablespoons rum
1 pint whipping cream	1 teaspoon sugar
3 tablespoons icing sugar	Pinch of cinnamon or nutmeg
	Chopped walnuts

Cut the sponge cake into chunks about the size of ice cubes. Slice the bananas. Whip the cream with the icing sugar and flavor it with the almond essence or rum. Put some of the cake in the bottom of a glass dish, cover with bananas and some of the cream. Repeat in layers. Decorate the top with what is left of the whipped cream. Sprinkle with a mixture of the sugar and cinnamon or nutmeg, and chopped walnuts. Chill well before serving.

QUEBEC APPLE DUMPLINGS

In Québec these were baked in deep brown earthenware pudding dishes and served on a hot wooden board or tray surrounded by autumn leaves or boughs cut from the Christmas tree. It was a tradition in our family to serve these dumplings after we had finished decorating our Christmas tree.

Pie dough of your choice	Rum
(a double batch)	Butter
Grated cheddar cheese	Sugar
12 medium apples, peeled and	¼ cup brown sugar
cored	¼ cup cream
Mincemeat	Grated rind of ½ a lemon

Make enough pie dough to roll into twelve 6″ x 6″ squares (about a double batch).* Sprinkle each square with a spoonful of grated cheese. Peel and core the apples and place one on each square. Fill the centre of each apple with a heaping spoonful of mincemeat, a teaspoon of rum, a dot of butter and 1 tablespoon sugar. Bring diagonally opposite corners of the dough over the apple to form ears at the top. Cover the ears with aluminum foil. Mix the brown sugar, cream and grated lemon rind. Brush the dumplings with this mixture and bake 35 to 45 minutes in a 400°F. oven. Remove foil, brush ears with cream mixture and return to oven until ears are brown. Serve warm with plain cream or sweetened cream, flavored with rum.

*A recipe of the Tourtière pie dough can be used.

OLD-FASHIONED VINEGAR CANDY

This economical taffy, creamy white in color, is fun to make and nice to eat. If you're too young to have heard about it, try it and see.

3 cups sugar	1½ cups cider vinegar

Place the sugar and the vinegar in a deep saucepan over low heat. Stir constantly until the sugar is dissolved, cover and simmer 3 minutes to melt the sugar crystals. Uncover, and continue to cook slowly until the syrup reaches the firm ball stage in ice water or 240°F. on a candy thermometer. Pour into a large buttered platter and let cool until the candy can be handled comfortably.

Butter your hands and pull the taffy until it is white and almost firm. Stretch into a rope about 1 inch in diameter, then roll it into a twist and snip off pieces with kitchen scissors. Place on a buttered dish or wrap each piece in transparent paper.

WHEN THE SAP BEGINS TO STIR

Every year, in the early spring, around St. Patrick's day, the sap from maple trees starts to run. To the farmer it means long hours of hard work. To the children it means fresh boiled sugar on snow. To the mother it means extra food to cook, bread to bake, tubs to wash, cans to fill and people to feed.

If you're an inveterate romantic like me, you listen to the first spring rush and roar of overflowing brooks, you delight in the mixed smell of wood smoke and maple syrup, and suddenly you're hungry for all the good things you can make with the maple's sap.

I remember how my husband and I were thrilled the first time we saw the sap running from our own maples at Noirmouton, our farm, and how eager we were to find out how the syrup of our trees would taste. I remembered my grandfather saying, "If you cook the first pail of early sap by itself on the stove, you have a syrup fit for the gods," so I decided to cook that first pail. It took patience but we were well rewarded.

I feel a little sad today to see the maple sap transported by plastic hose, and the sugar houses replaced by automatic evaporators. With everything streamlined and efficient, a bit of the old-fashioned romance and magic of sugaring off has been lost.

The "brown sweetness" as people used to refer to maple syrup in the old days, has a way of adding charm and flavor to any food. Pour a golden trickle on your morning cereal, enjoy it on grapefruit halves, glaze your ham with it, or simply heat it with chopped walnuts and pour it over ice cream for a hot maple sundae.

A FEW NOTES ON MAPLE SUGAR AND SYRUP

—If a recipe calls for maple sugar and you have only maple syrup, simply boil the syrup slowly until it threads or forms a soft ball in cold water. Then remove from heat, let it cool and beat until thick like fudge. Pour in a pan and let it harden. Two cups of maple syrup will yield 1 cup of sugar.

—If, on the other hand, a recipe calls for syrup and you have only maple sugar, simply grate or cut the sugar into pieces, add a small amount of water and simmer over low heat until the sugar is melted.

—Always store maple syrup in a dry cool place in small containers, preferably ones of glass. Once a gallon tin has been opened, transfer the syrup to glass jars or bottles.

— If maple syrup ferments slightly, or forms a white cloud on top, you can restore it to its normal flavor by straining through a sieve lined with cheesecloth or paper cloth, then heating it to a full rolling boil. Skim the scum as it forms, then pour into hot sterilized jars or bottles and store.

— Keep maple sugar in a cool place, wrapped in a double layer of foil paper.

LES TOQUETTES
(Sugar on Snow)

In a large saucepan place 4 to 5 cups maple syrup. Bring to a boil over high heat. Watch closely, as it easily boils over if the pan is not large enough. Then cook over medium heat until the candy thermometer registers 230°F.-232°F.

Have bowls filled with clean snow (or shaved ice). Dribble the hot syrup over the snow by spoonfuls. It sets quickly. Pick up with a wooden stick or a spoon and eat. After the sweetness, drink a large goblet of cold clear sap, right from the tree. A treat to be had once a year!

JAMBON DE LA CABANE A SUCRE

When baked for a sugar-house party, the ham is boiled in sap instead of apple juice. I usually freeze 6-9 quarts of pale sap at sugaring time to make this delight off-season.

8 - 10 lbs. ham	2 tablespoons ground cloves
3 quarts apple juice or maple sap	¼ cup water
2 cups maple sugar	2 cups raisins
1 teaspoon hot dry mustard	

Bring the apple juice or the maple sap to a boil and place ham in it. Cover and simmer over low heat for 3 hours, or until the ham is tender. Remove meat from liquid and trim off the rind only.

Place the sugar, mustard, cloves and water in a saucepan and add one cup of the cooking juice and 2 cups of raisins. Simmer 5 minutes, then place ham in dripping pan and pour sauce over it. Bake at 300°F. for 30 minutes.

Thicken the juice to taste with browned flour, blended with cold water. Serve the delicious raisin sauce with the warm ham (which is equally good cold).

HAM SLICE IN SYRUP

With its shiny, mahogany-colored sauce, this is as good to eat as it is to look at. It is a refined version of Indian venison cooked in maple sap. A thick slice of ham is essential.

1 ham slice, 1¼-1½ inches thick	2 teaspoons lemon juice or
Whole cloves	cider vinegar
2 teaspoons dry mustard	¾ cup maple syrup

Cut the rind from the slice of ham and slash the fat in several places to keep it from curling. Put a few cloves here and there in the fat. Mix the mustard with the lemon juice or cider vinegar until smooth, then add the maple syrup. Place the ham slice in a dripping pan, pour the syrup mixture on top. Bake uncovered at 350°F. for 50 minutes. Baste every 10 minutes with some of the maple sauce.

When the ham is cooked, remove from the baking pan and place on a warm serving platter. Put pan over direct heat and cook the drippings, stirring constantly, until the consistency is that of a thick gravy. Pour over the ham and serve with boiled potatoes and broccoli.

MAPLE SYRUP RUM BAKED BEANS

This is one of my family recipes. I have never seen the apple cover in any cookbook, and have no idea where my mother got the idea — maybe it was her own. These are very, very good beans.

4 cups dried navy beans	1 cup maple syrup
12 cups cold water	1 tablespoon coarse salt
1 teaspoon soda	4 cored apples, unpeeled
1 lb. fat and lean salt pork,	1 cup maple or light brown sugar
sliced	½ cup butter
1 large onion	½ cup rum (optional)
1 teaspoon dry mustard	

Preheat oven to 325°F.

Cover the beans with 12 cups cold water. Let soak overnight. In the morning pour the whole thing in a large saucepan. Add 1 teaspoon soda and more cold water to cover the beans if necessary. Bring to a boil, uncovered, then boil until some of the skins come off when you blow on the beans.

Line a bean pot with the sliced pork, then pour in the beans and their water. Roll the onion in the dry mustard until all of the mustard sticks to it, then bury it in the middle of the beans. Pour the maple syrup and coarse salt on top.

Bake 4-5 hours in a 325°F. oven. In the last hour of cooking, cover the beans with the whole apples, placed as close together as possible. Cream together the sugar and butter, then spread the mixture on top of the apples. This forms a most delicious topping when the beans are baked. Pour the rum on top just before serving.

MAPLE SYRUP PIE

Of all the maple syrup pies I've made, none was ever as good as this one. The recipe dates from Colonial days when crushed wheat was used to thicken the mixture.

Pastry for 2-crust pie	2 tablespoons cold water
½ cup water	2 tablespoons butter
3 tablespoons cornstarch	¼ cup nuts, chopped

Boil the maple syrup and ½ cup of water for 5 minutes. Blend the cornstarch with the 2 tablespoons of water and add to the syrup. Cook, stirring constantly, until mixture is smooth and transparent. Add the butter and chopped nuts and let it cool. Bake between two crusts at 400°F. for 25-30 minutes.

CREAMY MAPLE SYRUP PIE

This is an exquisite filling used for small tarts. Top them with a dab of whipped cream or chopped walnuts for dinner or buffet parties.

Pastry of your choice	**1 cup maple syrup**
2 tablespoons butter	**⅓ cup water**
2 tablespoons all-purpose flour	**½ cup chopped walnuts**
2 egg yolks	

Melt butter and stir in flour, mixing well. Beat egg yolks with syrup and water. Add to butter-flour mixture and cook over boiling water until thick and creamy, stirring most of the time. Add walnuts and let cool. Pour into an 8-inch pie shell or divide into 6 individual tart molds lined with pastry.

As a variation, sprinkle the nuts on top instead of mixing them in the filling.

To make chiffon maple tarts, beat 2 egg whites until stiff, fold into cooked and cooled maple cream, then pour into baked tart shells.

MAPLE CHIFFON PIE

Topped with whipped cream and a lavish sprinkling of grated maple sugar, this makes an elegant treat.

Pie shell, baked	**¼ teaspoon salt**
1 tablespoon gelatine	**2 egg yolks, well beaten**
2 tablespoons cold water	**1 cup whipping cream**
½ cup milk	**1 teaspoon vanilla**
½ cup maple syrup	**2 egg whites, stiffly beaten**

Soak the gelatine in the cold water. Heat milk, maple syrup and salt in the top of a double boiler, then slowly add the egg yolks. Add the gelatine, stir to dissolve and let the mixture cool.

Whip the cream, flavor it with vanilla and set half of it aside. Fold the rest, along with the egg whites, into the cooled custard. Pour into the baked pie shell, top with the remaining whipped cream and refrigerate until well chilled.

SUGAR PIE

Every summer, requests pour in for this sugary, yet creamy pie. People who travel, eat it in restaurants, then look for the recipe — which is almost as old as Canada. The following is made the way grand'mère taught me, though there are all kinds of recipes.

Pastry of your choice	**1 cup all-purpose flour**
½ teaspoon soda	**1 cup dark brown sugar**
¼ teaspoon vanilla	**Pinch nutmeg**
1½ cups maple syrup	**⅓ cup butter**

Line a 9-inch pie plate with pastry. Stir soda and vanilla into syrup and pour into pastry. Blend remaining ingredients with your fingertips until mixture is crumbly, then spread over syrup. Place a piece of foil under pan, because the pie often bubbles over. Bake at 350°F. for 30 minutes and let cool — it is best cold.

MAPLE SYRUP MOUSSE

This is a delightful frozen dessert when served in long fluted glasses or parfait glasses.

1 cup maple syrup	**1 pint whipping cream**
3 egg yolks, beaten	**3 egg whites**

Bring maple syrup to a fast rolling boil, boil 3 minutes and cool 5 minutes. Beat the egg yolks until light and pale yellow then pour the syrup slowly on top, beating constantly. Cook over very low heat until the ingredients have the texture of a custard. Stir constantly and do not boil.

Let the mixture cool and whip the cream and egg whites until stiff. Fold into the custard and pour into an oiled mould. Cover with foil paper and freeze. Take from refrigerator 15-20 minutes before serving. Top with a small macaroon or whipped cream.

SUGAR-HOUSE COOKIES

Because bacon and ham fat are plentiful in the larder at sugaring time, these old-fashioned cookies are made with one or the other. For added flavor toast the oatmeal in the oven. Whichever way these are made they are an unusual treat.

½ cup bacon or ham fat	**½ cup seedless raisins**
1 cup maple syrup	**1½ cups oatmeal**
1 egg	**1 teaspoon nutmeg**
1½ cups all-purpose flour	**¼ cup milk**
1 teaspoon salt	**½ cup nuts, chopped**
2 teaspoons baking powder	

Place the fat, maple syrup and egg in a bowl and beat until light and creamy. Sift together the flour, salt and baking powder. Fold in the raisins, oatmeal and nutmeg. Add the milk and nuts and blend thoroughly into the creamed mixture. Drop by spoonfuls on to a greased cookie sheet and bake 375°F. for 15 minutes.

SUCRE A LA CREME

In French Québec there are as many recipes for this maple fudge as there are bean recipes in Boston. This one is superb.

1 cup maple syrup	2 cups 15% cream
3 cups light brown sugar	Pinch of salt
1 cup sugar	1 tablespoon butter
2 tablespoons baking powder	2 teaspoons vanilla
1 cup milk and 1 cup 35% cream or	Nuts to taste

Place all ingredients except the last three in a large saucepan. Cook over medium heat, stirring constantly. The syrup will swell at the beginning of the cooking, but it will soon go down.

The fudge will be done when a candy thermometer reaches 240°F. or when a drop of it in cold water remains soft. Let the fudge cool, then add butter, vanilla and nuts, and stir until creamy. Spread into a buttered pan.

MAPLE SYRUP BROWN BREAD

This delicious bread is usually steamed, but it can also be baked. The baked version is very good, somewhat drier, of course, than the steamed. It should be served hot.

1 cup cornmeal	1 teaspoon soda
1¾ cups Graham or whole wheat flour	1 cup maple syrup
	2 cups buttermilk or sour milk
1 teaspoon salt	1 cup seedless raisins

Mix the two flours, salt and soda. Add the maple syrup to the milk and pour all at once over the dry ingredients.

Add the raisins and mix thoroughly. Pour into a well-greased 1½-quart mould, cover loosely with foil. Place in a steamer, or on a trivet in a saucepan large enough to leave a space all around the mould. Fill with water to halfway up the mould. Cover and steam over low heat for 3½ hours. Or bake at 325°F. for 1 hour, using 2 greased 4 x 8-inch breadpans. Cool on cake rack. Serve warm or warm up in the oven. It freezes very well. Not necessary to thaw out, simply place the frozen loaf in a 350°F. oven for 30 minutes or until hot.

PAIN AU SUCRE
(Sugar House Maple Toast)

A sugaring party spectacular, especially since I learned to make it at "grand'papa's" sugar house, with freshly beaten soft sugar. However grated maple sugar will do very well.

6 slices whole wheat or French bread	1-1½ cups soft or grated maple sugar
Butter	⅓ cup chopped walnuts
	Rich cream or sour cream

Toast the bread on one side. Butter the untoasted side. Sprinkle generously with the sugar, without going too near the edges. Place on broiler, 4 inches away from source of heat and broil until the sugar melts and bubbles. Set on a plate — each one sprinkles the nuts to taste on top and pours cream over all.

FROSTED MAPLE GINGERBREAD

Molasses, ginger and maple syrup are inextricably linked with early Canadian foods. The first two came as part of the English navy rations, the other from the Indians.

2⅓ cups all-purpose flour	1 cup maple syrup
1 teaspoon baking soda	1 cup sour cream
1½ teaspoons ginger	4 tablespoons melted butter
½ teaspoon salt	or bacon fat
1 egg	

Frosting:

2 - 3 cups icing sugar, sifted	1 tablespoon sour or
2 tablespoons soft butter	whipping cream
3 tablespoons maple syrup	

Sift together the flour, soda, ginger and salt. Beat the egg until it is foamy, then gradually beat in the maple syrup, sour cream, and butter or bacon fat. Gradually add the dry ingredients, beating until well blended.

Pour into a greased and lightly floured 11 x 7 x 1½-inch baking pan. Bake at 350°F. for 30-40 minutes, or until cake pulls away from the sides of the pan. Remove from the oven and let it cool.

Combine all the frosting ingredients in a bowl, beat with an electric mixer until smooth, creamy and of spreading consistency. Place the icing in big swirls on the cake and sprinkle to taste with chopped walnuts.

MAPLE CLOUD CAKE

This light feathery cake has a delicate flavor and a delectable icing. The cake by itself will freeze beautifully.

¾ cup maple syrup	1 teaspoon baking powder
4 eggs, separated	⅛ teaspoon ground
½ teaspoon vanilla	coriander (optional)
1 cup sifted all-purpose flour	¼ teaspoon salt

Icing:

1¼ cups maple syrup	2 egg whites

Boil syrup exactly 2 minutes. Beat egg whites until stiff and set aside. Beat egg yolks and vanilla until light, then gradually mix in boiled syrup.

Fold egg yolk mixture gently into egg whites. Sift remaining dry ingredients together 3 times and fold into egg mixture. Pour batter into an ungreased 9- or 10-inch tube pan. Bake at 325°F. for 50 minutes, or until done. When cake is cooked, invert pan on a cake rack and let cool for 1 hour. To unmould, pass a knife around the edges and ease cake out of the pan.

To make icing, boil syrup until it forms a firm ball when tested in ice water (328°F. on candy thermometer). Beat egg whites until stiff, then add hot syrup as in maple shortcake recipe. Continue beating until frosting stands in peaks, or cools. Spread on top and sides of cake.

MAPLE TOURLOUCHE

This is a sort of quick upside-down cake and a must in the sugaring season in Eastern Canada. It should be served hot with cold rich cream poured on top. As a variation, add some chopped walnuts to the hot syrup.

1 cup maple syrup	2 teaspoons baking powder
1 tablespoon soft butter	1/8 teaspoon salt
3 tablespoons sugar	1/4 teaspoon nutmeg or cinnamon
1 egg	1/2 cup milk
1 cup all-purpose flour	

Bring syrup to a boil and pour into a generously buttered 8 x 8 x 2-inch baking dish. Let stand in a warm place. With a large spoon or blending fork, beat butter, sugar and egg together until creamy.

Mix remaining dry ingredients and add with the milk to creamed mixture, stirring until well blended. Place as four large balls into hot syrup, then stretch dough with two forks until all are joined together. This is easy because the dough gets very soft when it comes in contact with the hot syrup.

Bake at 350°F. for 30 minutes, or until golden brown. When done, invert on a platter or serve directly from pan.

MAPLE SHORTCAKE

A very rich, sweet favorite at sugaring-off parties, this dessert goes well served after a thick slice of hot ham, with big mugs of steaming tea.

2 cups all-purpose flour	3/4 cup maple syrup
1 tablespoon baking powder	1 tablespoon butter
1/2 teaspoon salt	2 egg whites
1/8 teaspoon mace	1/2 cup whipping cream
1/2 cup soft butter	1/2 teaspoon vanilla
3/4 - 1 cup milk	

Mix flour, baking powder, salt and mace, then work in butter with fingertips. Add enough milk to make a soft dough, knead 5 or 6 times and divide in half. Grease two 8-inch pie plates and pat dough into each — as a cake, not as a pie crust. Bake at 400°F. for 15-18 minutes, or until brown. Unmould and set aside.

To make filling, boil syrup and butter until it forms a soft ball in ice water (238°F. on a candy thermometer). Beat egg whites until stiff and slowly pour hot syrup on top, beating constantly with an electric beater. If you use a hand rotary beater, pour in a little syrup, beat, pour more, beat until all syrup is used. Continue beating until filling is thick and smooth. Whip cream with vanilla and fold in. Spread between biscuit layers and on top.

LONG ON DUCK

Wild or domestic, a duck is a duck — the difference being that the domestic duck can be given a wild taste, but nothing can domesticate the elegant wild duck. If duck hunting is one of your husband's favorite sports, then you are in luck. If no such luck is yours, then replace the 2 or 3 wild ducks called for in a recipe by a 4- to 5-lb. domestic duck.

All across Canada a large Québec duck farm supplies nice, white, plump frozen domestic ducks. I find duck difficult to cook well, so we must get acquainted with basic instructions on duck preparation, cooking and carving.

HOW TO PREPARE A DOMESTIC DUCK FOR COOKING

If you have bought a 4-5 lb. (average weight of a drawn domestic duck) frozen duck, thaw it, unwrapped, in the refrigerator for 24-48 hours. This will thaw the bird gradually without affecting its flavor.

Do not wash the duck under running water. Instead, pat the inside of the duck with absorbent paper and then rub it, inside and out, with a cloth that has been dipped in fresh lemon juice or cider vinegar.

You may, if you wish, remove some of the inner fat from the duck before roasting by the following method: dry and rub the duck with lemon juice or cider vinegar and then brown on all sides in an enamelled cast-iron pan, over medium heat. This will release a good amount of the fat.

Remove the duck from the pan and cook it according to the recipe. Do not, however, throw away the fat. You may cool it and store it for later use in general cooking. You'll find that it gives an interesting flavor to many foods.

HOW TO PREPARE A WILD DUCK FOR COOKING

The advice that follows I have learned from the best duck hunting guide in Sorel, near Montreal.

— Whenever possible pluck the bird in the field. Never stuff it in a bag or hunting coat until it is cold.

— Cut the throat and hang the head down to bleed.

— Remove the feathers from the crop and the tail, pulling them gently towards the tail, so as not to break the skin.

— Slit the skin over the crop and remove it.

— Cut down to the vent and remove the entrails, separating the giblets and putting them back in the cavity. Carefully cut the oil sac at the base of the tail.

— Stuffing the cavity with fresh cool grass helps to keep some air circulating inside.

At home, pluck the duck. Never dip duck in hot water to pluck as the feathers are too well oiled.

Have a large pan of boiling water, at least 4 to 6 quarts. When boiling, add ½ lb. of paraffin and let it melt. It will stay on top.

Dip the duck in the water and paraffin. Lift — it will then be coated with wax, without being wet. It will take 6 to 8 dips to build up a sufficiently thick coat. Let the paraffin cool and harden. You may then scrape it off with a dull knife or roll it off with your fingers. The down and pin feathers will come off with it.

HOW TO ROAST A DOMESTIC DUCK

A shallow, enamelled or black cast-iron baking pan is best, but any pan about 10 x 14 inches and not more than 3 inches deep will serve well for roasting.

Place the duck, breast side up, on a large crust of dried bread. This will prevent drying. The crust of bread will absorb a good deal of the fat. Roast the duck in a 325°F. oven — 25 minutes to the pound for medium, and 35 minutes to the pound for well done. Do not cover, baste or prick the duck with a fork or knife during roasting. Piercing the duck will release the juices and cause drying.

When 1 hour of roasting remains, you may brush the duck with a mixture of 2 tablespoons of honey and 1 teaspoon of Kitchen Bouquet or soy sauce. This will give the skin a golden brown color and a crispy texture.

HOW TO ROAST A WILD DUCK

There are many ways to roast a wild duck, all equally good. The Québec way, adapted from the French cuisine, is easy and always a success. A 350°F. preheated oven is the right heat for wild duck — usually 35 to 50 minutes in all, depending on size.

2 **wild ducks**	½ **teaspoon salt**
2 **carrots, peeled and**	¼ **teaspoon pepper**
chopped fine	2 **large onions**
2 **stalks celery, diced**	½ **cup chicken stock**
1 **large onion, diced**	½ **cup white or port wine**
¼ **cup salad oil or melted butter**	**or Madeira**

Mix together in the dripping pan the carrots, celery, chopped onion and salad oil or melted butter. Place over direct heat and stir until the vegetables are well coated with the oil or butter. Spread in a roasting pan large enough to sit ducks on. Place onion in each cavity. Place ducks on vegetable bed. Brush top with some of the oil in the bottom of the pan. Add salt and pepper. Pour the chicken stock and wine around the ducks.

Roast in a preheated 350°F. oven 35 to 50 minutes. Arrange ducks on hot platter. Strain the pan juices. Use as is or thicken to taste with 2 teaspoons arrowroot or cornstarch blended with 2 tablespoons cold water.

STUFFED ROAST DUCK GRAND'MERE

This is an old family recipe that I always enjoy. Just before serving, grand'mère used to remove the stuffing from the duck and spread it on a thick, buttered slice of toasted homemade bread. To serve this, she sliced the bread in long fingers, set a finger on each plate and then poured a little gravy on top. It was superb.

4½ - 5 lb. domestic duck
 3 tablespoons butter or duck fat
 1 large onion, diced
 ½ cup celery, diced
 1 cup dry toasted bread, cubed
 ¼ cup fresh parsley, minced
 2 cups unpeeled apples, diced
　 Grated peel and juice of
　 1 lemon

 ¼ teaspoon cinnamon
　 Pinch of anise or caraway seeds
　 Pinch of cloves
　 Salt and pepper, to taste
 2 teaspoons butter
 1 teaspoon soy sauce
 1 tablespoon honey
 1 tablespoon flour
 ½ - ¾ cup apple juice

Clean the duck and prepare the stuffing. Melt the 3 tablespoons of butter in a saucepan, add the onion and the celery and simmer 10 minutes over low heat. This will soften the vegetables. Make sure they do not brown. Remove from heat and add the toasted bread cubes, parsley, diced apples, lemon peel and juice, cinnamon, anise or caraway seeds, cloves, and salt and pepper to taste. Blend the whole thoroughly and stuff the duck with this mixture. Place the duck in a roasting pan and spread it with a mixture of 2 teaspoons butter, soy sauce and honey. Roast duck in a 325°F. oven until cooked to taste.

To make the gravy, remove the excess fat from the pan. Add the 1 tablespoon flour to the drippings and stir over low heat until the flour is browned. Add the apple juice and stir until light and creamy. Serve separately.

PLUM PERFECT DUCK

Plums are as good with duck as oranges. In the fall plum season, use 10-12 stewed plums, in the winter, use canned ones. The little blue plums, freestone and slightly acid are the best to use.

⅓ cup bottled lemon juice
 1 crushed chicken bouillon cube
 ½ teaspoon tarragon or marjoram
5-lb. duck (domestic)
 1 large chopped onion
 2 tablespoons butter
10 - 12 stewed plums or
　 16-oz. can drained plums

 1 cup plum juice
 ½ cup bottled lemon juice
 ⅓ cup chili sauce
 2 tablespoons soy sauce
 1 - 2 tablespoons sugar
 1 teaspoon Worcestershire sauce
 1 teaspoon ground ginger
 ½ teaspoon dry mustard

44

Combine the ⅓ cup bottled lemon juice, bouillon cube and tarragon or marjoram. Prick the surface of the duck, then brush the cavity and the outside with the lemon juice mixture.

Roast in an open pan at 450°F. for 15-20 minutes. Turn the duck several times during this period, then pour off the excess fat. Reduce the heat to 350°F. and continue roasting for an additional 1½ hours. Prick occasionally and if necessary, pour off the fat.

In the meantime, sauté the onion in the butter. Make a purée of the plums and plum juice. Add it to the onion along with the ½ cup of bottled lemon juice, chili sauce, soy sauce, sugar, Worcestershire sauce, ginger and dry mustard. Simmer 15 minutes.

During the last half hour of roasting, brush the duck several times with the sauce. Serve the remaining sauce separately.

GLAZED DUCKLING

Very beautiful, very delicious and very easy. Use 3 wild ducks or 2 domestic ducks.

3 wild ducks or 2 domestic ducks	**1 cup black currant jelly**
Salt and pepper	**1 cup consommé**
¼ teaspoon rosemary or sage	**½ teaspoon ground ginger OR**
¼ cup maple syrup	**1 tablespoon grated fresh ginger root**
¼ cup fresh orange juice	**1 teaspoon curry**
1 cup orange juice	**¼ teaspoon nutmeg**

Clean the ducks and place them on a rack in a roasting pan. Sprinkle inside and out with salt and pepper. Rub rosemary or sage inside each duck. Roast until done or 30 minutes to the pound in a 400°F. oven. The ducks are done when the drumstick wiggles easily when moved. Pierce the skin once during the cooking period so that the fat will run out. Half an hour before they are done, stir together the maple syrup and ¼ cup fresh orange juice, pour off the fat from the dripping pan and brush the ducks with the orange juice mixture. Continue cooking. Then remove the ducks from the roasting pan. Keep in a warm place. To the juice in the pan add 1 cup orange juice, the currant jelly, the consommé, ground ginger or grated fresh ginger root, curry and nutmeg. Boil over direct heat, while stirring, until the sauce is reduced to a nice consistency. Cut the ducks into individual portions with kitchen shears or slice the meat if you prefer. Cover with boiling sauce.

CANARD A LA RHUBARBE
(Rhubarb Duck)

The first rhubarb was brought to Québec by the English. It had come to England in the 1700s by way of Padua in Italy. A guide who lived with the Indians for most of his life had learned and mastered many a way to cook duck. He believed that rhubarb restored a man's strength and he used lots of it.

2 **wild ducks or 1 domestic duck**	1 **cup cold water**
2 **teaspoons ground ginger**	2 **tablespoons butter**
6 **cups rhubard, diced**	2 **tablespoons flour**
1 **tablespoon cinnamon**	1 **cup apple or orange juice**
1 **cup sugar**	1 **tablespoon honey**
½ **cup honey**	**Salt and pepper to taste**

If you do not care for the flavor of wild or domestic duck, remove the skin and all visible fat and rub all over with the ginger, or leave the skin on and rub all over inside cavity with the ginger.

Mix the rhubarb, cinnamon, sugar and honey. Use 1½ cups of this to stuff the ducks. Place the ducks in a deep cast-iron saucepan. Pour the water on top, and fill the pan with the rhubarb mixture. Be sure to cover the entire duck at least one inch deep. Add more rhubarb if necessary. Cover tightly. Place in a 375°F. oven for 1½ hours. My guide used to leave the pot 6 to 8 hours buried in the breakfast embers. Lower the heat to 350°F. after 1 hour.

When done remove duck to a hot platter. Melt the butter, add the flour, stir together and add the apple or orange juice, honey, salt and pepper. Cook, stirring all the time, until creamy. Pour into the rhubarb in the pan. Simmer together for 10 minutes. Pour some over the duck. Serve rest of sauce in a bowl.

SAGE AND ONION STUFFING

Sufficient for 1 domestic or 3 wild ducks.

4 **onions, chopped**	1 **egg slightly beaten**
¼ **cup butter or bacon fat**	1 **teaspoon salt**
4 **cups soft breadcrumbs**	½ **teaspoon freshly ground**
6 **to 10 sage leaves, chopped or**	**pepper**
1 **teaspoon dried sage**	

Melt the butter or bacon fat, add the onions, and simmer a few minutes until browned.

In a bowl combine the breadcrumbs, onions and butter, sage leaves or dried sage, and egg. Toss until well mixed. Season with salt and pepper. Stuff the bird or birds lightly.

LIVER STUFFING

Sufficient for one small domestic or two wild ducks.

1 **or 2 duck livers, chopped**	1 **teaspoon marjoram**
2 **scallions, tops and all,**	2 **tablespoons minced parsley**
chopped	¼ **cup butter, melted**
3 **stalks celery, diced**	1 **egg, beaten lightly**
2 **cups soft breadcrumbs**	**Salt and freshly ground pepper**
½ **cup chopped walnuts, or**	
pignolia nuts	

46

Combine the liver, scallions, celery, and bread crumbs and mix thoroughly. Add the walnuts or pignolia nuts, parsley, marjoram, melted butter, and finally the egg. Season to taste. Toss together lightly, and stuff the ducks.

HOW TO CARVE A DUCK

Carving a duck is more difficult than carving a chicken, as the joints are tougher.

Before you begin carving, remember to remove all the juice from the inside of the cooked duck by standing the bird upright and letting it flow out. Then add it to the sauce.

The Three Ways to Carve a Duck

First method: The choicest slices are from the breast. Be careful, however, and more or less scrape the meat off the bone. Serve each guest half a breast, plus a drumstick or thigh section.

Second method: Place the duck breast upward, and point the legs to your right. With poultry shears or kitchen shears, cut through the top of the bird from end to end. Turn the duck over and proceed in the same manner along the centre of the back. Cut each half crosswise, just before the thigh. You will then have two portions with the drumsticks and thighs and a small amount of the breast meat, and two portions with the wings but a major part of the breast meat. My favorite piece is the drumstick and thigh.

Always serve a basket of paper napkins with duck carved this way because you will probably have to use your fingers some time during the meal.

Third method: First, remove the legs by making a circular incision with the point of a knife where they join the body. Insert the fork in the thigh, and with a quick movement lift the leg towards you and cut through the joint.

Insert the fork in the lower part of the carcass to get a good grip on the bird, and begin to carve slices from the breast on one side, beginning at the wing and finishing against the breastbone. A large duck should yield 4 to 6 slices on each side.

Separate the legs in two portions, cut at the joint between thigh and leg.

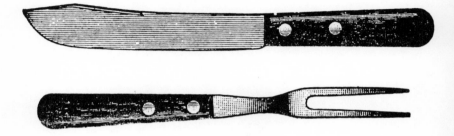

ONTARIO

Upper Canada, as Ontario used to be called, has a different type of cuisine than the provinces of the Eastern Seaboard. Much of it has been revived and kept alive by Upper Canada Village, so that our generation can see something of yesterday's life.

Erika Gaertner of Chalk River wrote a very interesting book *Harvest Without Planting,* which is an account of the table delicacies of our forefathers, all edible and many quite fascinating.

When you try some of the following recipes, you will wonder at how good cooking ideas were, and how these same ideas have lasted for generations. There is always something new for us in what is old.

UPPER CANADA REVISITED

TROUT IN CORN HUSKS

This recipe is an old idea, learned from the Indians who were masters at cooking small fish in this marvellous way. I found the recipe in a fascinating book with a long title: *The Family Doctor, containing a description of the principal diseases to which most persons in this country are liable, together with their treatment and cure supplied so that every man can be his own doctor. To which is appended the best health recipe for Upper Canadians by the doctor's Cook woman.* It was published in Toronto in 1874.

Because this is an open-fire cooking technique, it is suitable for the modern-day backyard barbecue as well as open fires on camping trips. You can use trout, or any pan fish, such as perch.

Clean and scale the fish, and place a lump of butter or melted salt pork in the cavity. Sprinkle with black pepper. Wrap each fish in a whole husk of corn, from which the corn and silk have been removed. Smooth down the husk and tie at the silk end. Place at edge of fire. Cover with live coals. It cooks to perfection in 15 minutes.

GAME AND BEANS IN A CLAY POT

This was described in Volume II of *Kemp's Travels* as being a favorite game dish of the Upper Canadian and northern trappers (about 1862-1871). For an Early Canadian family, thrift was the main reason this old and delicious dish was served so often. All each dish needed was a small piece of meat served atop a "big mess" of the most delicious beans. Sometimes a wild bird was replaced by a stewing hen. You might prefer to do this.

The night before, soak 2 lbs. of beans in enough cold water to cover. In the morning, boil, covered, without salting, in their soaking water for about an hour. Save the water.

Take 2 partridges (when using partridges, split them in two, or use a cut up stewing hen). If the bird is fat, pull excess fat out and melt it down. Cut bird into individual pieces and shake pieces in a bag with 4 tablespoons salted and peppered flour. Then brown chicken or partridge in fat over medium heat.

Cover bottom of a casserole or bean pot with layer of boiled beans. Top with a few slices of onion. Lay on top of onion a few pieces of chicken or partridge, then more beans, onion and chicken until all is used. On top, place a one pound piece of salt pork, either left whole or sliced. To the reserved bean water, add ½ cup molasses, 1 teaspoon dry mustard, 1 teaspoon savory (or 1 teaspoon pine needles (the Indian way), 1 tablespoon coarse salt. Pour over beans, and fill pot until you can see the liquid — if more liquid is required, use cold water. Cover, and bake in 250°F. oven 5-6 hours. The finished dish should have tender beans full of partridge or chicken flavor and be moist, but not watery.

ROAST YOUNG WILD GOOSE

I first read of this dish in an old journal *The Jesuit Relation,* in the Quebec City Archives. I include the Indian recipe here because Upper Canadians were considered best at cooking it — and also because they had the best wild goose. (Obviously, you will need a hunter handy to supply you with the bird.) The Indians used to say that the young wild goose was at its best when shot on its first flight south or to the far-north breeding ground. How right they were! In either case the geese were usually shot over a mud flat and were quite dirty. So the Upper Canada women cleaned them in a special way now used by French-Canadian women even for domestic goose.

Pluck and clean the goose. Singe off remaining down or pin feathers. Do not use the giblets. They are too gamey. Make a solution of mild soapsuds in warm water, and scrub the goose thoroughly, inside and out. Rinse with plenty of clear water and wipe dry with a towel. Rub the bird thoroughly inside and out with coarse salt and a half lemon. The bird is now ready to be cooked. The favorite Early Canadian way was stuffed and roasted. For the stuffing they used a mixture of crumbled stale bread, sage, black pepper, cloves and cinnamon, minced onions and dried celery leaves, well mixed. Then they added one cup of fried, diced salt pork, fat and all, along with a few cups of unpeeled sour apples (wild apples were favored). Then the goose was roasted the equivalent of 20 minutes to the pound in a 350°F. oven.

BAKED KETTLE OF POT-AU-FEU

I found this recipe in *Cook Book for Home Comfort — Army Posts and Steamboats* (published in Toronto, 1884). The text also mentioned the French-Canadian way of using pot-au-feu. This dish turns up on the menus of such hostelries as Belleville's Hotel Quinte, Toronto's Walker House Corner, and the New Union Station Dining Department in the 1890s.

As the name indicates, it was influenced by the French-Canadian idea of pot-au-feu: meat cooked in soup in a pot. It was eaten with large slices of bread as the evening meal. My version is a soup and boiled beef, a one-meal-in-itself dish. You make it with chuck or brisket (left in one piece), and lots of root vegetables. When well prepared, this dish is suitable for parties.

3-lb. piece of shoulder or rump of beef	**1 medium parsnip, peeled and cut in four**
1 lb. knuckle bone, sawed in two, lengthwise	**2 stalks celery, left whole**
Cold water	**3 leeks, whole (optional)**
1 tablespoon butter	**6 - 8 small onions, whole**
1 teaspoon sugar	**1 bay leaf**
1 onion, finely chopped	**1 whole clove**
3 - 6 whole carrots	**2 tablespoons coarse salt**
1 small turnip, peeled and cut in two	**A pinch of thyme**

Put in the soup kettle, the piece of beef and the knuckle bone. Cover with cold water, and bring it to full rolling boil. After boiling 5 minutes drain off water and cover with 4½ quarts cold water. Return to boil. Lower heat, and simmer, covered, for 1½-2 hours, or until tender.

Melt the butter in a frying pan. Add sugar. Stir together until sugar is dark brown, then add the onion, finely chopped. Fry onion in this colored butter until onion is well browned. Add it to soup after meat has cooked for one hour. Then add whole carrots, turnip, peeled and cut in two, parsnip, peeled and cut in four, celery stalks, left whole, leeks, left whole, and small onions, left whole, bay leaf, clove, coarse salt and thyme. Then simmer gently, covered, until meat and vegetables are tender. To serve, slice beef, and surround with vegetables. Serve one cup of hot, strained bouillon for each person.

VOYAGEUR BEAN SOUP

This soup is the voyageur version of Quebec pea soup. Very different, but equally good. It is traditionally served with hot cornbread.

1 lb. navy beans or yellow peas	**3 carrots, sliced**
3 quarts cold water	**1 tablespoon salt**
1 ham bone	**¼ teaspoon pepper**
1 cup celery, chopped	**½ teaspoon sage or savory**
2 cups raw potatoes, diced	**Small can of tomatoes**
1 large onion, finely chopped	**(optional)**

Place the beans or peas in a soup kettle with the ham bone and the cold water. Bring to a boil, cover and boil slowly for 2 hours. Add the rest of the ingredients, bring back to a boil. Cover and simmer over low heat for another 2 hours or until the beans or peas are tender.

This freezes to perfection, and reheats beautifully. In the old days, they never served this soup the day it was made; often it was kept frozen in a large vat, in the snow, and cut with an axe. When it got cold and thick, it was reheated and served.

THE OLD WAY WITH GREEN BEANS

The next two recipes come from a small booklet published in 1889 by Brown Bros., Ordonance Square, Halifax. They refer to them as "Upper Canada Traditional Dishes." In this same booklet they give recipes that "our English forefathers have left us" for "warming over cold fragments" (which, to us, are slices of cold roast beef). Another recipe is titled: "Read this — make it and cough no more" (our own ginger crackers)." Also "The good boys die young unless they eat our Graham bread."

Place fresh-picked green beans in a "bean cook pot," Cover with cold water and top with a good-sized piece of salt pork. Cover pot and start cooking slowly. Fry an onion in melted diced salt pork. Scrape contents of frying pan into bean cook pot. Cover, and cook about one hour. Don't let the pot cook dry, because the beans are served, undrained, in a considerable amount of their cooking liquid, with the sliced salt pork — and lots of freshly baked bread to mop it all up.

PICKLED WILD MUSHROOMS

This was a contribution of the English settlers to Upper Canada's traditional cooking. Gathering wild mushrooms is a lost art, but this old recipe can be used for cultivated mushrooms with equal success — and they make a most pleasant hors d'oeuvre or pickle.

Tie up in a piece of cheesecloth, several strips of parsley, pinch of thyme, a bay leaf, a whole clove, a dozen peppercorns. Put these in a saucepan with 2 cups water, 1 cup olive oil, ½ cup vinegar (I sometimes like to use lemon juice instead of vinegar). Let boil 5 minutes. Then add 1 lb. button mushrooms, the stems neatly clipped off, and let it all boil for 15 minutes. Remove from heat, take away spice bag, let mushrooms cool in juice. Pot, seal, and keep in a cool, dark place.

53

VICTUALS OF QUALITY

At a country auction in Quebec the auctioneer offered a torn straw basket full of "medicine books". I knew that such books of the 1800s and early 1900s were full of observations on food as well as remedies for the family and horses. So I made a bid and got the basket — and so received ten times my money's worth. Among the volumes was an 85-page book with a hard cover published in Upper Canada in 1901. Its title was *Victuals of Quality,* and it contained two chapters of unusual ideas. These are my favorites.

For Delicate Fingers

The hostess with delicate taste has an unusual way to offer a snack with champagne in a moonlit garden. She fills nasturtium flowers with fresh cream cheese made light by the addition of whipped cream.

Sweet Peace Applesauce

When you next serve a golden, fragrant roast of pork, serve it with applesauce made sweet with a liqueur glass of port wine, along with a pinch of sage and cinnamon. Top and beat with a piece of butter, but never, never add sugar.

Fruit Temptation

Cook enough of the fresh fruit of your choice in a minute quantity of water, over low heat in a covered saucepan, to make 2 cups of fruit purée after being put through a sieve. To the fruit add a syrup made with 1½ cups sugar and ½ cup water, the juice of 2 lemons or 2 oranges. Mix well and freeze until mushy.

Pleasant Raspberry

A Canadian trifle of raspberry. Layers of French macaroons soaked in Spanish sherry with a thick coating of custard on each layer, and on the custard, sweetened raspberries. A few hours in the cold room, and you have a most seasonal dessert.

THE MUSHROOM INDUSTRY

This is the magic story of mushrooms — how they grow, how they are processed, and how they may be used to enhance any dish, anytime.

For many, many centuries, mushrooms lived in a dark, mysterious world of their own. The wild varieties were known and enjoyed by the ancient Chinese who used them for medicinal purposes; by the early Greeks and Romans who considered them as food for the gods and for the enjoyment of the aristocracy only; and by the Egyptians who thought the common man so unworthy of these fragile fungi that only the Pharaohs were permitted to eat them.

It was not until the late 16th century, during the reign of Louis XIV, that the art of cultivating mushrooms was discovered. The Parisians experimented with decomposing organic matter (manure) and the growth of the mushroom plant. By 1749 mushrooms were being grown successfully in caves and cellars with better results than when they were grown outdoors. The quarries under Paris housed the mushroom beds and by 1900 about 1500 miles of these beds were winding their way through the caves under Paris.

Canadian mushrooms first came on the commercial market in 1912. By 1969 the Canadian Mushroom Growers' Association reported that approximately twenty-seven million pounds of mushrooms were produced in Canada: of this amount, between fifteen and eighteen million pounds were grown in Ontario alone.

Canadians, today, eat about one pound per person per year, approximately three times as much as fifteen years ago. New Canadians and an increased interest in gourmet cooking and foreign foods have made us more aware of the mushroom's flavorful pleasures.

Hints on How to Buy, Keep, and Prepare Mushrooms:

1. Eat mushrooms often for good nutrition:
   (a) They contribute substantial amounts of Viamin B — thiamine, riboflavin, and niacin to the diet, as well as limited amounts of Vitamin C, calcium, phosphorous, and iron.
   (b) They contain impressive amounts of protein and are low in fats and sugars — they are a weight-watcher's joy at only 66 calories per pound (a pound is 4-5 half cup servings).
2. Versatility is essential when serving mushrooms — they are just as delicious eaten raw in salads as they are broiled, sauteed, or barbecued and put next to steak.
3. Enhance the taste appeal of almost any meat, fish, poultry, egg, or vegetable dish by adding a few or many mushrooms. The Chinese have shown us how the small cost of mushrooms is more than worth the unique flavor they add to a variety of dishes.
4. Select fresh mushrooms carefully.
   (a) An obvious indication of freshness is a smooth, white, unblemished cap, with no space between the inverted rim of the cap and stem. As a mushroom matures and loses its moisture, the cap opens, exposing on its underside, a fluted formation called gills. These should be light in color, not black or brown.
   (b) The larger mushrooms are considered by connoisseurs to be the pick of the lot. Button mushrooms, a homemaker's delight, are simply at the infant stage of the mushroom crop, picked because of crowding. They lack the full flavor of more mature mushrooms.
   (c) Short stemmed mushrooms are preferred because although perfectly edible, stems sometimes lack the tenderness of the cap.
5. Handle mushrooms tenderly.
   (a) Mushrooms object violently to having a bath although they enjoy a quick shower if they're dried off well. Because of their

sponge-like capacity for any liquid, mushrooms will throw off any absorbed water at the first sign of heat. This loses valuable flavor and tenderness. Washing quickly under running water and drying thoroughly should satisfy the most fastidious cook and at the same time allows the mushrooms to retain their natural moisture when heated.

(b) Never peel fresh mushrooms. The most intense flavor lies in the skin. At the most, snip off only the sandy stem tips.

(c) Lighten or preserve the color of mushrooms by sprinkling lightly with lemon juice or white wine.

(d) Do not overcook mushrooms. Sauté small amounts at a time in limited amounts of butter, oil, or cream — 5-6 minutes is plenty of time.

(e) Refrigeration is needed to prolong the life of the mushroom. Unless they are maintained at a temperature of 30°F.-38°F. the veins open resulting in rapid dehydration and discoloration. Kept in an open container in the refrigerator vegetable crisper, mushrooms will keep for up to one week.

(f) Extra quantities of fresh mushrooms can be frozen successfully. They should be precooked first because of their high water content (85%-90%). Prepare the mushrooms as for immediate serving, package, and freeze immediately. Only small amounts of mushrooms should be done at one time, and these should NOT be thawed before reheating.

(g) To prepare canned mushrooms, drain thoroughly (except those in a cream or butter sauce, or gravy). Save liquid for use in soups and sauces. Dry mushrooms on paper towelling to get rid of excess moisture, then sauté as you would fresh mushrooms.

SOME TEMPTING WAYS TO USE MUSHROOMS

Alone or with an unlimited variety of other foods, cultivated mushrooms are delightful served raw or cooked, whole, sliced, or chopped. *Larousse Gastronomique,* the bible of French gastronomy, lists over 40 different ways to serve mushrooms, but any reliable recipe book will list a choice of interesting recipes.

Here are some suggestions for using our flavorful fungi.

Appetizers
— mushroom caps filled with cream cheese, eggs, seafood, or stuffing, then broiled.
— mushrooms dipped in a batter and fondued.

Soups
— plain or creamed mushroom or clam soup.

Sauces
— creamed mushrooms on toast, or baked or mashed potatoes, also mushrooms are almost indispensable to tomato sauces.

Salads
— raw mushrooms add that gourmet touch.

56

Main dishes
- add grilled, creamed or plain mushrooms to seafood, chicken, beef, or veal, left-overs, liver, or omelettes.
- excellent addition to broiled or barbecued kabobs.

Vegetables and Side dishes
- serve alone, broiled or stuffed.
- add to your favorite poultry stuffing.
- compliment green peas, or beans, squash, spinach, onions, potatoes, or broccoli.

Snacks
- add to pizza, chili, cheese and ham sandwiches.

Garnishes
- just use your imagination.

FINGERTIP FACTS ABOUT MUSHROOMS

1. 1 lb. fresh mushrooms, cooked and drained equals two (10 oz.) tins of drained mushrooms.
2. Stems and skin possess the greatest amount of flavor. Simmer them for consommé.
3. To reconstitute dried mushrooms, soak, covered, from ½-4 hours in lukewarm water. Drain, and use as for fresh mushrooms, saving the water for sauces or soups.
   3 oz. dried mushrooms, reconstituted = 1 pound fresh.
4. Never use a lid when sauteeing.
5. The definition of sauteeing is worth remembering: To sauté is to cook in a heavy frying pan with plenty of surface, using only enough butter to prevent sticking. Portions should not touch each other, or be stacked, or be moist, which will cause steam to form and will prevent browning. The pan should be HOT when mushrooms are added so they brown immediately.
6. Suitable seasonings to enhance the flavor of mushrooms are garlic, paprika, marjoram, chives, and parsley.

FROM PIG TO PORK

The Prairies are the Canadian bread basket, but Ontario — the food basket.

The pork chops or bacon on your table have come a long way from the pig on the farm. Through research and advanced technical know-how, Ontario's pork industry converted over 2,652,000 pigs into wholesome nourishing pork products last year. The chain from pork producer to meat packer to retail outlet to consumer to table is a long one involving a very superior product. It is much leaner, healthier, cheaper, and more prestigious than the pork available to our ancestors years ago.

APPLE-CROWNED PORK CHOPS

6 loin pork chops	¼ teaspoon nutmeg
1 medium red onion	½ teaspoon basil
2 - 3 tart red apples	⅛ teaspoon cloves
½ cup golden raisins	1 cup water
1 tablespoon brown sugar	2 tablespoons red currant jelly
1 teaspoon salt	
Few grains pepper	

Brown pork chops on both sides in their own fat. Transfer to a baking dish.

Cover chops with thinly sliced onion and add unpeeled apples which have been cored and cut into sixths.

Cover raisins with boiling water to plump. Drain. Scatter raisins over chops.

Combine brown sugar, salt, pepper, nutmeg, basil, and cloves. Sprinkle over surface. Pour water into baking dish. Cover.

Bake at 350°F. for 1½ hours. Remove cover during last half hour of baking time.

Arrange chops and topping on serving platter. Stir currant jelly into sauce in pan; pour over all.

MACDONALD INSTITUTE PORK CHOPS

Pork chops, baked slowly in seasoned canned tomatoes, are deliciously moist and tender in this recipe from the Food Department, Macdonald Institute, University of Guelph. Add seasonings according to your own taste.

Cover pork chops with canned tomatoes seasoned with:

Sugar	Bay leaves
Lemon juice	Celery, diced
Onions	Salt and pepper

Bake in a 350°F. oven, in a covered dish until chops are tender.

EVEN CHEDDAR IS EXOTIC

A fine cheddar cheese is one that is made of whole, unpasteurized, summer milk from cows which have drunk fresh, clean water and have fed on green grasses, free from any flora that might taint the milk. A good cheese should be aged slowly and lovingly until it is eighteen months to two years old. It will then be full in flavor and sharp, without any bitterness.

This is the way the renowned cheese man of Jermyn street in London described a large wheel of cheddar. He then asked me to taste a paper-thin slice of it. He was right. The moment it touched my tongue I could feel all the penetrating quality of this perfect cheddar.

Alas! It is not, and cannot always be perfect, but it is rarely not good. Most of us associate cheddar with Ontario. When I can find a good

"Ontario"-mild from summer milk, I always have some. With an apple and a glass of port wine, it is the perfect ending to a meal.

The art of cheese making was introduced to the early settlers of Eastern Ontario by the United Empire Loyalists. By 1854, some 2,000,000 pounds of domestic cheese were produced in Canada for home use, and for export to the United States.

By 1964, Cheddar cheese making in Ontario had become an 83,000,000 pound, $30,000,000 industry. Today — the entire cheese industry, including both Cheddar and specialty types, has reached the 110,000,000-pound, $60,000,000 mark.

Of all the cheese produced in Canada today, 50% of all Cheddar and 75% of the foreign and specialty cheeses are manufactured in Ontario.

STORING CHEESE

If it is improperly wrapped, cheese will lose moisture and take on "off" flavors from other foods.

To store, wrap small pieces of cheese carefully in moisture-vapor-proof foil or film.

Protect the cut surface of large pieces of cheese with a coating of paraffin, or press a heavy piece of waxed paper to the cut surface with a hot iron.

Keep cheese in a dry cool place.

COOKING WITH CHEESE

Don't cook cheese, just melt it. High heat, or overcooking makes cheese stringy and leathery.

Crumble it into a cream sauce.

Melt it into an omelet for breakfast.

Toast it in a sandwich for lunch.

Spread it on crackers for snacks.

Grate it over a casserole for a crispy topping.

Pile it on a tray with fresh fruit.

Use it as a low-cost meat substitute, with no waste factor to consider.

Enjoy it with an apple, watching TV.

To bring out the true flavor of any cheese, allow it to come to room temperature before serving.

To melt cheese, place it over hot water, or add grated cheese to a hot mixture.

When making a sauce, add the sliced or grated cheese after the sauce is cooked; heat only until the cheese is melted. Overcooking may cause a milk-egg-cheese sauce to curdle or separate.

To make a cheese omelet, add the cheese just before folding.

ONTARIO MILD CHEDDAR SOUP

For my tenth birthday, my father took me on a boat trip across Lake Ontario from the American side to Toronto. To me, at that age, it was a great adventure. I still remember some of the things I ate. The lake boat I was on happened to have a famous French chef who was working there as a rest from his usually heavy duties. I think he must have enjoyed it, to make so many good things. I liked this soup so much, I insisted my father ask for the recipe for me. We were successful in getting it.

3 tablespoons butter	2 - 3 cups Ontario mild cheddar
2 carrots, grated	cheese, grated
½ cup celery, diced	2 tablespoons butter
1 large onion, minced	4 tablespoons flour
1 small parsnip, peeled and	4 cups consommé
grated	2 cups milk
	Salt and pepper

Melt the 3 tablespoons butter in a saucepan, add the vegetables. Cover and simmer 10 minutes over low heat. Blend 2 tablespoons butter with flour and add to vegetables and consommé. Stir together until creamy and continue cooking over low heat for about 5-8 minutes. Add grated cheese. Stir until melted. Then, gradually add cold milk. Continue to cook for another 10 minutes. Do not boil after cheese is added. Season to taste with salt and pepper, add a big handful of chopped parsley, and serve.

TWO-CHEDDAR MACARONI
Cheesy, Easy and Tasty.

8 oz. elbow macaroni	3 cups canned tomatoes
½ teaspoon savory	Salt and pepper, to taste
½ teaspoon sugar	1¼ cups sliced Ontario mild or
3 green onions, finely chopped	medium cheddar
1½ cups grated cheddar	2 eggs, beaten
4 cups diced fresh tomatoes or	1 cup milk

Boil the macaroni according to directions on package, then drain and pour into a 2-quart casserole. Stir savory, sugar, salt, pepper, green onions and grated cheddar into tomatoes and pour over macaroni. Mix.

Place sliced cheese on top. Beat eggs with milk and pour over macaroni, but do not mix. Bake 40-50 minutes at 350°F.

CHEDDAR CHEESE SHORTCAKE
These piquant little biscuits are tasty by themselves and superb with salads, cocktails or lobster.

½ cup grated sharp Cheddar	1 teaspoon chutney
½ cup soft butter	1 cup or slightly more
¼ teaspoon HP sauce	all-purpose flour

Cream the Cheddar and soft butter until light and creamy. Add the HP sauce and the chutney. Mix well. Slowly add the flour until a smooth, soft dough is formed. Wrap dough in waxed paper and chill 1 hour. Shape into small balls and place on an ungreased cookie sheet. Bake in a pre-heated 400°F. oven about 10 minutes, or until light brown.

CHEDDAR CHEESE WAFERS

These crisp cheese wafers are easy to prepare and, if stored in a metal box in a cool place, they will keep for months. Serve them hot or cold.

1 cup grated strong Cheddar cheese	¼ cup soft butter
	½ cup all-purpose flour
1 cup crushed potato chips	1 teaspoon prepared mustard

Measure the cheese and potato chips after grating or crushing. Place the cheese in a bowl, with the remaining ingredients and blend. Place on an unbuttered baking sheet in small spoonfuls, flattening slightly with the bottom of the spoon.

Bake at 375°F. for 5-8 minutes, or until golden brown, then cool on a cake rack. To serve hot, reheat at 300°F. for a few minutes.

CHEDDAR RAREBIT

In his *Century of Good Eating* Pierre Berton refers to rarebit or Welsh Rabbit as "Klondike cheese" taken from the *Home Journal* November 1907. Even then Cheddar was appreciated.

½ lb. sharp or medium Cheddar, grated	¼ teaspoon dry mustard
	1 teaspoon brown sugar
1 cup flat or stale beer	Cayenne and salt to taste
1 egg, beaten	Crisped toasted buttered bread

Melt cheese in a chafing dish or in top of a double boiler, over hot, not boiling, water. Add beer gradually, stirring gently all the time. Mix egg with dry mustard, brown sugar, salt and cayenne to taste. Add to cheese mixture, while stirring. Keep stirring until thickened. Cut toasted bread into triangles and let everyone dip into cheese pot. Keep under low heat, while eating.

DUTCH TREATS

The Dutch and others who grow beautiful vegetables in large quantities offer Ontario a marvellous choice of recipes and foods.

WINTER CHOWDER

From a nutritional viewpoint, this chowder has everything. In addition, its taste, color and cost are very pleasing. You may add a cup of frozen green peas to make it look even better.

1 tablespoon butter	¼ teaspoon savory
2 cups shredded cabbage	1 bay leaf
2 large carrots, diced	2 cups chicken broth or consommé
3 medium potatoes, cubed	
1 onion, thinly sliced	4 cups milk, scalded
2 large celery stalks, diced	Salt and pepper, to taste

Melt butter in a large saucepan and add vegetables, savory and bay leaf. Stir to coat with butter. Cover and simmer over very low heat 20 minutes, stirring once or twice.

Add broth or consommé and bring to a boil, then lower heat and simmer 10 minutes. Add hot milk and season to taste.

CELERY SOUP

Made with crisp, deep green celery.

3 cups celery (stalks and leaves)	1 teaspoon salt
2 potatoes, medium-size	¼ cup parsley, chopped fine
4 cups water or consommé	3 tablespoons butter
½ teaspoon pepper	1 cup hot milk

Dice the celery fine. Grate the potatoes. Bring the water or consommé to a boil. Add the celery, potatoes, pepper, salt, parsley and butter. Cover and simmer for one hour over medium heat. When ready to serve, add one cup hot milk.

In the old days, celery soup was flavored with ½ teaspoon anise, added with the salt and pepper.

CELERY PEANUT BUTTER SOUP

Quick, rich and filling, this should be served with a light meal. It freezes very well and will keep 3-5 months.

2 cups diced celery and top leaves	2 cups milk
½ cup water	½ teaspoon salt
2 tablespoons butter	¼ teaspoon pepper
3 tablespoons flour	½ cup peanut butter

Place celery and water in a saucepan. Cover and boil about 20 minutes, or until celery is tender, but not too soft.

Make a thin white sauce with butter, flour, milk, salt and pepper. When creamy, add undrained celery and peanut butter. Stir until ingredients are well blended and sauce is smooth, then taste for seasoning.

CREAM OF TOMATO SOUP

1 can (20 oz.) tomatoes	A pinch of savory
1 onion	1 tablespoon cornstarch
A few celery leaves	2½ cups (not homogenized) milk
1 tablespoon sugar	

Pour the tomatoes into a saucepan; add the finely chopped onion, minced celery leaves, sugar and savory and simmer for 20 minutes.

Mix cornstarch with ½ cup cold milk. Add the 2 remaining cups of milk. Bring to a boil and cook over low heat until the liquid thickens slightly. When ready to serve, pour this hot milk into the hot tomatoes all at once and stir quickly. Do not boil after adding the milk. ½ cup cooked rice may be added. Do not salt before serving. Avoid using homogenized milk which has a tendency to curdle.

NIAGARA VALLEY FRUIT SOUP

This soup is a perfect beginning for a barbecue on a hot summer day. Serve in pottery or wooden bowls.

1 lb. pitted black cherries
2 peaches, peeled, thinly sliced
4 blue plums, pitted and cut in four
1 - inch stick of cinnamon
5 whole cloves
Juice and grated rind of 1 lemon

4 cups apple juice
3 tablespoons honey
2 tablespoons cornstarch
¼ cup cold water or white wine
½ teaspoon ratafia or almond extract
Toasted, slivered almonds

Place in a saucepan the cherries, peaches and plums. Add the cinnamon, cloves, juice and grated rind of lemon, apple juice and honey. Bring to a boil, then simmer gently for 10 minutes. Remove the cinnamon and cloves. Stir the cornstarch with the cold water or white wine until dissolved and add to hot fruit. Stir gently until slightly thickened and clear. Remove from heat and add ratafia or almond extract. Cover and refrigerate. Serve sprinkled with toasted, slivered almonds.

TOMATO SCALLOP

When fresh tomatoes are out of season, take the tomato flavor out of a can.

1 20 - ounce can tomatoes
1 onion, chopped
1 tablespoon sugar
½ teaspoon salt

¼ teaspoon oregano
Dash of rosemary
1 cup bread, cut in ½ - inch cubes
⅓ cup grated mild cheddar cheese

Combine tomatoes, onion, sugar and seasonings. Top with bread cubes and grated cheese. Bake at 350°F. until bread cubes are browned.

CREAMED SPINACH

Try this perfect way to cook and serve spinach.

1 lb. fresh spinach or
1 pkg. frozen chopped spinach
1 tablespoon butter
1 tablespoon flour

Salt, pepper and nutmeg, to taste
1 hard-boiled egg, chopped or sliced

If using fresh spinach, wash it, cook without adding extra water, then chop it up. Cook frozen spinach according to package directions. In either case, drain and save the juice.

Melt the butter, add the flour and cook gently for 1-2 minutes until thickened. Remove from the heat and add the spinach juice slowly, stirring constantly. Season with salt, pepper and nutmeg.

Pour over the spinach and heat again. Serve decorated with the egg.

ONION CUSTARD

A feathery, creamy and delectable way of serving onions. This is excellent with seafood, chicken, veal or turkey.

¼ cup butter or margarine	1 teaspoon salt
6 medium onions, diced	Pinch of pepper
2 beaten eggs	Pinch of nutmeg or curry
1 cup milk	powder

Melt butter or margarine in a saucepan and add onions. Stir until well coated with butter, then cook over medium heat until golden here and there.

Combine remaining ingredients. Add to onions and pour into a buttered 1-quart casserole. Bake uncovered 25-30 minutes at 375°F., or until set like a custard.

PICKLED TURNIP

Turn turnips into a tangy ginger pickle. Fresh ginger can usually be obtained from Oriental food stores or a supermarket specialty counter.

1 cup white sugar	½ teaspoon yellow food coloring
1 cup water	½ teaspoon grated fresh ginger
¼ cup vinegar	or ¼ whole ginger in syrup
3 tablespoons pickling salt	4 cups thinly-sliced turnip

Peel turnips; slice crosswise into thin slices.

Combine water, sugar, vinegar, salt, coloring and ginger. Pour over turnips. Place in a covered jar and leave in refrigerator overnight before serving.

TURNIP CASSEROLE

When cooking turnips, remember not to salt them as it extracts their sweetness into the stock.

2 lbs. yellow turnips	½ teaspoon pepper
1 large potato	3 tablespoons butter
1½ teaspoons salt	2 tablespoons brown sugar

Wash and peel turnip and potato. Cut in medium-sized pieces and cook in boiling water until tender. Drain. Add salt, pepper and butter, and whip until fluffy. Put in lightly greased casserole, sprinkle with brown sugar and bake at 350°F. for 20 minutes.

EASY CABBAGE ROLLS

The cabbage family includes dozens of varieties and is second only to the potato as the most commonly used vegetable in the world. Select cabbage with bright color and crisp outer leaves.

Cabbage is a versatile vegetable. Raw, it makes delicious salad; pickled, it becomes sauerkraut. Used in the recipe given below, it makes a delicious, filling, main dish.

1 medium cabbage	½ teaspoon salt
2 tablespoons butter	Rice filling
1 - 1½ cups tomato juice	

Remove cabbage core by cutting around it with a sharp knife. Place cabbage in a deep utensil and pour boiling salted water into the core until head is completely covered. Let stand until leaves are soft and pliable so they will not break when folded.

Drain cabbage and carefully take leaves apart without tearing them. Cut off hard center rib from each leaf. Cut the larger leaves into 2 or 3 sections.

Line the bottom of a pot with a few leaves, and place a generous spoonful of filling on each. Roll leaves lightly, using a toothpick as a skewer.

Arrange the rolls in layers, sprinkling each layer with pepper.

Combine tomato juice with melted butter and seasoning. Pour over rolls; the liquid should barely show between the rolls.

Protect the top layer from scorching by covering with a few large leaves. Cover pot tightly and bake at 350°F. for 1½ to 2 hours. To allow top layer to brown, uncover just before removing from the oven. Serve hot, garnished with sour cream and crisp crumbled bacon.

Rice Filling:

2 cups cooked rice	**4 or 5 tablespoons butter**
1 medium onion, finely chopped	**Salt and pepper**

Cook rice as directed on package.

Cook the onion in butter to a light golden color.

Mix with rice, taste to season with salt and pepper if necessary.

Cabbage rolls can be a tasty addition to the menu for the next camping trip. Here are the directions for their preservation and use at the campsite:

Prepare cabbage rolls beforehand, cook, and freeze in appropriate containers.

Allow them to thaw while traveling. Sauce may separate because of freezing but will be reabsorbed while heating.

Heat in a frying pan over the fire. Do not use a cast-iron frying pan because it will cause discoloration of the sauce. Convenient foil trays can be purchased and used for both heating and serving.

CABBAGE CASSEROLE

6 slices bacon	**4 oz. medium noodles (cooked,**
1 tablespoon sugar	**about 3 cups)**
1 teaspoon salt	**½ cup sour cream**
½ teaspoon pepper	**Parsley flakes or paprika**
6 cups cabbage, chopped	

In a large frying pan, cook bacon until crisp. Remove from frying pan, drain and crumble. Set aside. Stir sugar, salt, pepper into bacon drippings in frying pan. Add cabbage. Stir until cabbage is coated. Combine cabbage mixture, cooked noodles and bacon in a casserole dish. Cover and bake at 325°F. for 45 minutes. Uncover, spoon sour cream over top. Sprinkle with parsley or paprika. Return to oven and bake 5 to 10 minutes.

DUTCH COLESLAW

If you are going to give a harvest party, consider serving a large, cold boiled ham, hot boiled potatoes and this Dutch coleslaw. A big jar of good mustard, apple dumplings and cider will make the meal perfect.

4 - 5 cups thinly sliced cabbage	**½ cup rich cream**
2 diced celery stalks	**2 tablespoons cider vinegar**
2 thinly sliced onions	**½ - 1 teaspoon salt**
4 grated carrots, in medium shred	**¼ teaspoon pepper**
2 tablespoons sugar	**¼ cup minced fresh parsley**

Combine the cabbage, celery, onions and carrots. Place them in a large bowl and completely cover with ice water. Refrigerate for one hour, then drain thoroughly.

Combine the sugar, cream, vinegar, salt and pepper (the vinegar will thicken the cream). Pour over the vegetables when ready to serve and toss very well. Sprinkle the minced parsley on top.

GLAZED CARROT NUT CAKE

This will keep for three months in the freezer. I always like to have one on hand. If you don't want to make the orange glaze, put whipped cream on the cake when you're ready to serve it.

1¼ cups salad oil	**2 teaspoons cinnamon**
2 cups fine granulated sugar	**4 eggs**
2 cups all-purpose flour	**3 cups grated raw carrots**
2 teaspoons baking powder	**1 cup finely chopped walnuts**
1 teaspoon soda	**or pecans**
1 teaspoon salt	

Beat the oil and sugar with mixer for 5 minutes. Sift the next five ingredients together and stir half into sugar mixture. Blend thoroughly. Add remaining half of dry ingredients, alternately with eggs, one at a time, mixing well after each addition.

Add carrots and nuts, mix well and pour into a lightly oiled 10-inch tube pan. Bake at 325°F. for 1 hour and 15 minutes. When done, invert pan on cake rack and let it cool.

For the glaze: place in a saucepan: 1 cup of sugar, grated peel of ½ an orange, ¼ cup of cornstarch, 1 cup of orange juice and stir until well mixed. Then add 1 teaspoon of lemon juice, 2 tablespoons of butter and ½ teaspoon of salt. Cook over medium low heat, stirring constantly, until thick and glossy.

Let cool until tepid, then spread on unmolded cake. When cool, freeze cake on a tray, then remove cake, wrap, label and put back in freezer.

SPICED CARROT JAM

This is excellent with meats, especially ham and game.

4 cups finely chopped raw carrots	**½ teaspoon each cloves, allspice**
3 cups sugar	**and cinnamon**
Juice and grated peel of	
2 lemons	

Place all the ingredients in a saucepan. Slowly bring to a boil over medium low heat, stirring constantly. Then, stirring often, cook over low heat 30-40 minutes, or until mixture is as thick as jam. Pour into hot sterilized jars and seal. Yield: 4 jelly glasses.

HOW TO CHOOSE THE PERFECT PEACH

When you are shopping for peaches, the Food Council, Ontario Department of Agriculture and Food, advises that you look for firm undamaged fruit that is well-colored, with no evidence of green. Always select peaches with well-colored "ground" or under-color, which may range from creamy white to yellow, depending on the variety. A green tinge in the ground color indicates immature fruit which will not ripen completely. Although the "rosy blush" on peaches is lovely to look at, it is not necessarily an indication of peach flavor or maturity. The "blush" differs with the variety.

Store ripe peaches in the refrigerator in a covered container or perforated plastic bag. At this temperature, they will retain their high quality for about a week. If your peaches are slightly unripe, spread them out at room temperature, away from direct sunlight. When ripened, use them right away, or refrigerate them.

PEACH SOUR CREAM PIE

An equal quantity of well-drained canned peaches can be used for this open pie in the winter, but the velvety texture and blush color of fresh peaches will be lost.

1 cup dairy sour cream	2 egg yolks, well beaten
Grated peel of ½ an orange	Unbaked 8-inch pie shell
¾ cup firmly packed brown sugar	2 tablespoons flour
½ teaspoon salt	2½ cups peeled, sliced peaches

Blend the sour cream, peel, brown sugar and salt, then stir in the egg yolks. Sprinkle bottom of pie shell with 1 tablespoon of the flour.

Pour in peaches and sprinkle with remaining flour. Pour sour cream mixture over all. Bake at 425°F for 15 minutes, reduce heat to 350°F. and bake 30 minutes. Let cool.

APPLE OMELETTE

The apples may be replaced by peaches, pears or other seasonal Ontario fruits and prepared in the same manner. The recipe is easily doubled.

2 apples	6 eggs
1 tablespoon rum or lemon juice	1 tablespoon sugar
4 tablespoons fine granulated sugar	3 tablespoons cold water

Peel and core apples and slice paper-thin (the thinness of the apples is important as they barely cook). Add the rum or lemon juice and sugar. Mix well and let stand until ready to use.

Beat eggs with the sugar and cold water, then add the apple mixture. Cook according to directions, fold and serve.

To flame the omelette, sprinkle top with 2 tablespoons of sugar and pour 3-4 tablespoons of hot rum over it. Set the rum afiire and keep pouring it over the flaming omelette until the fire dies out.

SOUR CREAM CHERRY PIE

Deep red, smooth, tasty, and most attractive when covered with a lattice top, this is good alone or with ice cream.

2 cups pitted black or red cherries	¾ cup dairy sour cream
Pastry of your choice	½ - ¾ cup sugar
3 eggs	¼ teaspoon salt
	¼ teaspoon almond extract

Pour cherries into an unbaked 8-inch pie shell. Beat eggs well, add sour cream, sugar and beat until thick. Add salt, almond extract. Stir and pour over cherries.

Top with lattice strips and bake on bottom shelf of oven at 400°F. for 25-35 minutes.

STEWED PLUMS

Use any type of plums, whole or halved for this. If the plums are not freestone, it is easier to cook them whole and then remove the pits.

1 cup sugar	2 - inch cinnamon stick
1 cup apple juice or water or 1¼ cups red wine	2 lbs. pitted Ontario plums

Make a syrup of the sugar and apple juice, water or red wine by boiling them together for 10 minutes. Add the cinnamon stick. Place the plums one next to the other, in the syrup, then cover and simmer over very low heat for 20-25 minutes.

When cooked, gently place the fruit in a glass dish and pour the syrup on top. Cool, then refrigerate until ready to serve.

CANADIAN GRAPE JELLY

This uncooked jelly is made with Concord grape canned juice. Serve it with chicken or roast pork.

1 package powdered fruit pectin	6 - oz. can frozen grape juice concentrate (thawed but still cold)
2 cups lukewarm water	
	3¼ cups sugar

Pour the lukewarm water into a large bowl and add the powdered fruit pectin gradually, stirring constantly. Stir until it is completely dissolved, then let stand for 45 minutes, giving it an occasional gentle stir. Pour the undiluted grape juice concentrate into a bowl. Add 1½ cups of the sugar. Mix thoroughly and stir until the sugar is partially dissolved.

Add the remaining 1¾ cups of sugar to the pectin and stir until the sugar is dissolved. Add the juice mixture to the pectin and stir until its sugar is completely dissolved.

Pour into containers and cover with lids. Let stand on the kitchen counter for about 24 hours, or until set, then refrigerate. Makes 5-6 jelly glasses.

ONTARIO WINES

Ontario is an important producer of Canadian wines. Although somewhat young, they nevertheless can add new appeal to favorite old recipes and make ordinary food extraordinary, Beef Bourguignon is an example. Anyone can enjoy wine cooked dishes, because the alcoholic content of wine disappears in cooking leaving only the essential flavor to complement the food. If not specified in a recipe, the choice and quantity of the wine used should be a matter of personal preference.

If you want to make your own wine, write to the Ontario Department of Agriculture and Food for their booklet *Wine Making in Small Quantity*. The booklet is excellent and well suited to Canadian grapes and climate.

WINE JELLY

Serve with game or roast turkey or as a dessert with a custard sauce.

2 envelopes unflavored gelatine	¼ cup lemon juice
½ cup cold water	¼ cup orange juice
1 cup boiling water	2 cups Ontario red wine
⅔ cup sugar	
Pinch of salt	

Soften gelatine 5 minutes in the cold water. Dissolve in the boiling water. Add sugar, salt, lemon and orange juice. Stir until sugar is dissolved. Stir in the wine. Stir until blended. Pour into oiled mold. Refrigerate overnight or until well set. Unmold to serve.

JELLIED CHICKEN — WALNUT MAYONNAISE

4 - 6 chicken breasts	½ teaspoon tarragon or savory
4 tablespoons butter	2 cups hot water
1 garlic clove, halved	2 chicken bouillon cubes
1 onion, diced	1½ cups Canadian white wine
5 - 6 parsley sprigs	2 envelopes unflavored gelatine
2 carrots, sliced	¼ cup cold water

Cut each chicken breast into 4 pieces and roll lightly in unseasoned flour. Brown in the butter, with the two garlic clove halves, in a large frying pan. Remove the pieces to a saucepan as they are browned. Remove the garlic from the frying pan and add the onion, parsley, carrots, tarragon or savory, hot water, chicken bouillon cubes and wine. Simmer a few seconds and pour mixture into the saucepan. Cover and simmer until the chicken is tender. Strain the chicken, remove bones, and arrange meat in an oiled mould.

Measure 3 cups of the stock, and heat (if there isn't enough, add water; if there are more than 3 cups, boil uncovered until reduced.) Soak gelatine 5 minutes in the cold water, add to the hot stock and stir until melted. Season to taste and pour over the chicken. Refrigerate until firm. This should be prepared a day or two ahead of time.

Walnut Mayonnaise

Mix 1 cup mayonnaise, ½ cup sour cream, ½ cup very finely chopped walnuts. Add chopped green onions and parsley to taste.

MENNONITE CUISINE

Kitchener and Waterloo County in Ontario is Mennonite country. It was back in the 1800's that they first came to what was then the wilderness of Waterloo County. Just like the pioneers in French Québec, they had land-clearing and barn-rising "bees," where their wonderful foods were prepared by women to feed their working men.

A strong sense of community organization and a deep feeling for the simplicity of life have given their food a uniqueness all its own.

The Kitchener market has been a Canadian tourist attraction for a great many years, and even if some of their traditional costumes have almost disappeared, much of their home baked goods, pickles and sausages are still sold. And everywhere they are known for their delicious "Stuffed Goose."

MENNONITE SCHNITZEL

Fried onions, sour cream and thick veal steaks make this quite different from the Austrian Schnitzel.

6 small veal steaks, 1 inch thick	3 tablespoons flour
3 tablespoons melted veal or beef fat	3 medium onions, thinly sliced
½ teaspoon salt	½ cup boiling water
¼ teaspoon pepper	½ cup dairy sour cream

Melt veal or beef fat in a cast iron frying pan. Sprinkle steaks with salt and pepper, then roll in flour. Add onion to pan, stir until well coated with fat, then cook over low heat 5-8 minutes, or until soft. Remove, pressing as much fat as possible, and set aside.

Add meat to fat in pan and brown lightly on both sides over medium heat. Top with onions and pour boiling water over it. Cover and simmer 30-40 minutes, turning meat once.

Then add sour cream, cover and simmer at a very low heat for 20 minutes — the meat will be tender and the gravy creamy.

KITCHENER BAKED HAM

This makes a perfect buffet or cold supper "pièce de résistance".

10 - 15 lb. tenderized ham	2 tablespoons malt vinegar
½ cup brown sugar	Whole cloves
2 teaspoons dry mustard	1 pint light beer or porter
2 tablespoons rye or all-purpose flour	

70

Bake the ham in a 300°F. oven for 4 hours, uncovered. Remove from dripping pan, drain the fat accumulated in the pan. Remove the skin from the ham and put back in the dripping pan. Mix the brown sugar, dry mustard, flour and vinegar into a paste. Score the ham in large diamonds, dot the middle of each diamond with a whole clove. Spread the paste over the top of the ham. Return to the oven for 40 minutes, basting every 10 minutes with the beer, then with the drippings in the bottom of the pan. Bake the last 15 minutes in a 400°F. oven. Serve hot or cold.

BAKED BACON A LA MENNONITE

5 or 6 - lb. piece of back bacon	3 tablespoons brown sugar
10 or 15 whole cloves	4 tablespoons breadcrumbs
3 tablespoons horseradish mustard	1 cup apple juice

Remove the casing from the back bacon. Stick the cloves in rows along the length of it. Spread the top with the horseradish mustard and cover with the brown sugar, then with the breadcrumbs. Place the bacon on a piece of folded, heavy-duty foil in a dripping pan. Lift the sides and ends of the foil to partly cover the meat and form a shallow pan. Pour the apple juice around the meat and bake for 2 hours in a 375°F. oven, basting twice with juices from the foil container. Cool in the foil, wrap and refrigerate until ready to serve. Before serving, slice thinly and reconstruct the shape of the roll.

To reheat — if you wish — place in a 350°F. oven for 1 hour. Slice as you serve. Delicious hot or cold.

STUFFED GOOSE

A recipe inspired by the Mennonite cuisine, with a few additions of my own.

10 - 12 lb. goose
Juice of 1 lemon
¼ teaspoon pepper
¼ teaspoon nutmeg
½ lb. chicken livers
1 tablespoon parsley, chopped
2 onions, minced
1 clove garlic, crushed
½ teaspoon marjoram
1 bay leaf
1 cup red wine

2 tablespoons butter
2 egg yolks
1 cup orange juice
1 tablespoon prepared mustard
1½ cups finely sieved dry breadcrumbs
2 tablespoons red currant jelly
Grated rind of 1 orange
1 tablespoon brandy
1 can undiluted consommé

Clean the goose, wiping it with a cloth dipped in vinegar. Do not scald, nor soak in cold water, nor wash with soap. Rub inside and out with the lemon juice mixed with the salt, pepper and nutmeg.

Place in a saucepan the goose liver, chicken livers, parsley, onions, garlic, marjoram, bay leaf and red wine. Simmer 30 minutes, turning the liver from time to time. Drain off the wine and reserve it. Chop the liver and seasoning together, as finely as possible, add the butter and the egg yolks. Blend together. Taste for seasoning and place in the cavity.

Tie up the opening. Fold the skin back over the neck, cut and prick the skin all over with a fork so that the fat will exude during the cooking period. Place the goose in a roasting pan, breast side up. Add the orange juice to the reserved red wine. Pour into the roasting pan. Roast uncovered 25 minutes per pound in a 375°F. oven. Baste every 25 minutes with the liquid in the pan.

When the goose is cooked, remove from the roasting pan. Drain all the fat in a bowl. Place the goose back in the roasting pan.

Mix 3 tablespoons of the fat with the prepared mustard and use to rub the bird all over. Sprinkle with the breadcrumbs. Put back in the oven for 20 to 25 minutes or until the skin is crisp and brown.

To make the gravy, add to the drippings in the pan, the currant jelly, grated orange rind, the brandy and the consommé. Bring to a boil and serve.

HOT POTATO AND ONION SALAD

This creamy, warm, tasty potato salad is one of the best known of all the Mennonites' famous salads. Delicious served with cold ham or roast beef.

6 - 8 medium size potatoes
2 tablespoons bacon dripping
1 onion, chopped fine
¼ cup water
½ cup cider vinegar

1 tablespoon sugar
1 teaspoon salt
¼ cup butter
Pepper to taste

Boil the potatoes in their jackets. Drain and put back over heat to dry. Peel as hot as possible and slice, set aside and keep warm. Heat the bacon dripping, add the onion, stir until brown here and there, pour the whole over the potatoes.

Bring to a boil, the water, vinegar, sugar, salt, butter and pepper. Pour boiling hot over the potatoes and toss together lightly. Place in a warm dish. Sprinkle top with parsley.

SOUR CREAM AND CUCUMBER SALAD

Serve this in a glass dish if possible and decorate it with fresh dill sprigs. Dill is a must on any cold table and usually loved by all.

4 medium cucumbers	¼ cup salad oil
1 tablespoon salt	1 teaspoon sugar
1 cup dairy sour cream	3 tablespoons chopped dill
2 tablespoons white vinegar	Salt and pepper, to taste

Scrub the cucumbers, but don't peel them. Cut off ends, score lengthwise with the tines of a fork, then slice as thinly as possible.

Place slices in a bowl, sprinkle with the salt and let stand 1 hour at room temperature. Drain and rinse under running cold water to remove salt, then squeeze dry.

Combine sour cream, vinegar, oil, sugar, dill and pour over cucumbers. Salt and pepper, then refrigerate and toss just before serving.

HOT SLAW FOR SAUSAGES

A pleasant change from the sameness of cole slaw. Fried sausages or hot smoked sausages are placed on top of this hot slaw. Serve them with mashed potatoes.

3 tablespoons butter	1 teaspoon sugar
4 - 5 well-packed cups shredded cabbage	½ teaspoon pepper
	2 tablespoons cider vinegar
1 teaspoon salt	½ cup dairy sour cream

Melt butter in a large frying pan, add cabbage and stir until well coated with fat. Cook 5-8 minutes over low heat, stirring often — the cabbage should be softened, but not fried. Place in a warm bowl, add remaining ingredients and toss together until thoroughly blended.

SOUR CREAM GREEN BEAN SALAD

A superb dish prepared with fresh green or wax beans. To schnippel the fresh beans takes a little longer, but it's worth the trouble.

4 cups cold cooked beans	1 tablespoon cider or white vinegar
2 green onions or 1 small onion, finely chopped	½ cup dairy sour cream
1 tablespoon sugar	Salt and pepper, to taste

Schnippel the beans by cutting them on the bias in very long, thin slices. Place in a bowl and add onion.

Blend remaining ingredients, pour over beans and toss lightly.

MENNONITE GERMAN SUMMER SALAD

This is a very good meal in itself, but it's even better when served with thin slices of lightly buttered black bread.

2 cups finely chopped raw spinach	2 teaspoons fresh or bottled lemon juice
1 thinly sliced peeled cucumber	½ teaspoon salt
4 chopped green onions	¼ teaspoon freshly ground pepper
½ cup sliced radishes	Paprika, to taste
2 cups (1 pint) cottage cheese	½ cup minced fresh parsley
1 cup sour cream	

I like to wash the spinach the day before, then wrap it in a cloth and refrigerate it overnight.

Chop the spinach, add the cucumber, onions and radishes, then toss lightly. Arrange in a wooden salad bowl and place a mound of cottage cheese in the middle. Blend the sour cream with the lemon juice, salt and pepper and pour over the salad.

Sprinkle the paprika in the middle and the parsley all around. Toss when ready to serve.

QUICK HOT BUNS

The Mennonite coffee cakes, pies, "Fasnachts", doughnuts and cakes are justly famous. This recipe was given to me by a Mennonite house-wiife at the Kitchener market. She serves them hot with "café au lait".

3 cups all-purpose flour	½ cup lard
1 teaspoon soda	1 egg beaten
2 teaspoons cream of tartar	1 cup brown sugar
1 cup sugar	½ cup all-purpose flour
½ cup butter	1 egg, beaten

Sift together the 4 cups of flour, soda, cream of tartar and sugar. Cut in the butter and lard with two knives or a pastry cutter. Beat the egg in an 8-ounce measuring cup and add enough milk to reach the ¾ cup mark. Add to flour mixture. Toss to blend. If necessary, add a bit more milk. Put on a board, shape into a ball and roll to a sheet of 15 x 15 inches.

Combine the brown sugar, the ½ cup flour and beaten egg until creamy. Spread on top of the dough with a rubber spatula. Sprinkle cinnamon on top. Roll as for a cake and cut into slices about ¾ inch thick. Place each in well buttered muffin pan, or one next to the other on a baking sheet. Bake in preheated 375°F. oven for about 20 minutes or until golden brown. Serve hot with butter or syrup.

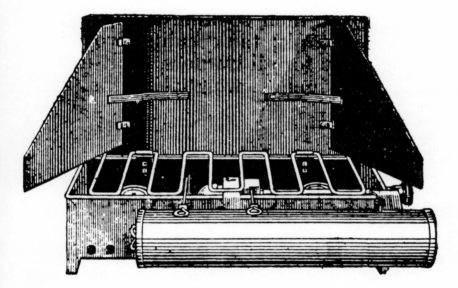

SHOO-FLY PIE

Although baked in a pie plate with a crust, this is not a pie but a very good molasses cake with a crumbly topping. The Mennonites serve it hot for breakfast but, for me, it is equally good any time of the day.

1 teaspoon soda	1 cup dark brown sugar
¾ cup molasses	½ cup lard
1 cup boiling water	¼ cup butter
Pinch of salt	½ teaspoon cinnamon
Pinch of ginger	Pastry of your choice
1½ cups all-purpose flour	

Stir soda into molasses until foamy. Add water, salt, ginger and set aside. Mix flour and brown sugar, cut in lard and butter, then add cinnamon. Stir until crumbly.

Line a 9-inch pie plate with pastry and pour in ⅓ of the molasses mixture. Sprinkle ⅓ of the crumb mixture over and continue alternating layers with crumbs as top layer. Bake at 375°F. for 35-40 minutes, or until golden brown on top.

KITCHENER RICE CREAM

I first ate this elegant pudding at a buffet luncheon in Kitchener, Ontario. Since then I've made it often for guests. I serve it on a tray with five bowls of garnish — whipped cream, thin slices of canned peaches that have been flavored with sherry or brandy, slivers of toasted almonds, shredded coconut and strawberry or raspberry jam. It delights everyone.

¼ cup rice	1 teaspoon vanilla
2 cups light cream or milk	2 egg whites
2 egg yolks	4 tablespoons sugar
4 tablespoons sugar	

To make a light pudding, use long grain rice. For a creamier pudding, use short grain rice.

Place the uncooked rice and the cream or milk in top of double boiler. Cover and cook about 45 minutes until rice is tender.

Beat the egg yolks until light yellow. Add 4 tablespoons sugar and beat until well blended. Add to the hot cooked rice, stirring all the time. Simmer 2 minutes. Keep stirring. Remove from heat and add the vanilla.

Beat the egg whites until stiff, add 4 tablespoons sugar; beat until well blended and fold lightly into the rice cream. Remove from heat. Pour into a nice serving dish and serve hot. Or cover and chill until ready to serve cold.

APPLE BUTTER

A Mennonite sweet, marvelous on toast or hot homemade bread, the ingredients for this are available all year around. But, for me, the very best apple butter is made with the first summer sour apples.

5 cups sweet apple cider or juice	**1 cup brown or white sugar**
cups apples (see below)	**1 cup corn syrup**
	1 teaspoon cinnamon

Boil cider or juice uncovered over high heat until reduced to about ½ cups. Pare, core and thinly slice apples, measure them well packed, then add to liquid. Simmer uncovered over low heat, stirring often, until mixture begins to boil.

Add remaining ingredients and continue to cook until mixture is quite thick, stirring often so it won't stick. When a little bit placed on a cold plate cools to a spreading consistency, it is ready. Pour into sterilized jars, cover and keep in a cool place. Yield: 4-5 jelly glasses.

PICKLED DAMSON PLUMS

On the market these plums are sometimes called Italian plums. The smaller they are, the more attractive they will be when pickled.

2 lbs. damson plums	**3 whole cloves**
1 cup brown sugar	**1 bay leaf**
1 cup cider vinegar	

Rinse plums under running cold water and rub dry with a cloth. Make a few holes in each plum with the point of a knitting needle, and place in earthenware or glass jar.

Boil together the sugar and vinegar, stirring until the sugar is completely melted. Pour this mixture, boiling hot, over the plums. Cover and let stand until the next day. Pour off the syrup from the plums, bring back to a fast rolling boil and pour again over the plums. Cover and let stand another day. Repeat this process a third time and let stand a day longer; then pour the syrup and plums into a saucepan and just bring to the boil without stirring. Pour into jars and cover. These will keep their flavor as well as other pickled fruits.

NOTE:

If you wish to know more about Mennonite cooking, I recommend the following books, all written by Canadian Mennonites.

Food that really Schmecks
Edna Staebler (Ontario)

Canadian Mennonite Cookbook
Altona Women's Institute (Western)

The Mennonite Treasury of Recipes
Favorite Recipes for Large Groups and Families,
Contributed by All Canadian Mennonites,
produced in Steinback, Manitoba.

NOVA SCOTIA

The early settlers of Nova Scotia were an industrious people us
reaping harvests and grazing their animals in a hard and dema
land. In their new country, the families became famous for re
harvests from the sea and making their land attractive as well as
ductive. They still have the persevering and proud nature of their
fathers. Some of the old customs and many of the old dishes are
very much alive. This in part creates Nova Scotia's charm.

To this we can add the elegance of the kilt, the nostalgic musi
the bagpipes, their many beautiful handicrafts, the scenic Cabot T
Lunenburg, the Acadians, and the Annapolis Valley. There is a lo
see, enjoy and love in the peninsula which juts, with Cape Br
Island, deep into the Atlantic Ocean.

The Scottish communities are close to the warm waters and sh
beaches of the Northumberland shore. The Northern country is rug
and similar to the highlands of Scotland. Gaelic is often heard in th
parts. On the Eastern shore, the coastline is penetrated by deep oc
inlets backed by granite cliffs, and the South shore is an artist's pa
dise. It is often said that the Bay of Fundy provides some of the rich
fishing grounds in Canada, while the Annapolis Valley has its app
exported as far as South Africa.

FEATS WITH OATMEAL

For a long, long time oatmeal was the main food of the Scottis
peasant, and in many areas it still is. We should thank the Scots wh
brought it with them when they came to Canada from their hill
countryside.

Scottish, Irish or Canadian oatmeal, rolled or flaked oats, groats o
grits, and quick, or no-cooking oatmeal are all oats. But there are
important differences between them.

Oatmeal is the husked meal of the oats, ground and kiln-dried.
The most superior type is the Scottish, followed by the Irish. To sample
these, just ask for imported oats at specialty shops.

Scottish and Irish oatmeal need careful cooking in order to break
down the starch cells and, of course, the larger and coarser the meal,
the longer the boiling required.

Rolled or flaked oats are oats that, once dried, husked and softened
by steam, are rolled flat and carefully dried by a special process.

Quick, or no-cooking types of oatmeal are mill-processed and
produced from the rolled or flaked oats.

Groats or grits are the seeds or kernels of oats, either left whole or
cut in two or three pieces. If ground, they are referred to as prepared
groats. The whole groats are used to make pilafs and casseroles. The
cut types are chiefly used to make soup, or as a thickener for consommé.

80

SIX BREAKFAST OATMEALS

Oatmeal is still one of the world's best breakfasts. In order to get the full value out of your porridge, let the oatmeal soak in a glass or stainless steel pot overnight and cook it in the morning. To further enrich porridge, let it stand covered for 5 minutes after cooking.

There are six basic ways to cook oatmeal, each giving slightly different results. The following recipes require 1½ cups rolled oats, ¾ teaspoon salt, 3 cups water and serve four. Quick- or no-cooking oats may also be used, but for these, follow the directions on the box.

Quick Method: Bring water to a boil, add salt, then stir in oats. Cook 10 minutes, stirring occasionally.

Cold Water Method: Stir oats and salt into cold water, bring to a boil over medium heat and cook 10 minutes, stirring occasionally.

Double Boiler Method: Stir oats and salt into boiling water in top of a double boiler over direct heat. Cook 2 minutes, then place over boiling water and cook 15-20 minutes, stirring occasionally.

Oven Method: Place oats in a casserole, then add boiling water. Cover and bake 25 minutes at 350°F.

Night-Before Method: Stir oats and salt into boiling water in top of a double boiler over direct heat. Remove from heat, cover and let stand overnight. In the morning, place over boiling water and heat to serving temperature, stirring frequently.

Cooked-in-Milk Method: Follow any of the previous cooking methods, using 1½ cups fresh milk and 1½ cups water, or mixing ¼ cup of instant skim milk powder with the oats.

PORRIDGE MEAT LOAF

This is an excellent way to use up leftover porridge. You may find it worthwhile to cook extra porridge just to make this tasty, moist Aberdeen specialty.

½ lb. minced beef	2 teaspoons salt
½ lb. minced pork or veal	½ teaspoon pepper
1 finely chopped onion	½ teaspoon savory
1 thinly sliced leek (optional)	⅛ teaspoon thyme
2 cups cold porridge	½ cup consommé or red wine

Thoroughly mix all ingredients in a bowl. Grease a loaf pan, sp
with flour, and shake out excess. Pack in mixture and place in
filled with hot water until water comes 1 inch up side of loa

Bake at 325°F. about one hour, or until top is golden brown.
hot or cold.

SWORD AND ANCHOR OATMEAL BREAD

The Sword and Anchor was one of the most attractive inns I
ever seen in Canada, and I'm sorry to say it is no more in Ha
Their fresh cod casserole and oatmeal bread recipe given to me b
maître d' years ago, I have made and enjoyed ever since.

2 cups boiling water	½ teaspoon ground ginger
1 cup rolled oats	½ cup warm water
2 tablespoons butter or margarine	3 cups whole wheat flour
½ cup molasses	¼ cup wheat germ (optional)
2 teaspoons salt	2 to 3 cups all-purpose flour
1 envelope active dry yeast	

Pour the rapidly boiling water over the oats. Add the butte
margarine. Stir to mix and let stand until cool. Add the molasses
salt. Dissolve yeast and ginger in the ½ cup warm water, let s
10 minutes. Add to oatmeal mixture. Mix well. Start adding the w
wheat flour and wheat germ beating hard at each addition. Then
just enough white flour to make a soft dough. Turn on a genero
floured board and knead until smooth and satiny. Turn into a grea
bowl. Cover and let stand in a warm place until double in bulk, ab
1 hour. Shape into 2 loaves. Place in greased bread pan. Cover, let
until double. Bake in a preheated 350°F. oven, for about 50 to
minutes or until well browned. Unmold and cool on rack.

POT HAGGIS

Of course it is not like the traditional haggis, but it is quite close to
and is much less work. Also it is easy to find the needed ingredier

½ lb. lamb liver	1 cup rolled oatmeal
1 lamb heart	1 cup beef or lamb stock
¼ lb. beef suet	Salt and pepper to taste
2 medium onions, finely minced	

Place liver and heart in a saucepan. Cover the meat with hot wat
Bring to boil, then cover and simmer for one hour. Cool. Mash t
liver and chop the heart in very small pieces. Chop the suet.

Place the oatmeal in a large baking pan and toast in a 350°F. ov
until the whole has turned a nutty brown color. Stir once or twice.

Mix the liver, heart, suet, onions and oatmeal together with a cu
of stock, (use the one from the liver and heart). Salt to taste and ad
pepper generously. Turn into a greased round-bottom bowl, such as

pyrex bowl. Cover with two layers of foil paper. Place on a rack in a pan of boiling water for 2 hours, adding more water, if necessary, as it cooks. Serve piping hot. Serve with "neeps and nips" mashed turnips and nips of whisky.

SADIE'S OATMEAL MACAROONS

In Digby, Sadie was everybody's friend. Wherever she went she brought a batch of her chocolate oatmeal macaroons or her super buttermilk biscuits. She always said that it was a hundred-year old family recipe.

1¼ cups sugar	5 tablespoons cocoa
⅓ cup butter	2 teaspoons baking powder
1 egg	½ teaspoon salt
1½ teaspoons vanilla	⅓ cup milk
½ teaspoon almond extract	2 - 2½ cups rolled oatmeal
⅔ cup flour	

Cream the sugar, butter and egg until light and fluffy. Blend in the vanilla and almond extract. Sift together the flour, cocoa, baking powder and salt. Add to creamed mixture alternately with the milk. Mix well and stir in the oats. Drop by tablespoons on greased baking sheet. Bake in a 350°F. oven for 12 to 15 minutes, cool on wire cake rack.

OATMEAL CRUSTY TOP APPLE PIE

This unusual pie is full of crunch and nut-like flavor.

¼ cup rolled oats	¼ cup pure lard
1 cup all-purpose flour	3 tablespoons cold water
½ teaspoon salt	

Filling:

4 cups peeled, sliced apples	¼ teaspoon cinnamon
¾ cup brown sugar	

Topping:

¼ cup rolled oats	¼ teaspoon cinnamon
¼ cup all-purpose flour	¼ cup margarine
2 tablespoons brown sugar	

For pastry, stir oats, flour and salt, then cut in lard until mixture resembles coarse crumbs. Blend in water and form into ball of dough with fingertips.

Let stand 5 minutes, then roll to fit an 8- or 9-inch pie plate. It is a bit tender to lift, so pass a spatula under as you fold it in two. If it breaks, simply join it together.

To fill, stir apples, brown sugar, and cinnamon. Pack into pie shell.

83

To top, mix oats, flour, brown sugar and cinnamon. (
margarine until mixture is crumb-like, then cover apples.

Bake for 35 minutes at 375°F., or until golden brown on top

CREAM CROWDIE

To get the best result with this very old Scottish dish which m
to our shores, I recommend that you take the trouble to lo
authentic Scots oatmeal. It makes a difference. If you must
substitute do not use quick-cooking oats, but the old-fashionec
cooking type. Early in the day spread 2-3 cups of it on a cooky
Place in a 300°F. oven until toasted to a golden brown. Stir
times to ensure it will be toasted throughout. Let it cool.

To serve, whip a pint of cream, sweeten to suit your taste, anc
with either vanilla, almond essence, a spoonful of whisky or Dra
Add the oatmeal and serve. The toasted oatmeal gives this de
wonderful flavor.

ATHOL BROSE

Now for a wee nip.

2 cups water   **4 tablespoons heather honey**
3 cups of oatmeal

Stir 2 cups of water into 3 cups of oatmeal. Cover and set a:
one hour, then press through strainer until you have one cup of
liquid. Add the honey and stir until the two are well mixed. P
mixture into a 26-ounce bottle and fill with whisky. Cork the
tightly. Shake it vigorously and serve.

SMOKED, DRIED AND FRESI
FROM THE SEA

I never knew what true Finnan Haddies were before I ate
Skink at a friend's farm in Scotland, surrounded by big black
through which moaned the fierce winds of the North Sea
I learned that Finnan (or Findon) Haddocks were named after
village near Aberdeen.

In the old days, they were smoked, dried over seaweed, and s
with salt water during the smoking.

Our Scots ancestors brought the delicacy to our shores. As
I remember my mother serving "Scots Fish." And since it h
brought to Canada, we should all try to learn how to cook it to
tion. And we can.

84

during the Second World War, eaten a "Poached Finnan"
ny remembrance of the Scottish type — in Halifax.
, Finan Haddocks can be grilled, steamed, poached or made
They have an affinity to butter, milk and potatoes. They are
em and seem to please even those who care little for fish.

ST. ANDREW'S GRILLED FINNAN

In Scotland, the St. Andrew type is heavily smoked and usually
served grilled. Topped with a poached egg, it is a treat I often enjoy.

1 lb. Finnan Haddie, cut in 4 portions	3 tablespoons unsalted butter or margarine
1 cup hot milk	4 poached eggs (optional)
	¼ cup parsley, minced

Place the fish in a dish and pour the hot — but not boiling — milk
on top. Cover and let stand 4 hours. (This will tenderize the fish and
will prevent the drying effect of direct heat during the grilling period.)
Remove from the milk and wipe as dry as possible with absorbent
paper towels.

Cream the butter and spread 2 tablespoons of it on one side of the
fish. Place, buttered side up, on a grill and set 4 inches from the source
of heat. Grill 4 minutes, then turn, spread with remaining butter and
grill 2 minutes. Poach the eggs while the fish is cooking. To serve, place
the fish on a hot plate, top each piece with a poached egg and sprinkle
the whole with the parsley. Add 3-4 tablespoons of the milk used for
soaking to the melted butter in the bottom of the grill pan. Warm over
direct heat and pour over the fish.

CULLEN SKINK

A traditional soup in Scotland, Cullen Skink is sometimes served
quite thick, as a meal, or thinner, as a hearty soup. I like to float a piece
of unsalted butter on top when I serve mine.

1 lb. Finnan Haddie	1 tablespoon butter
3 cups boiling water	Salt and pepper, to taste
1 onion, thinly sliced	2 cups milk
3-5 medium-sized potatoes	

Place the fish in a pan, and pour the boiling water on top. Spread
the sliced onion over the fish. Cover and simmer 20 minutes over very
low heat. This will make the fish tender and creamy. When done,
remove the fish to a plate, cool slightly and flake, removing any bones
or hard parts. Cover and simmer the cooking liquid for 20-40 minutes.

In the meantime, peel and boil the potatoes. Drain, dry over medium
heat and mash thoroughly with the butter, salt and pepper. Set aside.

Strain the cooking liquid and heat the milk. Mix together the cooking
liquid, hot milk and flaked fish. Simmer very gently, for a few minutes

so everything will be very hot. Add the mashed potatoes, then beat until well mixed. Taste for seasoning, and serve with a pat of butter on each plate.

FINNAN SAVORY

Old Country people use leftover Finnan Haddie for a creamy breakfast dish, or they serve it on toast as an after-dinner savory. Use chutney or curry powder to flavor the breakfast dish and cayenne for the savory served on squares of hot buttered toast.

1 - 1½ cups Finnan Haddie, cooked and flaked	2 tablespoons cream
1 tablespoon butter	1 teaspoon capers
Cayenne to taste, or	Salt, to taste
½ teaspoon curry powder	Fresh parsley, chopped

Melt the butter, add the cayenne or curry powder. Stir until the butter is light brown, add the flaked fish, cream and capers. Simmer over low heat until the fish has absorbed most of the cream. Add salt to taste and sprinkle with parsley.

FINNAN FARMHOUSE SCRAMBLE

Serve this on a cold night with hot buttermilk biscuits.

1 lb. Finnan Haddie	¼ cup parsley, minced
1 cup milk	4 eggs
2 - 3 tablespoons butter	Juice of ½ lemon
Salt and cayenne, to taste	

Pour the milk over the fish in a shallow pan. Simmer, covered, over low heat for 10 minutes, or until the fish is tender. Remove the fish from the milk, and flake.

Melt the butter in a frying pan, add the flaked fish, salt, cayenne and parsley. Stir over low heat for 2-3 minutes.

Beat the eggs in a bowl and pour over the fish mixture. Cook slowly to make scrambled eggs. Do not overcook. When ready, remove from the heat, pour the lemon juice on top and serve.

The remaining milk can be thickened with 1 tablespoon cornstarch mixed with 2 tablespoons cold water, to make a parsley sauce to serve with the scramble.

Add salt and pepper to taste and as much minced parsley as you like. This should be done before scrambling the eggs. The fish can be kept warm while you make the sauce.

FINNAN PUDDING

A green salad is all that is needed to make an elegant, tasty meal of this light, soufflé-type pudding.

86

1 lb. Finnan Haddie	1 small onion, minced
2 slices bacon	½ teaspoon celery salt
1 tablespoon butter	3 tablespoons parsley, minced
2 cups potatoes, mashed	¼ teaspoon savory
Salt and pepper to taste	3 tablespoons butter, melted
Juice of ½ lemon	3 eggs

Place the fish in a shallow pan. Top with the bacon and just enough water to cover the bottom of the pan. Cover, and steam 10 minutes over medium heat. Remove the fish to a plate. Rub with 1 tablespoon butter. Cool. Flake the cooled fish and stir it into the mashed potatoes. Add the salt, pepper, lemon juice, onion, celery salt, parsley and svory. Beat until the whole is thoroughly mixed. Add the 3 tablespoons melted butter.

Separate the eggs. Beat the yolks until light and stir in. Beat the whites until stiff, then fold them gently into the fish.

Butter a casserole or soufflé dish, pour in the mixture. Bake at 350°F. for 30-40 minutes or until golden and puffed up.

RAW FINNAN HADDIE

1 thick slice Finnan Haddie	Unsalted butter
2 lemons	Dill pickles
Hot toast	

Using a very sharp knife, cut the uncooked fish on the bias, into paper-thin slices. Place on a plate. Squeeze the juice of the 2 lemons and pour over the fish. Cover and refrigerate an hour or so.

Serve with a basket of hot toast and a bowl of unsalted butter.

HOW TO BOIL LIVE LOBSTER

Many cookbooks will tell you to "plunge live lobsters head first in boiling water to cover." But when I was a teenager, an Indian from Laprairie in Quebec taught me a much better way. I have used this method to cook live lobster ever since.

First, choose a large saucepan or soup kettle. Place the lobster on a large piece of clean cotton or cheesecloth, tie the corners together at each end. (This is not absolutely necessary, but it gives a deeper red to the lobster as it cooks, and it makes removal a simple matter by lifting the cloth bag with long forks slipped in each knotted end.)

Cover the lobster completely with cold water and add 1 tablespoon coarse salt. If you're lucky enough to be near the sea, use sea water and omit the salt.

Bring the water to a boil over high heat and let it boil 3 to 4 minutes, then lower the heat to simmer and cook another 12 to 18 minutes, depending on the size of the lobster. An overcooked lobster will have stringy meat.

As soon as the cooking period is finished, remove the lobster from the water and dip briefly into a bowl of cold water. This will stop the cooking without cooling the meat.

THE BEST LOBSTER

An old seaman living in Covey Cove, Nova Scotia, proved to me that the only way to cook fresh lobster is to start it in icy cold sea water with a good handful of seaweed. Bring it to a boil over a roaring fire built on the shore. When the lobster becomes deep red, fish it out and eat it. I got around this by using very cold water and sea salt purchased at the drugstore. With a tinge of sadness I replaced the fire with my stove's fastest heat. I got the seaweed easily enough from the market where I bought the live lobster. A dish of hot melted sweet butter and a big bowl of watercress complete this lobster treat.

SWEET CREAMED LOBSTER STEW

This makes a delicious meal to serve in the garden, with a basketful of hot buttered crackers, and followed by strawberries, thick cream and maple sugar.

2 select or 3 quarter live lobsters	**4 cups milk**
3 tablespoons butter	**½ pint whipping cream**

Steam the lobsters. Remove the meat from the shell. Cover and cool.
Melt the butter in an enamelled cast-iron saucepan or a flameware saucepan. Add the lobster meat and simmer over low heat for a few minutes, add the milk and stir most of the time until hot, add the cream and keep on stirring. When hot, simmer for a few minutes, but do not boil. Cool. Cover and refrigerate 12 to 24 hours before serving, to develop the full flavor of the lobster. Reheat, without boiling, and, just before serving, season to taste with salt and pepper.

COVEY COVE CRAB QUICHE

I learned to make this while spending a few days with a fisherman's family in Covey Cove, N.S. This is my variation of his wife's lobster pie.

Pie crust of your choice, thinly rolled	**¼ lb. Swiss or mild Cheddar cheese, grated**
1 cup mushrooms, sliced	**3 eggs**
2 tablespoons brandy or lemon juice	**1 tablespoon all-purpose flour**
	⅛ teaspoon nutmeg
1 cup canned crab	**½ teaspoon salt**
	1 cup cream

Line 8 2-inch aluminum tart pans with the thinly-rolled pastry.
Preheat oven to 375°F.
Combine and stir the mushrooms with the brandy or lemon juice,

then shred the crab, removing any hard parts. Fill each tart with alternate layers of sliced mushrooms, crab and grated cheese.

Beat together the eggs, flour, nutmeg, salt and cream, then pour equally over each tart. Place in a baking pan and bake for 20-30 minutes, or until the custard is set and the top golden brown.

If you are preparing this in advance, cool thoroughly and wrap each tart individually in a square of foil. Refrigerate or freeze. To reheat, unwrap and place in a 375°F. oven for 10-15 minutes.

CRABMEAT CHOWDER

3	slices salt pork	1 - 1½	lbs. frozen crabmeat
1	large onion, sliced thin	1	teaspoon salt
2	cups sliced potatoes	¼	teaspoon savory
1½	cups hot water	2	tablespoons butter
2	cups hot milk		

Cut the salt pork into 1½-inch squares. Melt and brown over medium heat in a large saucepan.

Make alternate layers of potatoes and onion slices in the pan. Add the hot water. Cover. Bring to a boil and simmer from 10 to 15 minutes or until the potatoes are tender. Add the milk, crabmeat, salt, savory and butter. Do not mix, simply keep warm until ready to serve.

FISH BROTH

I often buy a bag of cod's heads and tails for pennies, then use them to make a delicious fish broth that can serve as a bouillon.

6 - 8	cups water	½	teaspoon thyme
3	stalks celery	1½ - 2	lbs. cod heads and tails
1	bay leaf	2	tablespoons vinegar
1	onion, sliced	2	tablespoons butter
1	carrot, sliced		Salt and pepper, to taste
8	peppercorns		

In a saucepan bring first 7 ingredients to a rolling boil and add fish. Cover and simmer 40 minutes, then strain through a fine sieve or a coarser one lined with cheesecloth. Pour fish stock back into pot, and add vinegar, butter, salt, and pepper just before serving.

To serve as a soup, add 1 cup fine noodles, 1 firmly chopped unpeeled tomato and simmer until noodles are soft. Or serve the Italian way by placing 1 tablespoon of grated Parmesan cheese in each soup bowl and pouring hot fish stock on top. Sprinkle with parsley.

This fish stock freezes well and will keep 3-4 months.

HERRING IN A POT

12 small fresh herrings	2 blades of mace
2 cups cider or wine vinegar	1 bay leaf
1 cup water	12 whole peppercorns
1 teaspoon coarse salt	6 coriander seeds
½ teaspoon pepper	2 tablespoons butter
6 whole cloves	Pinch of cayenne

Clean herrings and remove heads, scales and fins. Do not bone. Wash well and dry in absorbent paper. Salt and pepper insides lightly. Lay fish heads to tails, in glass casserole. Place bay leaf in middle. Pour vinegar and water over. Add other ingredients, cutting butter in small pieces. Cover tightly, place in 400°F. oven until liquid boils, then lower heat to 200°F. Bake 3 hours. Cool without uncovering. The long cooking in vinegar almost dissolves all the small bones. Refrigerate overnight. When cold, the liquid forms a nice jelly. When boned or rolled, much of the flavor is lost.

HERRING SALAD

1 medium salt herring or 1 lb. pickled herring fillets	4 tablespoons cider vinegar
	2 tablespoons water
1½ cups boiled potatoes, diced	2 tablespoons sugar
1 cup pickled beets, diced	Pepper to taste
1 medium onion, diced	2 hard-boiled eggs, quartered
⅓ cup dill pickles, diced	¾ cup minced parsley
½ cup peeled apples, diced	

If using salt herring, clean, remove head and soak overnight topped with cold water in a covered container. Then drain, skin and fillet.

With either type of fish, dice, add vegetables, pickles, apples and blend with a fork. Mix vinegar with water, sugar, pepper, add to fish mixture and blend thoroughly. Rinse a ring mold or mold of your choice in cold water and pack salad into it. Cover and chill a few hours or overnight.

To serve, unmold, garnish with eggs and sprinkle parsley over all.

SOLOMON GUNDY

Mrs. Deal gave this authentic recipe in the *Dutch Oven,* a cook book of recipes from the kitchens of Lunenburg.

| 2 | salt herring | Vinegar to cover |
| 1 | large onion | |

Clean herring thoroughly, remove skin, fillet and cut in 2 inch pieces. Soak in cold water for 5 hours, changing the water frequently (or soak overnight if desired). Drain. Heat vinegar, add 1 tablespoon sugar, little pepper and cool. Pour over onion and herring and let stand for a few hours.

NOVA SCOTIA HADDOCK HASH

1	lb. haddock	2	slices salt pork (or 4 slices
2	slices of lemon		bacon)
1	bay leaf	3	cups cooked potatoes
¼	cup cream or milk	1	cup cooked beets

Place the haddock in a saucepan with the lemon and bay leaf and enough cold water to cover. Bring to a boil and then simmer 10 minutes. Drain and flake, add diced potatoes and beets and chop the whole together. Cube the salt pork and brown in the frying pan. Meanwhile blend the cream into the fish mixture, then add to the pork in the pan. Cook over low heat about 15 minutes. It will be crispy brown at the bottom. Serve with sweet pickles or homemade chili.

This makes an excellent brunch for six. All you need to finish it off is some hot corn bread and English currant jam.

NOVA SCOTIA BOILED COD

The Nova Scotia woman has many culinary tricks. When she boils fresh cod, for example, she first places the fish under cold running water for an hour. This gives the cod a firm, interesting texture. Why not try it in this recipe?

6 - 7	cups water	1	tablespoon salt
½	teaspoon ginger	2 - 3	lbs. fresh cod
1	bay leaf		Garnish and sauce (see below)
2	slices unpeeled lemon		

In a saucepan bring first 5 ingredients to a fast rolling boil. Cut cod into slices just over 1 inch thick. Gently lower them into boiling mixture and boil 5-7 minutes. Do not just simmer.

Lift cod from water to a hot platter with a perforated ladle and sprinkle with parsley or dill. Serve with a mixture of butter melted carefully until light brown and 2 chopped hard-cooked eggs, or with mustard sauce:

Melt 3 tablespoons butter, stir in 3 tablespoons flour and 3 teaspoons dry mustard. Mix well and add 2 cups stock from fish. Simmer until creamy and smooth, stirring constantly, then add ¼ teaspoon sugar and 2-4 teaspoons prepared horseradish. Taste for seasoning and serve as is, or beat in 1 egg yolk for a golden sauce, or add ¼ cup rich cream for an ivory sauce.

LUNENBERG DUTCH MESS
(Salt Cod and Potatoes)

½ lb. salt dry cod
6 large potatoes
2 oz. salt pork
  Butter, size of egg

2 onions
1 tablespoon vinegar
2 or 3 tablespoons cream

Tear cod in small pieces. Wash thoroughly and soak in cold water 3 or 4 hours. Peel potatoes and cut in six or eight strips. Remove fish from water and cook potatoes in water in which fish has been soaked. When potatoes are half done add fish and cook until potatoes are tender. Drain. Place on platter and sprinkle with pepper. Dice pork into small pieces and fry until brown. Add onions cut on the round and fry until light brown. Add butter, vinegar and cream, let come to a boil and pour over fish and potatoes. Serve with applesauce.

SPICED SALMON

Salmon prepared in this way is a traditional dish in Liverpool and Lunenburg. You can use any salmon, but I especially recommend that from Nova Scotia's Medway Lake. Or, you can spice fresh young speckled trout in the same fashion — try it out of their Ponhook Lake.

2 cups white or cider vinegar
3 tablespoons coarse salt
2 tablespoons honey
¾ cup water

2 tablespoons black peppercorns
2 cinnamon sticks
2 - 4 lbs. fresh salmon or
  speckled trout

In a large frying pan, stainless steel if possible, mix all ingredients except fish and bring to a boil.

Cut fish into slices about 1½ inches thick and place in boiling vinegar mixture. Cover and simmer 20 minutes over low heat. Remove to a nonmetal dish and pour vinegar mixture over — it must cover fish completely. Remove cinnamon sticks but leave peppercorns in.

Let cool, cover tightly and keep refrigerated. Serve cold with hot boiled potatoes or a salad. Pickled fish will keep refrigerated 3 weeks.

PICKLED SALMON

Eat cold with bread and butter, beer or tea — or use as part of a buffet, served with mayonnaise.

1 quart water
½ lemon, unpeeled and thinly
  sliced
1 teaspoon salt
¼ teaspoon pepper
1 bay leaf
2 - 4 lbs. fresh salmon

4 cups white vinegar
4 cups of water used to cook
  salmon
20 whole peppercorns
10 whole allspice
4 blades of mace

Bring the water to a boil, add the lemon, salt, pepper and bay leaf. Add the piece of fresh salmon, bring back to the boil. Cover and simmer 20 minutes per pound. When done, carefully remove from the water and place on a dry cloth. Let it stand at room temperature for 2 hours.

To pickle, bring to the boil the white vinegar, the water used to cook the salmon, whole peppercorns, whole allspice, mace. Boil one minute and cool. When cooled, pour over the salmon which can be left whole if you have a large covered container to keep it in. Otherwise cut it into pieces. Cover and keep refrigerated.

SCOTTISH MOLDED SALMON

Here is an attractive way to use those leftover bits and pieces of a good poached or baked salmon, or start with a thick slice of poached salmon.

2 - 3 cups cooked salmon	1 teaspoon curry powder
1 envelope unflavored gelatine	Capers
¼ cup cold water	Lemon wedges
1 cup mayonnaise	Shredded lettuce
2 teaspoons prepared mustard	

Remove skin and bones from salmon, pack pieces into an oiled mold of your choice. Cover and refrigerate for a few hours. Sprinkle gelatine over the cold water to soften for 5 minutes. Set over a pan of hot water to melt. Mix together the mayonnaise, prepared mustard and curry powder, add the gelatine slowly while beating constantly. Refrigerate for 10 minutes.

Unmold the fish on a service platter. Spread generously with the jellied mayonnaise. If any is left, spread it around the unmolded fish. Decorate the top with dots of capers and lemon wedges. Surround with a thick layer of shredded lettuce. Refrigerate until ready to serve.

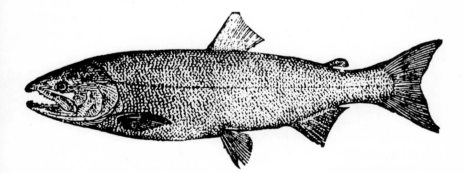

NOVA SCOTIA SMOKED SALMON

If prepared early in the morning, this can be refrigerated until serving. The delightful part of this entrée is cold scrambled eggs. Include a pepper mill and lemon wedges in your service.

½ lb. smoked salmon, sliced
   paper thin
8 eggs
4 tablespoons each, milk and
   cold butter

2 teaspoons chopped parsley
¼ cup chopped pimiento
3 tablespoons capers

Place separated slices of salmon on a plate and refrigerate. (Smoked salmon can be replaced with 3 cans of imported French sardines.)

Break eggs into a saucepan, then add milk, butter, salt and pepper to taste. Over low heat, stir mixture by pushing butter with a fork until it softens. Continue stirring until eggs begin to scramble, remove from heat while still soft and quickly add parsley and pimiento. Pile a tablespoon or so of egg on each salmon slice, roll lightly, and place two on each small service plate. Sprinkle with some capers and refrigerate.

If using sardines, place a tablespoon or so of mixture between two sardines on each plate, and sprinkle with capers.

SMOORED, STOVIES AND OTHERS

In 1953, Lunenburg, N.S., celebrated its 200th anniversary. In 1959, Liverpool, N.S., did the same. Each city produced a commemorative cookbook, *Dutch Oven* and *Perkins' Hearth* respectively, containing recipes that have been handed down from one generation to another.

Because of the early trade routes, Nova Scotia and Quebec have more food traditions than the rest of Canada. The difference between the two provinces is definite — the Quebec palate was determined by the French and English colonials and their tastes turned more to meat and the goods of the land. Nova Scotia, on the other hand, a port inhabited and trading with New England and the West Indies, had more fish, homemade bread and slaw.

SMOORED PULLETS

In the Lowlands of Scotland chicken is "smoored" (boiled) or stovies (baked). Undoubtedly those who built Nova Scotia, coming from the Old Country, brought the ways and the words with them.

1 3 - lb. broiler
3 tablespoons flour
½ teaspoon salt
¼ teaspoon pepper

2 tablespoons butter
2 tablespoons bacon fat
3 tablespoons parsley
½ cup clotted (sour) cream

94

Remove ends of wings, neck and giblets, split chicken in four. Place giblets in saucepan with 1 bay leaf, ½ teaspoon salt and 1 onion cut in four. Add 2 cups water. Simmer 2 hours, covered. Mix the flour, salt, pepper. Roll pieces of chicken in it.

Melt the butter and bacon fat in a cast-iron frying pan. Brown chicken on both sides. Cover and cook or "smoore" over very low heat about 1 hour, or until chicken is tender. When ready, add the parsley and the cream to the juice in the pan, (as the chicken will form its own juice). Stir together until hot but do not let it boil. Serve at once.

Strain the giblets, chop the meat, add to the sauce and reserve the stock to make a soup or add to a soup or use instead of water to dilute canned chicken soup.

STOVIES

A sort of scalloped chicken and potatoes cooked on top of the stove.

1 broiler or 2 lbs. chicken legs or wings	**1 bay leaf**
4 large potatoes	**¼ teaspoon sage**
2 large onions	**⅓ cup butter**
2 teaspoons salt	**1 cup water or chicken stock**
¼ teaspoon pepper	**3 tablespoons flour**
	¼ cup milk or cream

Cut the chicken in individual pieces. Peel and slice the onions thinly. Arrange alternate layers of chicken, potatoes and onions in an enamelled cast-iron saucepan. Dot each layer with butter and sprinkle with some of the salt, pepper, and sage. Place the bay leaf in the middle of the dish. Add the water or chicken stock. Bring to boil, then cover and simmer over very low heat 1 hour.

To serve, remove pieces of chicken from stock and thicken broth with 3 tablespoons flour mixed with ¼ cup milk or cream. Pour the whole over the chicken.

SCOTCH BROTH

My mother was taught how to make this by a dear Scottish friend who came to settle in Canada in the 1920s.

8 cups cold water	**1 diced large leek (optional)**
1 bay leaf	**1 cup diced turnips**
½ teaspoon pepper	**2 diced celery stalks**
2 lbs. lamb's neck or shank or mixture of both	**2 cups finely chopped green cabbage**
2 teaspoons salt	**¼ cup minced fresh parsley**
4 tablespoons pot barley	**3 tablespoons butter**
2 sliced carrots	**½ cup rolled oats**
2 diced onions	

To water in a large saucepan, add bay leaf, pepper and meat. Slowly bring to a boil, skimming it just before it boils. (This part is important — it improves the soup's color and flavor.)

Add salt, boil a few seconds and skim again. Add remaining ingredients, except butter and oats. Slowly bring to a boil, then cover and simmer 2 hours.

Melt butter in a frying pan, add oats and stir over medium heat until nutty brown. Add to soup and cook 10-15 minutes more.

HAM STEAK WITH APPLES

In 1953, I bought the **Dutch Oven** cookbook — it was the first of nine or ten successful editions. This was the first recipe I tried and I have been making it ever since. It is signed by Mildred Potter.

2 - inch slice cooked ham	¾ cup port
10 - 15 whole cloves	4 apples, cored and sliced
¾ cup brown sugar	

Stud the ham fat with cloves, place steak in a shallow roasting pan and bake at 350°F. for 25-35 mintes.

Take from the oven and spread ham with sugar, then slowly drench with port. Return to oven, set now at 400°F. and bake 20-30 minutes, basting once. Remove ham to a hot platter and stir apple slices in syrup left in pan. Bake for 10 minutes, stir again and pour on top of ham.

MOLDED CHICKEN

This will keep for weeks if well covered and refrigerated. If you let the chicken set in a ring mold, you can fill the centre with a salad of fresh green peas, or thinly sliced cucumbers tossed with chives and sour cream.

3 - 4 lb. chicken	1 teaspoon salt
2 tablespoons butter	¼ teaspoon pepper
5 cups hot water	¼ teaspoon thyme
1 onion, quartered	1 bay leaf
1 carrot, sliced	½ teaspoon dry mustard
½ cup coarsely chopped celery leaves	

Melt the butter in a deep saucepan and brown chicken all over. Add hot water and bring to a boil, then add remaining ingredients. Cover and simmer over low heat about 1½ hours, or until chicken is tender.

Set chicken in a bowl to cool and strain broth, skimming off as much fat as possible. Boil broth uncovered until there are 2 cups left.

Remove meat from cooled chicken, chopping skin as finely as possible, then cutting meat into small pieces. Add skin and meat to broth, taste for seasoning and pour into an oiled mold of your choice. Refrigerate until set.

To serve, unmold, garnish to taste and serve with a bowl of Nova Scotia Boiled Dressing.

NOVA SCOTIA BOILED DRESSING

In Nova Scotia, boiled dressing is always preferable to mayonnaise.

4 eggs	**4 - 6 tablespoons sugar**
6 tablespoons all-purpose flour	**¼ cup butter**
2 cups hot water	**4 teaspoons dry mustard**
1 cup cider vinegar	**2 teaspoons salt**

Beat the eggs in the top of a double boiler, then add flour and hot water gradually while beating. Add remaining ingredients and cook over boiling water until smooth and creamy, stirring occasionally.

Pour into a jar, cover, let cool and refrigerate. If dressing is too thick for your taste, thin to desired consistency with light cream.

BEAN PORRIDGE

When the Scots migrated to Canada, they traded the split green peas of their "Pease porridge hot, pease porridge cold, pease porridge in the pot nine days old" for bean porridge.

2 lbs. beef or lamb shank	**1 cup dried navy beans, precooked**
1 teaspoon salt	**¼ teaspoon pepper**
1 bay leaf	**2 tablespoons cornmeal**
8 cups water	

Place the meat in a pot with the salt, bay leaf and water. Cover and cook over the lowest heat until the meat is ready to fall from the bone. This may take 2-3 hours.

Drain the water from the precooked beans, but reserve it. Add the beans to the meat broth. Pick the meat into small pieces, discarding the gristle and bone.

Cover, simmer over low heat until the beans are tender. If more water is needed, use some of the reserved bean water.

Stir the pepper and cornmeal with some of the reserved water to make a paste. Stir into the hot broth when the beans are almost done. Cover and simmer another 30 minutes. Serve hot with molasses or maple syrup.

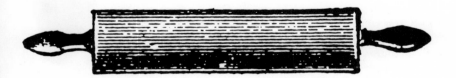

PIGS IN CORN

This old-time Nova Scotia favorite used to be made with fresh corn, grated from the cob. Today, canned corn niblets make the work easy.

1 lb. sausages	**⅔ cup cracker crumbs**
14 - oz. can corn niblets	**3 tablespoons minced parsley**
Milk	**¼ teaspoon sage or marjoram**
2 eggs, lightly beaten	**Salt and pepper, to taste**
1 small onion chopped	

Place the sausages in a cold frying pan without any fat. Set pan on medium low heat, and cook until sausages are a golden color, shaking pan often to rotate them. Remove from accumulated fat and set aside.

Drain corn niblets, pour juice into measuring cup and add enough milk to make 2 cups. Mix with corn and remaining ingredients in a bowl, then pour into a buttered shallow casserole and arrange sausages on top. Bake at 350°F. for 35-45 minutes, or until corn cream is well set.

ACADIAN RICE CASSEROLE

No matter how you vary this casserole, it always turns out successfully. You can replace the cheese with 1 cup medium white sauce. And you can sandwich left-over chopped beef or ham between the rice and cabbage.

1 cup uncooked long grain rice	**2½ cups hot water**
1 chopped onion	**3 tablespoons chili sauce or**
¼ teaspoon summer savory	**catsup**
2 tablespoons butter	**4 cups finely shredded cabbage**
1 teaspoon salt	**1 cup mild grated cheese**
¼ teaspoon pepper	

Place in a casserole: the rice, onion, savory, butter (in little pieces), salt, pepper, hot water and chili sauce or catsup. Mix with a fork. Top with finely shredded cabbage. Do not mix it. Cover and bake at 350°F. for 40 minutes or until the rice has absorbed the water. Uncover and top with the mild grated cheese. Brown under the broiler or cook 10 minutes longer.

HODGE PODGE

The original Hodge Podge was a summer dish of new vegetables; the following recipe, popular in the Lunenburg district, is the same thing, but with a salt pork sauce.

½ lb. fresh green or wax beans	**¼ cup flour**
6 - 8 new carrots	**1 cup light cream**
1 lb. fresh green peas	**3 tablespoons chopped chives or**
6 medium potatoes	**green onions**
1 small cauliflower (optional)	**¼ teaspoon pepper**
1 cup finely diced fat and lean	**Salt, to taste**
salt pork	

Split the beans in half lengthwise, cut carrots into long sticks, shell peas and place all together into unsalted boiling water. Boil fast uncovered 8 minutes, then drain, reserving 1 cup of cooking water.

Peel potatoes and slice into matchsticks. Cook covered until just tender, then drain, reserving water, and set aside. Break cauliflower into flowerets, place in a saucepan and, using potato water, boil uncovered 8-10 minutes. Drain and set aside.

Mix vegetables in a warm dish, cover and let stand in a warm place.

While vegetables are cooking, prepare sauce. Melt diced salt pork in a cast iron frying pan over medium heat. When golden brown, discard enough fat so that only about ½ cup remains.

Add flour and stir over medium heat until it turns a light brown color. Pour in cream, vegetable water and stir until creamy. Add chives or green onions, pepper, then taste for salt, as the salt pork is sometimes sufficient. Pour over the vegetables.

POTATO PIE

Pastry for 2 - crust pie	**½ - 1 lb. cooked salmon**
5 - 6 potatoes	**or**
1 teaspoon minced green onion	**1 (6 or 12-oz.) can salmon**
or onion	**1 can creamed corn or kernels**
¼ teaspoon savory	**or**
Salt and pepper to taste	**2 onions, minced and fried**

Line a pie plate with a crust of your choice.

Peel and cook the potatoes, mash and add green onion or onion, savory, salt and pepper. Blend together and spread over the pie crust. Cover with the flaked salmon and then add the corn or mince 2 onions, fry and place over the salmon. Cover with the second crust.

Bake in a 400°F. oven 30 or 35 minutes, or until golden brown. Serve hot. Also very good served at room temperature.

WILTED SPINACH SALAD

In this light but nourishing fare, the eggs and cottage cheese give good protein value. The salad's color and flavor will revive the appetites of even the most disinterested.

⅓ cup salad oil	**1 halved garlic clove**
3 tablespoons cider vinegar	**1 lb. fresh spinach**
Juice of ½ a lemon	**8 bacon slices**
¼ teaspoon dry mustard	**3 cubes bread slices (optional)**
½ teaspoon salt	**4 - 6 hard-boiled eggs**

In a bottle, blend oil, vinegar, lemon juice, mustard, salt and garlic. Set aside for a few hours to let flavors blend (it can even be prepared the day before).

Remove spinach stems. Wash leaves in cold water and let drain very well in a colander. Then roll in absorbent paper and refrigerate 20-30 minutes. Meanwhile, fry bacon until crisp, drain on absorbent paper. If using bread cubes, fry them golden brown in the bacon fat and place on absorbent paper.

When ready to serve, put spinach in a large bowl, shake dressing and add to taste. Toss lightly.

Cut eggs in half, remove yolks, cut whites in rings over salad, sprinkle with crumbled egg yolks and bacon, then sprinkle croutons over all. Toss salad at table.

Serve with a bowl of cottage cheese stirred with lemon juice.

CUCUMBER SALAD

Peel 3 medium sized cucumbers. Slice very thin and cover with 1 teaspoon salt. Press with heavy weight for about 2 hours. One small onion (cut fine) may be added to the cucumbers before pressing, if so desired. Then drain liquid off cucumbers.

Add 4 tablespoons of cider vinegar.

½ cup white sugar   **¾ cup thick sour cream**
¼ teaspoon pepper

Mix well with the drained cucumbers. More sugar and vinegar may be added to suit the taste.

SOUR CREAM SALAD DRESSING

A Nova Scotia specialty which has a feeling of spring. Use with thinly sliced cucumbers or fresh garden lettuce.

3 tablespoons cider vinegar   **¼ teaspoon pepper**
4 tablespoons sugar   **½ cup sour cream (commercial)**

Mix until well blended. Keep refrigerated. Blend into salad or cucumbers.

CLOVER AND ROSE HONEY

A Digby hostess with a lot of personality served this delectable summer jam and was kind enough to give me the recipe.

Gather 6 red clovers, 30 white clovers and 4 fully bloomed roses, red, if possible. Then, we boil 5 cups sugar with 1¼ cups water and 1 teaspoon alum, until syrup is clear. We pour the hot syrup over the flowers (without the stems). We stir the fragrant liquid and let it stand for 10 minutes, then pour into clean glass jars, flowers and all. It is sheer delight to smell, to look at, and to eat. Try it the first time you have tea in the garden. Spread it on small triangles of hot crumpets or hidden in tiny hot muffins.

QUALITY LEMON BUTTER

¼ cup sweet butter	Juice and grated rind of
2½ cups fine granulated sugar	4 lemons
6 eggs, well beaten	

Mix together the butter, granulated sugar, well beaten eggs and the juice and grated lemon rind. Cook on top of boiling water until thick. Pour into a clean glass jar. Cover and keep cold. Use with your afternoon hot bread or for tartlet filling. This is very easily made in the winter.

BAKING WITH CROFTERS

Rhubarb is with us most of the year: from the garden in the spring, and from the hothouse in the winter. It is sometimes called "wine plant", because it is used to make wine, and "pie plant" because for many years, it was used only to make pie.

And, if you remember your childhood days, you will bite into a stick of it and still enjoy the tartness.

When fresh, rhubarb is firm, crisp and bright. In fact, its color is brighter in winter than in spring, and the winter ruby pink with young immature leaves is one of the best rhubarbs.

A little girl I know calls rhubarb "winter sunshine," and she's right. It almost brings the summer sun to your table, in so many delightful and colorful pies, sauces, puddings and jellies.

BUTTERMILK BISCUITS

It is hard to give the exact amount of liquid for biscuits because flours differ — just add enough to achieve a rather soft dough.

2 cups all-purpose flour	4 tablespoons pure lard
1 teaspoon salt	¾ cup (approx.) buttermilk
1 teaspoon baking powder	or sour milk
½ teaspoon soda	

Sift together dry ingredients, then cut in lard (always use the very best fat for hot biscuits) until you have a mealy mixture. Add enough buttermilk or sour milk to mix into a rather soft dough. Turn on to a floured board and knead gently 5-6 turns — never knead too much.

Roll out gently to about a ¾-inch thickness. Cut into rounds and place on a greased baking pan. Bake at 425°F. for 15-18 minutes, or until golden brown.

NEWLYWED HOT CAKES

Here is a recipe so simple that an Early Canadian bride, or even a modern one, could manage it.

1½ cups buckwheat flour	1 egg
1 cup graham flour	2 cups buttermilk (or sour milk)
1¼ teaspoons soda	¼ cup cream
2 teaspoons salt	

Sift together the buckwheat flour, graham flour, soda, salt. Beat the egg with the buttermilk (or sour milk) and the cream. Stir into the flour mixture, beating until well blended. Pour on a hot griddle or large black frying pan, spreading the batter to the edge. When bubbly, turn and cook the other side. As cakes are cooked pile them on a hot plate in the oven, keeping them covered with a cloth. When ready to eat cut into squares and serve with butter and molasses, or — for a more filling meal — with hot pork and applesauce.

FORTY FATHOM CORNCAKE

This thin crisp corncake served with cod is a century-old recipe I copied from an old battered notebook one night when I had supper at a fisherman's house in Nova Scotia. It was a wonderful potluck meal.

1 cup yellow cornmeal	1 egg, beaten
¼ cup dark brown sugar	1 cup rich milk (I use cream)
½ teaspoon salt	2 tablespoons melted butter
1 cup flour	or bacon fat
3 teaspoons "tartaric and soda" (baking powder to us)	

In "steady succession" mix 1 scant cup yellow cornmeal, the dark brown sugar, salt, flour, "tartaric and soda" (baking powder), beaten egg, rich milk (or cream), melted butter or bacon fat. When these have become "thoroughly acquainted" pour in a thin layer in a greased pan, top with small pieces of crackling (if none available use diced bacon or omit altogether). Bake 25 minutes at 350°F. Unmold and serve hot with a "mess of creamed cod" (fresh cod poached in a medium white sauce flavored with onions and lots of parsley.)

SOFT OR CRISP MOLASSES COOKIES

A molasses, ginger, lard or bacon fat and soda cooky is almost a must on Scottish tables. They are soft or crisp, depending on how thick you roll out the dough.

1 cup lard or bacon fat	½ teaspoon anise seed
1 cup sugar	3 to 4 cups all-purpose flour*
1 egg, unbeaten	1 teaspoon salt
½ cup molasses	1 teaspoon baking soda
½ cup cold water	

Cream the lard until light. Add the sugar and beat until very creamy. Add the unbeaten egg and blend thoroughly. Stir in the molasses, cold water and anise seed. Mix thoroughly. Sift together three times the all-purpose flour, salt and baking soda. Gradually add to the batter and mix to a soft dough with your hands, kneading as little as possible. Refrigerate 6 to 12 hours. Roll out to ½-inch for soft cookies or ⅛-inch for crisp cookies. Cut with a 2-inch round or star cutter. Place on a lightly greased cooky sheet and bake 10 minutes in a preheated 375°F. oven. Cool on rack.

*For a very crisp cooky use just enough flour to bind the whole and refrigerate covered, for 6 to 10 days.

CARROT OATMEAL COOKIES

These old-fashioned cookies are big, soft, spicy and "very good keepers" as they used to say.

1 cup firmly packed light brown sugar	1 teaspoon baking powder
½ cup soft shortening	½ teaspoon soda
2 eggs	½ teaspoon salt
½ cup milk	½ teaspoon each cinnamon and nutmeg
1 cup grated raw carrots	2 cups quick-cooking oatmeal
1½ cups all-purpose flour	1½ cups seedless raisins

Cream the sugar, shortening and eggs until light and creamy. Add milk, carrots, and stir until well mixed. Sift together flour, baking powder, soda, salt, cinnamon and nutmeg. Add remaining ingredients and stir until raisins are well coated with flour mixture.

Mix with creamed mixture — this again is a fairly stiff batter. Drop by tablespoonfuls on to a greased cooky sheet and bake at 375°F. about 15 minutes, or until brown all over.

PINK RHUBARB PUDDING

Served cold in a round cut glass bowl, with macaroons and lady fingers or langues de chat, this is truly a company dessert for lunch or dinner.

2 cups rhubarb, in 1-inch pieces	⅓ cup sugar
¼ cup fresh orange juice	1 package sliced frozen strawberrie

Stew rhubarb with orange juice and sugar, cooking over low heat, barely simmering, about 20-25 minutes, or until rhubarb is tender. Add strawberries, cover and let stand over very low heat until they're thawed. Stir the whole gently, refrigerate until ready to serve.

PIE-PLANT PIE

You may use your favorite pie dough for this, but the French type is superb. And you may add an egg white topping that puffs up between the lattices, giving a very nice effect.

French pie dough:

2 cups all-purpose flour	⅓ cup cold pure lard
½ teaspoon salt	6 - 8 tablespoons ice water
⅓ cup cold unsalted butter	

Filling:

2 tablespoons all-purpose flour	Grated peel of ½ a lemon
⅓ cup sugar	12 rhubarb stems

Crust: Sift together flour, salt. Cut in cold butter with a pastry blender until well mixed. Cut in lard until mixture has consistency of small peas. Chill 2 hours (this unusual step gives the pastry its special flakiness).

Sprinkle top of dough with ice water, 1 tablespoon at a time, blending gently with a fork until well mixed. With your hands, gather dough into two balls.

Gently roll one ball into a circle — about 11 inches across for a 9-inch pie plate. Fit dough into the plate without stretching and trim with scissors so only an inch hangs over edge.

Roll second piece of dough into a rectangle about 9 x 11 inches. Cut with a pie crimping wheel or a knife into strips of dough ½ inch wide. About 18 strips are needed for a 9-inch pie.

Filling: Mix the 2 tablespoons flour, ⅓ cup sugar and lemon peel, and sprinkle into lower crust. Cut rhubarb into ½-inch pieces with a sharp knife and pour into pie plate.

Fit top crust by placing 9 strips ½-inch apart in one direction. Then cross and weave remaining 9 strips. Trim ends, fold the lower crust over strip ends and flute all around with your fingertips.

Dust the top of the pie plate lightly with sugar. Bake 15 minutes at 450°F., then reduce heat to 350°F. and bake 15 or 20 minutes, or until crust is browned.

If you wish to add the topping, do the following after you have poured the rhubarb into the pie plate.

Beat 2 egg yolks with ⅔ cup sugar, 2 tablespoons all-purpose flour, juice of ½ a lemon, pinch of salt and ¼ teaspoon almond flavoring.

Beat 2 egg whites and fold into yolk mixture. Pour over rhubarb, then put on lattice strips and bake.

CARAMEL BREAD PUDDING

¾ cup brown sugar
1 egg beaten
2 slices heavily buttered bread

1½ cups milk
1 teaspoon vanilla

Pack sugar in a buttered casserole, cut bread in small pieces and place buttered side down on sugar. Mix egg, milk and vanilla and pour over mixture. Put in oven and bake until nicely browned. Serve with or without cream.

BAG PUDDING

2⅔ cups all-purpose flour
½ teaspoon salt
1 teaspoon soda
2 teaspoons cream of tartar
¼ teaspoon mace or nutmeg
1 egg
1 cup sugar

½ cup cream (sour or fresh)
½ cup milk
½ teaspoon almond essence
  or vanilla
2 cups thinly sliced apples or
  stoned cherries or sliced
  peaches

Sift together the flour, salt, soda, cream of tartar, mace or nutmeg. Beat the egg, sugar and cream until creamy and fluffy. Add the milk, almond essence or vanilla and apples, cherries or peaches. Mix well, then add the sifted dry ingredients. Stir just enough to combine. It should be rather a soft dough.

Wring out a piece of cotton, or better still a cotton bag, in cold water. Fill not more than ⅔ full with the batter. Tie securely, leaving room for rising. Place the bag in a large saucepan of boiling water. Cover tightly and boil gently for 1 hour. Remove the bag to a platter, drain the excess water, cut the string and slide the pudding out. Serve hot with hard sauce, vanilla sauce or brown-sugar sauce.

OLD-FASHIONED HOT GINGERBREAD

This may be baked early and warmed up at 300°F. Our grandmothers used to call it soft gingerbread. The cooky was the snap, or hard gingerbread. It is delicious served with beaten butter and green applesauce or stewed rhubarb.

½ cup sugar
½ cup molasses or
   English treacle
¼ cup melted butter or
   bacon fat

2¼ cups all-purpose flour
1 cup hot water minus
   2 tablespoons (⅞ cup)
½ - 1 teaspoon ginger
1 teaspoon baking soda

Mix the sugar, molasses or treacle and melted butter or bacon fat. Add the flour and stir until thoroughly mixed.

Mix the hot water, ginger and baking soda and add all at once to the flour mixture. Mix enough to blend everything together.

Pour the batter into a well-buttered 8 x 8 x 2-inch pan. (If you use a Pyrex or pyroceram dish, it won't have to be unmolded.) Bake at 350°F. for 30-35 minutes, or until well done.

MOTHER'S APPLE CAKE

Joan Balcom's mother from Annapolis Valley created this unusual delicious cake.

¾ cup shortening
1 cup white sugar
2 eggs
1 large orange, juice and grated
   rind

2 cups flour
2 teaspoons baking powder
½ teaspoon salt
¼ cup jam of your choice
2 unpeeled apples grated

Cream shortening and sugar together. Add eggs, then sifted dry ingredients and orange juice alternately. Put one half of mixture in loaf pan, spread with jam and grate the apples over the jam (grate coarsely). Put remainder of mixture on top and sprinkle with ¼ cup sugar and ½ teaspoon cinnamon mixed with ½ cup chopped nuts. Bake 45 minutes in 350°F. oven.

APPLE BREAD OF THE VALLEY

The unpeeled grated apple gives the flavor and replaces the liquid. This quick bread will keep for 1 month wrapped in foil and refrigerated.

½ cup shortening
1 cup sugar
2 eggs
½ teaspoon salt
1 teaspoon vanilla
1 cup grated apple with skin
   left on

2 cups all-purpose flour
1 teaspoon baking powder
1 teaspoon baking soda
¼ cup walnuts

Cream shortening, sugar and eggs together until very light and creamy. Add grated apple and sifted dry ingredients. Mix well. Stir in walnuts. Bake 1 hour at 350°F. Cool on rack. Serve with butter and marmalade.

106

APPLE BLANCMANGE

A homemade applesauce gives something special to this old-fashioned dessert.

2 cups milk	**3 tablespoons sugar**
2½ tablespoons cornstarch	**½ teaspoon vanilla**
Few grains salt	**1 cup prepared applesauce**

Scald 1½ cups milk. Mix cornstarch and sugar with ½ cup of cold milk. Pour the hot milk over the cornstarch mixture, stirring until smooth. Cook over low, direct heat until thick and smooth. Add the salt. When nearly cold add the vanilla and stir in prepared applesauce. Turn into individual moulds which have been rinsed with cold water. Serve with cream, or other desired sauce. A variation of this dessert is to put the blancmange into a serving dish; when firm, top with applesauce and whipped cream.

GLAZED BAKED APPLES

This is one of the best Canadian desserts. When buying apples select the variety that is in season and best suits the intended use. In the summer, use the Duchess; in September the Lodi or Wealthy; in winter, the King or Baldwin or Greening; late in the season use the Golden Delicious or the Rome Beauty.

6 baking apples	**¾ cup water**
½ cup sugar	**1 tablespoon sugar**

Wash and core apples; peel ⅓ of the way down from stem end; place in baking dish. Combine ½ cup sugar and water; boil gently 5 minutes. Pour syrup over apples. Bake uncovered at 375°F. until apples are almost tender (approx. 30 minutes), basting frequently. Remove from oven; drain off syrup. Sprinkle each apple with sugar and return to oven until sugar melts. Pour a little syrup over apples and return to oven (repeat this 2 or 3 times until apples are glazed). Chill and serve with remaining syrup and rich cream.

MARIANE APPLES

Here is another of Joan Balcom's special recipes — tasty and attractive.

6 cooking apples	**2 tablespoons butter**
½ cup brown sugar	**⅓ cup raisins**
½ cup pastry flour	**6 teaspoons orange juice**
¼ teaspoon cinnamon	

Wash, pare and core apples; with tines of fork go round and round apples, making deep indentations. Combine sugar, flour and cinnamon; rub in butter. Press this mixture into creases until apples are completely coated. Place apples in shallow casserole; fill each core with raisins; pour 1 teaspoon orange juice in each. Bake at 350°F. until tender (30 to 40 minutes). Serve cold with light cream.

CANADIAN APPLESAUCE

Wash and cut some apples. It is not necessary to remove the cores. Measure by cupfuls and place in a saucepan. Remove blue Concord grapes from their stems, measure a quantity equal to the apples. Add to the apples, then add canned apple juice to cover just half of the fruits. Boil uncovered, stirring a few times until the fruits are soft, about 8 to 10 minutes. Pass through a sieve or food mill. Sweeten to taste with half sugar, half honey. Serve very cold.

APPLE AND TOMATO RELISH

A ruby red marmalade with the most pleasant tang.

3 lbs. apples	**2 tablespoons whole cloves**
5 lbs. ripe tomatoes	**2 lemons**
5 lbs. brown sugar	

Peel and slice apples and tomatoes; add sugar; boil, stirring frequently, until mixture becomes thick. Add lemons sliced thinly, and cloves. Simmer gently until mixture becomes clear. Pour into sterilized jars and seal.

NEW BRUNSWICK

New Brunswick, like all the other provinces, has much to offer. Potatoes are the aristocrats of New Brunswick agriculture, and their quality is well known. Their blueberry bogs produce a fruit of exceptional flavor. The cultivated type are easy to clean but lack a great deal of the flavor of natural blueberries.

In the spring, if we see the green fiddleheads with their fronds tucked in and their heads curled like violin heads, we think of New Brunswick. They are so much a part of the province. We can find them all year around on the Canadian market, frozen, and of excellent quality. Did you know too that New Brunswick pork ranks among the best in Canada? Their dairy produce too is of the very highest quality.

As for fish — New Brunswick's oysters, lobsters and other seafood are well known and enjoyed by many.

And the French touch is also there with the Acadians.

New Brunswick's cuisine is devoid of fuss and feathers. But taste her home cooking and you will understand that the secret of its goodness lies in its simplicity.

ACADIAN FARE

Like all traditional recipes, there are many variations on one theme. Women cook them as they like, or make use of available ingredients.

I once made a Rappie Pie with Jim Bennet, guest on my T.V. show — one of the best I ever made. His recipe called for a "quite fat chicken" — "two thirds of a pail of big potatoes" — "heavy on the onions", and so on. When finished the pie was the best of them all. For a treat make Acadian clam pies and fritters. The potato is important in Acadian cuisine.

PÂTÉ À LA RÂPURE
(Rappie or Râpé Pie)

Râpé in French means grated, so in either case "râpure" or "rappie" indicates that fact. A great deal of French and English is mixed together in the Acadian language.

5 - 6 - lb. fat boiling chicken	1 carrot, grated
5 lbs. potatoes	¼ teaspoon thyme or
2 medium onions, chopped	1 bay leaf
1 celery stick, diced	Salt and pepper

Cut chicken in individual pieces. Place in saucepan. Cover with cold water, bring to boil. Add onions, celery, carrot, thyme or bay leaf, salt and pepper to taste. Cover and simmer 1½ to 2 hours or until chicken is tender.

Peel and grate potatoes over a bowl of cold water. When chicken is cooked squeeze 1 or 2 cups potatoes at a time in a piece of cotton until quite dry. Place in a saucepan. When potatoes are all squeezed dry add as much boiling broth from the chicken as needed to almost cover the potatoes. Stir until thoroughly mixed. Salt lightly. Simmer over low heat about 10 minutes.

Grease generously an 8″ square baking dish. Spread half the potatoes in the bottom of the pan. Bone the hot chicken and spread over the potatoes, cover with the other half of the potatoes.

Mince one small onion very finely, add ¼ teaspoon pepper and two slices fat salt pork cut into very small dice. Blend well together. Spread on top of the potatoes. Bake ½ hour in a 350°F. oven or until top is golden brown and crisp. Serve hot.

PATÉ ÂUX BUCARDES
(Acadian Clam Pie)

A sort of hot bread shortcake filled with buttered small clams. When fresh ones are not readily available, use drained canned baby clams.

2 cups all-purpose flour
3 teaspoons baking powder
1 teaspoon salt
⅓ cup margarine or shortening
  Enough cold water to make dough

2 cups small clams
½ cup melted butter or margarine
4 crushed crackers
  Salt and pepper, to taste
1 onion, thinly sliced

Sift together the flour, baking powder and salt. Cut in the shortening and add just enough cold water to make a soft biscuit dough. Cut in two equal portions. Roll each one to fit a well greased 8-inch round cake pan. Place one round in the pan.

Blend together the clams, melted butter or margarine, crushed crackers. Season to taste. Spread over dough. Top with onion broken into rings.

Remove a one-inch round from the top. Place over clams and onion. Brush top with milk.

Bake in a preheated 375°F. oven for 35 to 40 minutes or until golden brown on top. Serve hot with coleslaw.

BUCARDES FRITES
(Bar Clam Fritters)

Clam fritters, a long glass of cold Canadian beer, cheddar cheese and salad — What can beat it for a good lunch?

1 cup clams, fresh or canned	1 teaspoon baking powder
⅔ cup or more milk	½ teaspoon salt
1 egg	¼ teaspoon pepper
⅔ cup flour	⅛ teaspoon mace

Drain clams and measure, chop or pass through meat chopper.
Measure the juice and add enough milk to make ⅓ cup liquid.
Beat the egg, add the clam juice mixed with milk.

Sift together the flour, baking powder, salt, pepper and mace. Add the egg mixture, blend, adding just enough of the remaining milk to make a dough stiff enough to hold the clams. Add the clams, mix well. Drop by spoonfuls in 1-inch of hot bacon fat or melted salt pork fat. (The salt pork is the traditional way). Fry 3 to 5 minutes or until brown on both sides. Serve with grated sweet pickled beets and sour bean relish.

PÂTÉ EN PÂTÉ A L'ACADIENNE
(Acadian Meat Pie)

"Pâté en pâté" means a many layered pie or casserole with dough between layers. A traditional Christmas dish. Each family follows its fancy as to the meat — wild birds, hare, rabbit, chicken, pork, veal — in any combination it chooses.

2 cups all-purpose flour	4 cups uncooked peeled diced potatoes
2 teaspoons baking powder	2 cups minced onions
¼ teaspoon soda	1 3 - lb. chicken
1 teaspoon salt	1 hare or rabbit
2 tablespoons shortening	3 lbs. pork steak or fillets
⅔ to 1 cup buttermilk or sour milk	Salt and pepper, to taste
	¼ cup minced parsley

Sift together the flour, baking powder and salt. Cut in the shortening and quickly stir in the buttermilk or sour milk. Add more milk if necessary until the dough is soft and light but not sticky. Turn on lightly floured board, knead gently, just enough to make a smooth ball. Roll ¼ inch thick, cut into 2-inch strips. Set aside.

Take a large deep earthenware or cast-iron pan. Place in the bottom a layer of each uncooked meat, boned and cut into thick slices or cubes. Add a layer of diced potatoes (cut about 1 inch square), then a layer of onion, salt and pepper. Cover with a layer of prepared strips of biscuit dough. Repeat the layers until all is used and the casserole is ¾ full. Pour chicken consommé or water to the level of last layer of onion. Cover the whole with strips of dough, placed near each other to cover everything. Make an incision in the center of dough. Bake in a 200°F. oven for 4½-5 hours. Serve hot or cold. Sprinkle top with parsley when ready to serve.

POUTINES RÂPÉES
(Meat and Potato Pie)

A mixture of boiled and grated raw potatoes, garnished with diced

112

crisped salt pork. Most unusual, to be enjoyed by those who like dumplings.

5 lbs. potatoes	**⅓ cup milk**
2 lbs. onions, grated	**Salt and pepper, to taste**
1 lb. salt pork, cut in 1-inch cubes	**¼ teaspoon celery seeds**

Peel the potatoes, boil half and grate the other half in a bowl of cold water. Drain cooked potatoes, dry over medium heat, then mash until no lumps remain. Squeeze water out of grated potatoes by pressing in a cloth. Add to mashed potatoes. Add onions, milk, salt, pepper and celery seeds. Blend thoroughly.

With 1 cup of mixture form a flat pattie about ½-inch thick.

Fry the salt pork until each piece is crisped and browned. Drain on absorbent paper. Reserve the fat for other use (such as for cooking the clam fritters). Place 1 tablespoon fried pork in center of each potato cake, close, forming a ball. Roll each one in flour and place gently in salted boiling water. Cover and simmer 2 hours. Serve hot with wild berry jam or sausages or brown sauce or buttered cabbage.

HOME FARE OR BIG FEED

In New Brunswick, whether you are looking for the first green of spring or the homey smell of freshly baked crusty bread, or flocking in search of fish and birds or participating in a "big feed" of lobster, you are sure to find good homespun fare.

BOILED LOBSTER

The lobster recipes and cooking directions which follow are the very best. They are prepared and tested by the New Brunswick Home Economists Association and were offered to me by "Hélène" of C.K.C.W.-T.V. in Moncton. Their book *New Brunswick Recipes* is full of good ideas and good foods.

Lobsters when taken from the water are usually of a very dark mottled bluish-green color, unless they come from a sandy watershed, when they may be reddish brown in appearance. Lobster meat is prepared for use by boiling the lobster whole while it is still alive. Use sea water if obtainable. If it is not obtainable, have ready a large pan containing an abundance of furiously boiling water to which 2 tablespoons of salt for each 2 quarts of water have been added. Plunge the lobster head first into this and cook for 20 to 30 minutes according to size. (Beware of overcooking, as it renders the meat tough and stringy.) As soon as the lobster touches the water it turns a brilliant red. After cooking, place on a platter, claws down, to drain. Then wipe dry and set aside until cool enough to handle.

Place the boiled lobster on its back and remove both large and small claws. If it is to be broiled, split lengthwise from the head right down through the body to the top of the tail, using a large sharp knife.

If it is to be used for entrées or salad, separate the head or body portions from the tail, at the point where these join, by giving a sharp twist with the hands. With a sharp knife, open the tail by cutting through the thin cartilage beginning at the body and working downward. After removing the thin shell of cartilage, the meat in the tail portion is exposed and can be readily lifted out of the shell. The only part to be discarded from this section of the lobster is the intestinal cord which runs right down the very centre of the back and which may be a dark greenish color or may have very little color.

Open the body by splitting down the centre. Remove the feathery gill-like portions (sometimes referred to as "fingers") which lie around the meat close to the shell and also the sandbags. This sandbag is found in the centre of the body. It is tough and cartilaginous and grayish green in color. The female or hen lobster usually contains "coral" as the eggs are called. This should be kept and used for garnishing.

The meat is best separated from cartilage by means of a sharp pointed knife and nut pick. The soft grayish green substance found in the lobster is fat and should be saved. Crack the large claws carefully with hammer or nut cracker and remove flesh. The small claws contain very little meat and are generally used as a garnish or in a soup pot. If they are to be opened, split them lengthwise with scissors and remove the meat.

LOBSTER EN COQUILLE

"Coquille" is French for a shell filled with food.

Pick up some shells on a New Brunswick beach and after washing them thoroughly, use them as a container for the cooking and serving of lobster or other fish.

Grease inside of the shell, spread over the surface a thin layer of well seasoned mashed potatoes. Cover the potato with flaked fish seasoned with salt and pepper. Spread over the fish 1 to 2 tablespoons of hollandaise sauce (or white sauce) — the amount of sauce depending on the size of the shell. Cover the sauce with buttered bread crumbs. Using a canvas bag and ornamental tube, flute mashed potatoes around the edge of the shell in a fancy design. Bake shells in a 375°F. oven until the contents of the shell are hot and the crumbs a golden brown color.

SCALLOPED LOBSTER

1½ cups lobster meat	½ teaspoon prepared mustard
1 cup soft bread crumbs	1 teaspoon lemon juice
1 cup top milk or thin cream	Few drops onion juice
1 egg, well beaten	½ teaspoon salt — pepper
2 tablespoons melted butter or	if desired
margarine	Crumbs for topping

Mix in order given. Put into greased baking dish and cover with buttered crumbs. Bake 30 minutes in moderate (350°F.) oven.

NOTE: Canned lobster may be substituted for the lobster meat.

114

FRIED NEW BRUNSWICK OYSTERS

Wonderful for cocktail parties, in a white towel set in a basket.

1½ pints oysters	4 tablespoons flour
2 eggs	½ teaspoon salt
4 tablespoons milk	¼ teaspoon pepper

Drain the oysters. Beat eggs well. Add the milk and beat again. Dip each oyster in the egg mixture, then dip each slightly into seasoned flour. Fry in deep fat 375°F. for 2½ minutes.

FISH ROE

It is difficult to find a good explanation of "how to" when it comes to fish roe, but you can trust these.

Fish roe, which consists of thousands of tiny eggs clustered together, is an excellent food and generally considered a delicacy. Shad roe is best known but that of other fish is also good.

BAKED ROE: Dip the roe in milk. Sprinkle with salt and pepper and roll in dry bread or cracker crumbs. Dot generously with butter or other fat and bake in very hot oven (450°F.) for 10 to 15 minutes.

BROILED ROE: Brush the roe with melted fat and sprinkle with salt and pepper. Place on greased broiler and cook about 5 minutes, turning once.

FRIED ROE: Sprinkle the roe with salt and pepper. Roll in flour. Dip in beaten egg, roll in crumbs, and fry in deep fat 360°F. for 3 to 4 minutes. It may also be pan fried. Serve with lemon.

OYSTER STUFFED HALIBUT

Not every day fare, but a truly elegant dish — perfect for a buffet supper.

2 slices halibut 1 inch thick	Oyster stuffing:
1 cup oyster stuffing	½ pint oysters
¼ teaspoon salt	½ cup bread crumbs
⅛ teaspoon pepper	2 tablespoons butter
2 tablespoons lemon juice	1 teaspoon salt
½ cup white wine	2 tablespoons lemon juice
	1 teaspoon onion juice
	¼ teaspoon mixed herbs

Wipe fish. Place one slice in a lightly buttered fireproof baking dish which can be sent to the table. Cover with oyster stuffing. Top with a second slice of fish and sprinkle with salt, pepper and lemon juice. Cover with wine. Bake for ½ hour in 375°F.-400°F. oven.

BOILED BEEF AUX BOULETTES

So many dishes of New Brunswick have double names, part English, part French. Boulettes are dumplings. The meat is also delicious cold, thinly sliced and served with green tomato chow and New Brunswick potato salad or with Squash Bake.

4 lbs. rolled brisket or	1 small turnip
chuck roast	2 teaspoons salt
4 - 5 celery stalks with leaves	3 whole cloves
6 carrots	½ teaspoon pepper
6 onions	2 bay leaves
1 parsnip	Dumplings or potatoes

Place the meat in a large saucepan, cover it with cold water and bring to a boil uncovered. Boil for 10 minutes, then skim the water.

Cut the celery into 1-inch pieces and chop the leaves; peel the carrots and cut them into chunks; peel the onions and leave them whole; peel the parsnip and dice it; peel the turnip and cut it into thick slices.

Add all the vegetables to the boiling meat along with the remaining ingredients. Bring back to a boil, then cover and simmer for 2½-3 hours, or until the meat is tender.

The simmering will make tender, tasty meat and vegetables that retain their original color and shape. The dumplings may be replaced with 6-8 medium potatoes, peeled, left whole and added in the last hour of cooking.

Dumplings

1 cup all-purpose flour	1 tablespoon shortening or
2 teaspoons baking powder	minced suet
½ teaspoon salt	1 egg
	Milk
	2 tablespoons chopped parsley

Sift together the flour, baking powder and salt. Cut in the shortening or mix in the suet. Break the egg into a measuring cup, add enough milk to make half a cup, and stir to mix.

Add to the flour mixture, along with the parsley. Stir until mixed to a soft dough. Dip a tablespoon into the hot boiled beef broth, scoop up a spoonful of the dumpling batter and slip it on top of the meat and vegetables. Repeat, cover and simmer for 15 minutes without uncovering.

Depending on the size of the saucepan, the dumplings may have to be cooked in two batches. Keep the first ones hot while the others are being cooked.

SAUSAGE BAKE

This is the name the Welsh give to this dish, which is served at what they call a "big feed", an expression also used by New Brunswickers referring to a lobster or chicken beach party. The Germans also prepare Sausage Bake, using frankfurt sausages.

1 lb. fresh pork sausages	2 cups thinly sliced cooked beets
Prepared mustard	1 cup beer, preferably ale
Nutmeg, salt and pepper	

With a sharp, pointed knife, split the pork sausages lengthwise, just enough to open them. Spread each with prepared mustard, then sprinkle with nutmeg, salt and pepper to taste. Place them in a shallow baking dish in a single row, then cover with a thick layer of beets. Pour the beer over all and bake at 400°F. for 30 minutes.

Serve with toasted or hot buttered French bread and a side dish of buttered green beans.

OXTAIL VINAIGRETTE

The oxtail can be served as a main course, the bouillon as a light, tasty consommé, to be garnished as you please. The "vinaigrette" provides the French touch.

1 oxtail, cut in pieces	¼ teaspoon thyme
1 onion, sliced	1 teaspoon salt
1 carrot, peeled and sliced	¼ teaspoon pepper
2 stalks celery, coarsely cut	2 thick slices lemon, unpeeled
1 bay leaf	2 quarts water

Place all the ingredients in a saucepan and bring to a full, rolling boil. Cover and simmer 3-4 hours over low heat, or until the oxtail is tender. Let it cool in its consommé.

To serve, prepare a simple vinaigrette by shaking together in a bottle: 4 tablespoons cider vinegar, ¼ teaspoon dry mustard, ½ teaspoon salt, ¼ teaspoon pepper, a pinch of sugar and 8 tablespoons salad oil. Dice 3 cups cooked potatoes. Add a few spoonfuls of vinaigrette to them and place on a serving platter. Place the cooked oxtail in a bowl and blend with vinaigrette to taste. Sprinkle with finely minced parsley or green onion tops.

FIDDLEHEADS

You will find an excellent description of this New Brunswick specialty in our own Sylvia Boorman's *Wild Plums in Brandy,* a book written, she says: "for those people who enjoy roaming the fields and woods". I warmly recommend this wonderful book, which is in itself an adventure filled with pleasures. It has some excellent recipes.

BAKED FERNS OR FIDDLEHEADS

Fiddleheads	½ cup cream
Salt	1 egg yolk
Butter	2 tablespoons Parmesan cheese
3 tablespoons flour	½ cup breadcrumbs
1 cup stock or vegetable water	

Wash your fern heads (incidentally, they seem to be a very clean, insect-free vegetable.) Cook in boiling salted water for ten minutes, until partly cooked. In the meantime, make a sauce by melting two or three tablespoons of butter; into which stir three tablespoons of flour, a pinch of salt, a cup of stock (or the water in which the ferns are cooking) and half a cup of cream. Then stir in the yolks of one or two eggs and finally two tablespoons of grated Parmesan cheese. Stir until all the cheese melts. Do this over a low heat.

Now, into a buttered oven-dish put the fiddleheads carefully in layers. Pour sauce over each layer; sprinkle a little Parmesan on each layer of sauce. Cover the top layer of ferns with sauce and sprinkle that with breadcrumbs. Put in a hot oven or under a grill for about twenty minutes, which should be long enough to brown the crumbs.

DANDELION POT

Similar to what they call a "mess of greens" in New England. Advice: Young spring dandelions are tedious to clean. Start early.

½ lb. lean and fat salt pork	9 medium size potatoes
3 onions, sliced	A branch of fresh savory or
6 - 8 cups dandelion greens	1 teaspoon dry savory

Place salt pork in a saucepan, cover with cold water, bring to boil. Then boil 30 minutes. Remove from the pot, cool slightly, cut 3 to 4 slices and dice. Place in frying pan and cook until browned and crisped. Add the onions and fry until golden brown.

Add the washed and cleaned dandelions to the salt pork water. Place pork in the middle. Pour the onions on top. Peel and halve the potatoes and add to salt pork. Sprinkle with savory. Cover and simmer 20 to 25 minutes or until potatoes are cooked. Serve with a few slices of salt pork on each plate, topped with the potatoes and a bowl of mustard pickles or sour green beans.

SQUASH BAKE

I like it hot for a light lunch or as a vegetable with roast pork. It is best at room temperature with cold cuts.

3 cups diced uncooked yellow squash	2 cups medium white sauce
½ cup diced celery	2 tablespoons butter
1 green pepper, chopped	½ cup breadcrumbs

Arrange vegetables in a casserole in layers. Top with white sauce. Sprinkle with the buttered crumbs. Bake at 375°F. about 1 hour or until squash is tender.

PARSNIP BALLS

This is a delicate, interesting vegetable dish, even for those who hate parsnip. The secret of a tasy parsnip is to eat it after it has had a touch of frost, which means late autumn and winter, and to boil it unpeeled, cut in half if necessary, then drained and peeled as the recipe demands.

Boil the parsnips until tender, about 20 to 25 minutes. Drain, peel and mash. Add a little salt, beaten egg, small piece of butter and a little cream. Form into balls. Dip in egg and breadcrumbs and fry in bacon fat or deep fat.

GLAZED PARSNIPS

4 - 8 parsnips, boiled	4 tablespoons brown sugar
4 tablespoons butter	1 pinch cinnamon

Boil the parsnips, peel and refrigerate until cold. Cut into pieces.

Place in a frying pan the butter, brown sugar, cinnamon and parsnips. Stir over low heat until the parsnips are browned and coated with the sauce.

COTTAGE CHEESE BISCUITS

Lightly textured inside, crispy and crusty on top, these biscuits can be served for breakfast, with fruit and salad or soup — or with the main course instead of bread.

1 egg, lightly beaten	2 scant cups all-purpose flour
3 tablespoons milk	4 teaspoons baking powder
1 cup cottage cheese, any kind	1 teaspoon salt
2 tablespoons butter, melted	¼ cup fresh parsley, minced

Preheat the oven to 450°F. Mix the egg, milk, cottage cheese and butter thoroughly.

Stir together the flour, baking powder, salt and parsley. Add to the first mixture and blend with the fingertips. If necessary, add more milk, a few drops at a time, to make the dough hold together.

Turn on to a floured board and knead for 30 seconds. Pat into a shape ½-inch thick, then cut into 18 squares.

Place on a greased baking sheet and bake for about 12 minutes or until golden brown.

RAISIN BROWN BREAD

Here is a recipe I have appreciated for years. It was given to me by a most cooperative motel owner when I stayed in Moncton. Every morning we could get this fragrant hot bread right out of the oven. Make the whole recipe. It freezes beautifully.

2 tablespoons lard	3 envelopes active dry yeast
1 tablespoon butter	½ cup warm water
1 cup brown sugar	9 to 11 cups all-purpose flour
2 teaspoons salt	2 teaspoons cinnamon
2 cups hot water	½ teaspoon nutmeg
1 cup molasses	¼ teaspoon allspice
½ cup tepid water	2 - 3 cups seedless raisins

Dissolve lard, butter, sugar and salt in the 2 cups of hot water. Add the molasses. Use the ½ cup water to rinse the cup, then mix everything until cool.

Dissolve yeast in the ½ cup warm water until foamy, about 10 minutes. Add to first mixture.

Sift 3 cups of the flour with the cinnamon, nutmeg and allspice. Add to liquid mixture along with the well stirred yeast and beat until the whole is thoroughly blended. Then add enough flour to have a soft dough. Stir in the raisins. Turn on floured board and knead until smooth and satiny. Place in greased bowl, cover and let rise in a warm place until doubled in bulk, about 1½ to 2 hours. Knead and let rise a second time, about 40 minutes. Cut in 3 or 4 equal pieces. Shape in loaves. Place in greased bread pans, let rise until dough is rounded above edge of pans, about 30 to 40 minutes. Bake in oven preheated to 400°F. for 35 minutes or until well done. Unmold as soon as out of oven and cool on cake rack.

BROWN BREAD

This authentic New Brunswick special was sent to me by a Fredericton reader.

2½ cups boiling water
1½ cups oatmeal
1 cup scalded milk
½ cup shortening
4 teaspoons salt
⅔ cup molasses

½ cup sugar
2 yeast cakes
¼ cup lukewarm water
1 cup whole wheat flour
9 - 10 cups all-purpose flour

Pour the boiling water over the oatmeal. Add the scalded milk to which the shortening and salt has been added. Then add the molasses and sugar. Stir, then cool to lukewarm. Meanwhile, soften the yeast cakes in the ¼ cup lukewarm water. When oatmeal mixture has cooled, stir in the whole wheat flour and 3 cups of all-purpose flour. Beat well and stir in the rest of the flour, reserving about 2 cups to use when kneading.

To knead, toss ball of dough onto floured board and press the dough away from you with the palm of your hand — fold back with finger tips, and continue for ten minutes, using the rest of the flour and dough until it is well blended and smooth. Place in a bowl, cover and let rise until double in bulk — at a temperature of about 75 degrees — no draughts, for about 1½ hours. When it has risen, remove from bowl, cut into 4 pieces, punch to remove gas. Shape into loaves, place in greased bread pans, and let rise until light, or double in bulk. Bake at 425°F. for 15 minutes. Reduce heat to 375°F., for the rest of the hour. Turn pans once while baking.

NOTE: All white flour may be used and raisins added if desired.

BERRY BLUFF

A "perfect bluff" for the well-known blueberries of New Brunswick.

2 cups flour
1 cup sugar
¼ teaspoon cinnamon or
   nutmeg
2 teaspoons baking powder
2 eggs, beaten

1 cup milk
2 cups blueberries
Grated rind of 1 lemon
Juice of 1 lemon
2 tablespoons sugar

Sift flour once, measure and sift again with the sugar, cinnamon or nutmeg and baking powder.

Combine the eggs and milk. Add to flour and stir until smooth, adding more milk if necessary, to obtain a soft biscuit dough. Stir in the berries and grated lemon rind. Turn batter into generously buttered and floured pudding mold. Cover with a layer of paper and a cover. Steam for 1½ to 2 hours. When done, unmold on a warm plate and pour lemon juice on top. Sprinkle with the sugar. Serve hot with thick cream.

BATHURST JAM CAKE

An old-fashioned dessert that is always a favorite. I am asked for the recipe whenever I serve this.

2 sponge layer cakes,
  home made or bought
1 cup blueberry jam
2 bananas or peaches

1 cup heavy cream
2 tablespoons icing sugar
½ teaspoon vanilla or ¼ teaspoon
  rosewater

Use the store-bought sponge cakes that are usually sold in pairs. On one cake spread the berry jam of your choice and top with thin banana or peach slices. Whip cream until stiff, sweeten with icing sugar and flavor with vanilla or rosewater.

Spread a thin coating of the cream on top of the bananas or peaches. Place second layer on top and cover with remaining cream. This will keep 4-6 hours refrigerated.

BLUEBERRY JAM

Use small natural New Brunswick blueberries, since they have more flavor than the large cultivated kind.

½ cup powdered fruit pectin
4 tablespoons sugar
2 cups blueberries

1½ cups sugar
4 tablespoons corn syrup
4 tablespoons lemon juice

Place the pectin and the 4 tablespoons of sugar in the bowl of an electric mixer. Stir together with a spoon until well mixed. Add the blueberries and crush, in the sugar, then beat at low speed for 7 minutes.

Add the 1½ cups of sugar, the corn syrup and the lemon juice. Beat at low speed for 3 more minutes. Pour into freezer containers and cover with lids. Let stand on the kitchen counter for 12 hours, or until set into a soft jelly, then freeze. Makes 4 half-pints.

PUMPKIN JAM

Pumpkin jam is unusual and tasty enough to warrant the use of one half a cup of gin. In the original recipe, it was made with the sweet Dutch gin liked in Quebec and New Brunswick. I still think it best. Fresh ginger root is essential.

4 lbs. pumpkin, diced	½ teaspoon allspice
4 lbs. sugar	Peel of 3 lemons, grated
2 oz. fresh ginger, grated	Juice of 3 lemons
	½ cup sweet Dutch gin

Peel and clean the pumpkin, remove seeds, dice and weigh. Place in a large dish in alternate layers with the sugar. Cover with a cloth and let stand 2 days in a cold place.

Place in a large saucepan with the ginger, allspice, lemon peel and juice. Simmer over medium heat, stirring often, until the pumpkin is tender and transparent. Remove from heat, cool slightly and add the gin. Stir well. Pour into hot sterilized jars and seal. Yields 6-8 quarts.

PICKLED PUMPKIN

Pumpkin makes an interesting sweet pickle, particularly good with tasty New Brunswick pork and poultry dishes or as a garnish for fruit salad.

5 - 6 lbs. pumpkin, pared	1 tablespoon cinnamon stick,
1 pint cider vinegar	broken
3 lbs. sugar	2 pieces crystallized ginger
1 teaspoon whole cloves	

Cut the pumpkin into 1-inch cubes. Bring the vinegar and sugar to a boil and simmer until the sugar is dissolved. Place the cloves, cinnamon and ginger in a bag. Add to the syrup and boil 5 min. Add the pumpkin and bring the mixture back to a fast rolling boil. Boil over low heat exactly 25 minutes, stirring often. Remove the spice bag. Put the pumpkin into sterilized jars, pour the vinegar syrup on top to completely cover, and seal. This yields 5 to 6 pints of pickles.

GREEN TOMATO CHOW

Years ago, my sister-in-law, a native of Fredericton, gave me this fascinating recipe.

½ peck green tomatoes	2 red peppers
6 large onions	3 lbs. brown sugar
6 medium cucumbers	3 tablespoons pickling spices
1 head celery	tied in a bag
4 sour apples	

Cut tomatoes fine. Add ½ cup salt and leave overnight. Next morning drain, and add other ingredients. Nearly cover with vinegar (about a quart of cider vinegar). Boil gently 1 to 1½ hours. Pour in sterilized jars and seal.

PRINCE EDWARD ISLAND

I cannot tell you what the exact annual potato harvest of Prince Edward Island is because I do not know, but I can tell you that ever since I have seen its beautiful red earth making the green grass and trees even greener, and the potatoes even redder, P.E.I. potatoes were for me. They are so good — and there are so many ways we can and should eat them, apart from boiled, baked or fried. Do not avoid eating potatoes just because of calories. Instead be aware that a medium potato, or an average serving of ⅓ pound, has a caloric value of less than 100, less than 1 grapefruit or 2 tablespoons of sugar. Another point for dieters is that potatoes are real food, heavy, satisfying and bulky enough to give the feeling of having dined not dieted. A large baked potato topped with a good helping of cold cottage cheese, the whole generously sprinkled with chives or parsley makes a very good light dish and is low in calories. Also this potato will supply half your body's daily Vitamin C requirement — plus the B Vitamins it contains and all the other nutrients. Most important, potatoes contain practically no fat, and butter or cream on top are not at all essential. There are many other ways to enjoy them.

This said, let's now enjoy the versatility of our Canadian potatoes and serve them often.

A WHIRL OF POTATOES

HOW TO BOIL NEW POTATOES

Boil enough water to cover potatoes. Salt it. Wash potatoes but don't grate or peel. Put in boiling water and bring to boil quickly. Boil steadily until tender and drain at once. After draining, place clean cloth on top of potatoes and put on low heat to "dry" them for a few minutes.

HOW TO BOIL WINTER POTATOES

Wash well and place in saucepan. Cover with cold water. Add enough salt to make water decidedly salty. Cover and bring to boil. Boil steadily until tender. Drain at once. Dry by placing a towel on top for a few minutes, the same as for new potatoes. Serve at once (potatoes, new or old, should be cooked only to be served as soon as ready).

BEST MASHED POTATOES

Through the years, I've tried many ways of preparing mashed potatoes. These are my winners, very smooth, white and creamy. I prefer to pressure-cook my potatoes, but they can also be boiled.

8 potatoes, peeled and halved	**¼ teaspoon savory**
4 tablespoons instant skim milk powder	**1 green onion, minced (optional)**
½ to ¾ cup commercial sour cream	**Salt and pepper, to taste**

Boil the potatoes until they're tender, then drain and put pan back over heat until the potatoes are dry. Put them through a potato ricer over the cooking pan, add the remainder of the ingredients and beat until light and smooth.

Variations:

— To serve with roast pork or sausages, add 2 cups of cooked mashed turnips to the above recipe, replace the savory with sage.
— To serve with chicken, fish, or eggs, add 1½ cups cooked, mashed carrots to the above and replace savory with basil.
— To serve with lamb, beef or hamburger, add 1 cup of onion, fried in bacon fat and mixed with the savory, to the above.

PERFECT HASHED BROWNED POTATOES

I've cooked hashed browns many ways in my years of cooking, but never as well as when I made them with baked potatoes and sour cream. In the summer, I serve them covered with minced chives mixed with fresh basil.

6 large potatoes, baked	¼ teaspoon pepper
2 tablespoons butter or bacon fat	1 tablespoon butter, melted
	4 tablespoons sour cream
1 teaspoon salt	Chives or parsley, minced

Bake the potatoes the day before and refrigerate with the skins left on. The next day, peel and grate potatoes on a medium grater. Heat the bacon fat or butter, or a mixture of both, in a heavy iron frying pan. Sprinkle the potatoes over the entire surface lightly, but do not pack them down. Sprinkle with the salt, pepper and melted butter.

Cook over low heat for about 20 minutes until brown underneath and loose from the pan (without stirring, lift up the edge to see if they are ready). When browned, turn once by sections and cook until second side is brown. When ready, place half on a hot serving dish, spread with sour cream and cover with balance of potatoes. Sprinkle to taste with chives or parsley.

HASHED BROWN WESTERN STYLE

A piece of beef suet and a spoonful of vinegar give a very special flavor to these potatoes. Serve them with pot roast or cold roast beef.

4 medium size potatoes	¼ teaspoon celery salt
2 tablespoons diced beef suet	Pepper, to taste
1 tablespoon butter	1 tablespoon finely chopped parsley

Boil the unpeeled potatoes, until just cooked, drain. Peel as soon as cool enough to handle. Cut into ½-inch squares.

Melt the beef suet until only small pieces remain. Add the potatoes and fry over medium heat until brown here and there. Drain the excess fat and add the butter, keep browning for another 10 minutes, by which time the potatoes should be tender. Add the vinegar, celery salt, pepper and parsley. Toss together until blended and very hot. Serve.

POTATOES MATELOTE

Serve with all types of roast meat or poultry. Leftover potatoes are interesting warmed up in this manner.

6 potatoes, peeled and sliced	**Salt and pepper, to taste**
2 tablespoons butter	**½ cup undiluted canned**
3 tablespoons minced parsley	**consommé or water**
1 teaspoon dehydrated onions	**1 egg yolk**

Boil sliced potatoes until barely tender. Drain and dry over heat. Add the rest of the ingredients except the egg yolk. Cook, uncovered, about 10 minutes. Beat the egg yolk, add a few tablespoons of the consommé and, stirring, put back in rest of potatoes. Stir. Do not let this mixture boil after adding the egg. Serve with a platter of celery and carrot sticks and a few radishes.

FANTAN POTATOES

Bake around the meat or in a separate dish.

Choose medium size potatoes of equal size. Peel and cut the top into thin slices without going right through so that the cut will stay attached. Roll in melted fat of your choice. Set on a shallow baking pan. Bake 40 to 50 minutes in a 375°F. oven.

SUNSHINE POTATOES

These quick, crunchy, golden brown potato cakes can be served with bacon and eggs for a quick top-of-the-stove luncheon.

4 large potatoes	**½ teaspoon salt**
	Salad oil

Peel potatoes, grate them on a large grater (new potatoes can be scrubbed with a stiff brush, then grated with the peels left on) and mix with salt. Pour enough salad oil into a large iron frying pan to cover the bottom and heat.

When hot, pour grated potatoes by spoonfuls into the oil. Spread as thinly as possible with a spoon. Brown on both sides, turning once only — they take just a few minutes to cook.

SPRING VEGETABLE POTATO CAKES

Delicate and tasty prepared with fresh potatoes, also nice to give zest to leftover mashed potatoes.

4 - 6 (3 cups) mashed boiled potatoes	3 green onions, minced
1 tablespoon melted butter	2 fresh tomatoes, peeled and chopped
Salt and pepper, to taste	6 tablespoons all-purpose flour
2 tablespoons chopped parsley	

Mix all the ingredients together. Knead lightly and shape into oval balls. Place on buttered baking sheets and bake in a preheated 400°F. oven until golden brown.

ISLAND POTATO SALAD

Cold cuts or pickled pig's feet or eggs and a good family type of potato salad is always a welcome meal. A salad for 6 to 9 people.

8 large potatoes	1/3 cup water
1 cup diced celery	1/4 teaspoon prepared mustard
3 small onions, thinly sliced	2 teaspoons salt
3 tablespoons minced parsley	1/4 teaspoon pepper
1/2 teaspoon celery seeds	4 - 6 slices bacon
2/3 cup cider vinegar	

Boil the potatoes, in their jackets, making sure they are all the same size, until tender but not overcooked. Drain, dry over medium heat for 2 to 3 minutes. As soon as cool enough to be handled, peel and slice about 1/8 inch thick or cut into 1-inch squares. Place in a bowl. Add the celery, onions, parsley and celery seeds. Toss gently.

Heat the vinegar with the water and mustard and pour while hot over the potatoes. Add salt, pepper and toss until well blended. Use a rubber spatula not to break the potatoes.

Fry the bacon. Drain on paper and pour bacon fat on potatoes. Mix thoroughly. Crumble the bacon and add to potatoes. Let stand 2 to 4 hours at room temperature before serving. This salad must not be served refrigerated.

GARDEN HERB POTATO SALAD

It is a good thing to know that 2 pounds of potatoes make about 4 cups of cubes or slices; and 2 pounds of medium potatoes usually yield 6 to 8 potatoes.

6 - 8 potatoes	Salt and pepper, to taste
2 tablespoons chives or green onions	2 tablespoons chopped parsley or savory
1/3 cup mayonnaise	2 tablespoons chopped mint
2 tablespoons milk or cream	1 hard cooked egg

Boil potatoes with their jackets. Drain, peel, dice. Sprinkle with the minced chives or green onion tops.

Thin the mayonnaise with the milk or cream, enough to make a light mixture. Pour over the potatoes. Toss gently, add salt and pepper. Toss again, add the herbs and toss. Place in a bowl and grate the hard cooked egg on top.

GREEN POTATO SALAD

This actually is a specialty of Nova Scotia and a very interesting one. Use only the leaves of the spinach and make sure the water is truly boiling.

Pour boiling water over one pound cleaned spinach. Let stand exactly 3 minutes, not over heat, and uncovered. Drain thoroughly, wrap in absorbent paper if necessary. Chop lightly, add 3 to 4 cups cold sliced potatoes and ½ cup long thin slivers of mild cheddar cheese. Dress with 3 tablespoons sour cream and the juice of 1 lemon, salt and pepper to taste.

BACON FRIED POTATOES

Good Canadian fare to serve with a platter of scrambled eggs or fried ham.

6 slices bacon	Salt to taste
6 - 8 potatoes	¼ cup water
1 medium size onion, chopped	2 tablespoons cider vinegar

Fry the fat remaining in the pan, add the potatoes peeled and cut in 1½-inch cubes Press the potatoes in the fat and cook over medium heat until the bottom is brown and crisp. Sprinkle the top with the onion and salt to taste. Cut into wedges and turn each one, reshaping the potatoes. Cook over medium heat until bottom is brown. Add the water, cover the pan and simmer over low heat for 10 minutes. Add the vinegar. Remove pan from heat. Keep covered for 15 minutes. To serve, sprinkle crumbled bacon on top. Serve very hot.

CRUSTY BAKED POTATO PANCAKES

Try it first for a Sunday brunch with ham and eggs, or serve with whipped butter, maple syrup or warm applesauce.

2 large or 4 medium potatoes	½ teaspoon salt
3 whole eggs	2 cups milk
¾ cup flour	¼ lb. salt pork or bacon

Peel and grate the potatoes on medium grater. Add the eggs, flour, salt and milk. Beat thoroughly well mixed. Dice salt pork or bacon and fry until crisped and browned, in an iron frying pan. Leave fat in the pan, remove salt pork or bacon. Add the batter, spread in the pan. Scatter fried salt pork on top. Bake in 350°F. oven for 30 to 35 minutes.

SIMPLE — HONEST POTATO PUDDING

During a summer I spent at Summerside, our hostess was named Dolly. She was vivacious, always neat as a pin, and a good cook to top it. She gave me this recipe.

2 cups grated raw potatoes	¼ teaspoon pepper
1 cup thinly sliced onions	¼ teaspoon savory or marjoram
1 cup grated carrots	2 tablespoons cream
½ teaspoon salt	2 tablespoons butter

Mix together the potatoes, onions, carrots, salt and pepper. Mix and add the cream. Place in a generously buttered pudding dish. Dot with the butter. Cover and bake in a preheated 350°F. oven 45 minutes. Uncover and bake another 15 minutes or until a thin golden crust has formed.

DOUBLE BOILER CREAMY POTATOES

In the spring top with fresh dill; in the winter try dried crushed mint. Either way, or without herbs, it is good. This is another of Dolly's creations.

4 medium size potatoes	⅛ teaspoon pepper
1 small onion	2 tablespoons butter
½ teaspoon salt	2 tablespoons sour cream
A pinch of nutmeg or grated rind of ½ lemon	

Pare and quarter the potatoes, cover with boiling water, add the onion, salt and pepper. Boil 15 minutes over direct heat. Drain well, add the butter, sour cream and nutmeg or lemon rind. Place on top of boiling water and simmer 40 minutes. Serve.

INDIAN POTATOES

For this one you must dig the potatoes in your garden. When the potatoes were dug, the Indians always set aside the tiny ones, no larger than a walnut, clinging near the larger tubers. They cook them as follows, over a slow fire.

Wash them well and put (when possible) in a cast-iron saucepan. Add 2 to 4 tablespoons water (no matter what amount of potatoes you have). Cover and cook them over very low heat, shaking pan often, but not uncovering it. They are perfect when the skin is lightly browned here and there. When tender, which may take from 15 to 25 minutes, remove the cover and leave them over the heat until absolutely dry, shaking the pan 4 or 5 times.

Then pour into a dish. Add a generous piece of butter — but no salt. Put pepper to taste and all you want of minced chives or green onions. Gobble them whole, skins and all. A real treat I enjoy every September when the potatoes are dug up.

POTATO CASSEROLE

Prepare in the morning to serve at night. Serve with cold cuts or roasted duck or lamb. In the spring — a real treat is to make it with tiny new potatoes.

6 medium size potatoes	½ cup beef bouillon
or	½ cup light cream
24 tiny new potatoes	2 tablespoons chopped parsley
1 large onion, thinly sliced	2 teaspoons fresh dill or dill seed
4 tablespoons butter	Salt and pepper, to taste
2 tablespoons flour	Grated cheddar cheese

Boil the unpeeled potatoes, drain, peel and place in a shallow buttered casserole. Fry the onion in the butter until golden brown, add the flour, stir and cook until the flour is ivory color. Add the bouillon and cream all at once. Whisk together, with a wire whisk or a blending fork, until creamy, add the parsley and dill. Salt and pepper to taste. Pour over the potatoes and top with the grated cheese.

Bake in a preheated 450°F. oven for 15 to 20 minutes. Serve.

SEABOARD POTATO CAKES

4 large or 8 medium boiled potatoes	1 teaspoon baking powder
2 teaspoons salt	4 tablespoons butter, melted
½ cup flour, sifted	⅓ cup milk

Mash potatoes. Add salt, flour and baking powder and mix well. Add melted butter and milk and knead lightly. (The dough should be soft enough to roll.) Roll out half-inch thick on lightly floured surface. Cut into rounds with cooky cutter. Brown in lightly greased cast-iron frying pan for 5 to 8 minutes on each side. Shake griddle occasionally to prevent burning. Place as ready on a hot platter, but do not overlap. Keep warm in a 200°F. oven.

COLCANNON

A gift from Ireland to us, and a perfect vegetarian lunch.

3 cups shredded green cabbage	Salt and pepper
1 onion, minced	6 to 8 medium sized potatoes
1 cup hot milk	

Place in a saucepan the finely shredded green cabbage and the onion. Pour the hot milk on top. Salt and pepper generously. Cover and simmer 15 minutes.

In the meantime, peel and slice the potatoes, boil until tender. Drain, dry over medium heat. Add to the cabbage and pound or break with a blending fork until the whole is well mixed. If too liquid simmer uncovered for a few minutes. Serve with a nice square of butter melting in the middle.

POTATO CHAMP

Also from Ireland — to be served in the late spring when chives and fresh green peas are with us.

6 - 8 medium sized potatoes	1 or 2 cups cooked green peas
¼ cup minced chives, green onions or parsley	Salt and pepper, to taste
	2 tablespoons butter

Peel, boil, dry and mash the potatoes rather coarsely. Add minced chives, green onions or parsley and the green peas. Salt and pepper to taste. Add butter and beat until well mixed. To serve, give everyone a soup plate of champ, make a hole in middle and put in large lump of butter. The champ is eaten from outside with fork or spoon, dipping it in melted butter in centre. Serve freshly churned buttermilk as a beverage with this. A treat!

130

NEWFOUNDLAND

"Let's have a boil-up on the bogie". In good Newfoundland language this means "Let's warm up near the small stove" — which has close similarity to the Nova Scotia "Little Cod" small cast-iron stove which heats beautifully. With only a few logs it is forever simmering the water kettle to "thin out" the tea or make another batch of good strong black tea, a favorite of the island people — when the dash of rum is not around.

So let's talk about Newfie cuisine. After all it is not every day that we can have "hashins on our plate", which means plenty of food around. We may not fully appreciate some of their native dishes any more than they would appreciate some of ours, but we should be aware of those that are most typical, such as the "Fish and Brewis". Well done it can be very nice. The little "scrumchions" or pieces of salt pork browned to a crisp in a black iron "bake-pot" give a very nice Canadian flavor to the fresh caught cod, which is browned and simmered in them. Then the hard tack biscuits, or Brewis, are pounded to a powder and added in the required quantity to the fish juice, so that the whole becomes a sort of fish porridge. Believe me, when the cod is fresh it is a very interesting dish. However, made with soaked salt cod, I feel you must have some sea wind in your blood to really appreciate it.

Do make the "Dressed Cod Fillets", a truly tasty dish — inexpensive and filling. To a Newfoundlander fish means cod. One day I asked at the hotel where I was staying: "Have you any fresh fish on the menu?". The Maître D' said "No, but we have very good steamed salmon"!

Another native dish — "Newfoundland Flippers", which are the fore-paws of the seal. As we have to catch the seal first, let's forget it.

Their "Bake-pot" is often used to make beans — similar to the Québec way, with salt pork, molasses, dry mustard. At times they add pork chops which slowly bake in the beans. In Québec we use partridges. Both are delicious.

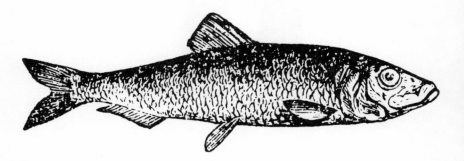

We cannot talk of Newfoundland cuisine without a mention of their "Lob-scause" — a very thick stew of salted pork or beef, parsnip, turnip, carrots, onions and potatoes, the whole thickened, with the powdered "hardtack". As a sort of take off to this one make the "Bubble and Squeak" — a tasty, nourishing vegetable meal.

With meats, they offer us the big moose, the small caribou, their many ways of dealing with big and small rabbits, their fat sea bird the "Turr". If these are not within reach — try their beef heart stew and cold liver loaf, sliced and fried, or settle for the Corned Beef Chowder.

Their sweets and cakes are much like ours, but how I envy them their partridge berry, their bake-apple, a yellow berry resembling a raspberry, also popular with the Finnish people, eaten as a jam called "Cloudberry Jam".

Here we go. "Long may your big jib draw" (a wish of good luck). May there always be wind in your sails.

COD AND HERRING IN A POT

PICKLED COD

Pickled and marinated fish, should be prepared with fresh fish. Frozen fish do not give satisfactory results. In this recipe, halibut or cod steaks can replace the fresh cod.

3 lbs. cod	3 bay leaves
Pepper	1 cup pitted olives (green
Flour	or ripe)
1 cup salad or olive oil	½ cup cider or wine vinegar
2 medium onions, sliced	1 teaspoon salt
10 peppercorns	

Rub the fish on both sides with pepper, then dredge with flour. Heat the salad or olive oil in a large frying pan and quickly brown the fish. When the fish is done, arrange it in a symmetrical pattern in a deep glass dish.

To the oil left in the pan, add the onions, peppercorns, bay leaves, olives, vinegar and salt. Simmer for 3 minutes, then pour over the fish while still hot. Cover, cool a little and refrigerate at least 24 hours.

Garnish with tomato wedges, lime or lemon quarters and parsley and serve with mayonnaise to taste.

CODFISH CAKES

A well-prepared codfish cake is a treat, just as a poorly-prepared one is a real mess. Try the Newfoundland idea of adding parsnips to the mashed potatoes; they sweeten the salt cod and give a golden color to the cakes.

2 finely chopped onions
2 - 3 tablespoons cold water
2 cups codfish (see below)
6 potatoes
3 medium parsnips
1 cup water

¼ teaspoon pepper
½ teaspoon sugar
1 beaten egg
½ cup fine breadcrumbs
4 diced fat salt pork slices or
¼ cup bacon fat

Place onion in a dry frying pan and stir occasionally over medium heat. When it browns here and there, add the 2-3 tablespoons cold water and stir. Pour into a deep saucepan.

If using boxed salt codfish, soak, bone and shred it according to directions on box. If using fresh codfish, soak it and it will shred itself. Add potatoes, parsnips and 1 cup water to onion and simmer until vegetables are tender.

Drain, add codfish, pepper, sugar and egg. Mash well, shape into cakes and roll in breadcrumbs. Refrigerate until ready to cook.

Melt salt pork until light brown or heat the bacon fat. Add fish cakes and fry over medium heat until golden brown on both sides, turning only once.

DRESSED COD FILLETS

This cod has an everyday dress and a company dress. Both are very nice.

1 lb. cod fillets
2 cups soft, crustless bread cubes
½ teaspoon sage
1 chopped small onion
1 teaspoon salt
¼ teaspoon pepper
2 tablespoons cold margarine
1 beaten egg
Flour
2 tablespoons melted margarine

2 tablespoons melted bacon fat
2 tablespoons flour
2½ cups milk
Salt and pepper, to taste
¼ teaspoon savory
Company version:
2 - 3 thinly sliced tomatoes
½ teaspoon sugar
2 diced bread slices
2 tablespoons grated cheese
2 tablespoons melted margarine

If using frozen fillets, thaw just enough to separate them. Mix next 5 ingredients well, then cut in cold margarine and mix in egg.

Place a thin layer of this dressing on each fillet, roll up like a jelly roll and fasten with a pick. Roll each fillet in flour, place in a shallow dish next to one another, and pour a bit of melted margarine over each. Set in a 400°F. oven 10-12 minutes, or until lightly browned.

In the meantime, make a white sauce with fat, flour, milk, salt, pepper and savory. When smooth and creamy, pour over fish rolls and bake another 20 minutes.

Company version: Proceed as above to point of pouring on white sauce. Top sauce with tomatoes and sprinkle with sugar. Mix bread cubes, cheese and margarine, pour over tomatoes and bake 20 minutes.

134

COD AND OYSTER PIE

This recipe was sent to me by a fisherman's wife. She said it had been their traditional New Year dinner for three generations.

2 cups cold cooked cod	1 small onion, grated
½ cup melted butter	Cream
12 fresh oysters	Salt, pepper to taste
8 potatoes	

Flake fish from bone, remove skin and break into small pieces. Lay in a pie plate, add the oysters and their juice, (canned oysters can be used, but it is not as delicate). Pour the melted butter over all.

Boil the potatoes, drain, mash with the onion, cream, salt and pepper. Put on top of fish. Sprinkle top with paprika. Bake in a 375°F. oven 30 minutes or until potato crust is golden color.

COD TONGUES AND CHEEKS

The heavy jowls of the cod have in them lots of good meals, such as the tongues and cheeks. These rolled in cornmeal or fine breadcrumbs, fried in bacon fat or butter until light brown, are quite a treat. Did you know that the tongue is not really the tongue, as a Newfoundlander taught me, but the blob of meat at its base. The cheek is the meat that is cut from the jaw bone. When fishermen fry the cheeks they call them "pork chops".

FISHERMAN'S CHOWDER

Of course, it is a cod chowder!

8 cod heads	6 potatoes, peeled and diced
¼ lb. salt pork	Butter
2 large onions, sliced	Salt and pepper

Wash the heads, remove the eyes.

Dice the salt pork, melt in a cast-iron frying pan. Add the onions and fry until golden brown. Add the cod heads. Add enough cold water to cover. Add the potatoes. Season to taste with salt and pepper. Cover and simmer until potatoes are done. Serve in a deep soup plate with a good chunk of butter on top — and a pinch of dried parsley.

FRESH HERRING, MARINATED

Any type of small fresh herring will do, or use thawed frozen smelt.

1½ lbs. small fresh herring	2 tablespoons tomato paste
2 tablespoons cider vinegar	1 teaspoon salt
6 tablespoons salad oil	½ teaspoon pepper
1 teaspoon sugar	

Clean the herring or ask the fish dealer to do it. Wash thoroughly in cold, salted water and drain on absorbent paper. Place them side by side in baking dish (do not use a metal one). Stir together the rest of the ingredients and pour over the fish. Cover with a lid or foil paper and simmer over low heat for 10 minutes. Cool and refrigerate for 24 hours before serving.

These are very good with a bowl of unseasoned greens and a plate of cucumber sticks. Let each person use some of the fish liquid as a salad dressing.

MARINATED SALTED HERRING

12 small salted herring
Milk
1 tablespoon peppercorns
3 bay leaves
1 onion, minced
4 whole cloves

3 slices unpeeled lemon
2 teaspoons mustard seeds
½ cup cider vinegar
½ cup water
1 tablespoon sugar

Soak herring in enough milk to cover, for 12 to 24 hours. Wash under running cold water.

Place in a pyrex dish, placing here and there, between the fish, the peppercorns, bay leaves, onion, cloves, lemon and mustard seeds. Pour on top, the vinegar, water and sugar mixed together. Cover and marinate 24 hours refrigerated. They are then ready to serve.

MARINATED HERRING FILLETS

5 - 7 fresh herring fillets
2 large onions thinly sliced
2 carrots, thinly sliced
½ cup water
½ cup cider or malt vinegar

10 peppercorns
¼ teaspoon thyme
3 bay leaves
½ cup salad oil

In an earthenware or pyrex dish, make alternate rows of herring and onions.

Place the carrots and the water in a saucepan, bring to a boil, then simmer, covered for 10 minutes. Add the vinegar, peppercorns, thyme and bay leaves. Simmer another 10 minutes. Cool.

Add the salad oil and pour over the herring. Let stand 3 to 4 days covered, in refrigerator, before serving. Herring marinated in this manner will keep 8 to 10 days. Delicious served with potato salad.

HERRING IN SOUR CREAM

6 - 8 fresh fillets of herring
Juice of 4 lemons
24 peppercorns

1¼ cups sour cream
(commercial type)
1 onion, thinly sliced

Place the fillets of herring in a pyrex dish. Pour the lemon juice on top. Cover and refrigerate 24 hours. The lemon juice "cooks" the fish.

136

To serve, remove the fillets from the lemon juice, blend them with the peppercorns, sour cream and onion rings. Refrigerate 4 to 6 hours. Serve garnished with sliced hard-cooked eggs and tomatoes.

TURNIPS AND THE SWEETS

TURNIPS GRATINÉS

A meal in itself.

2 cups mashed turnips
1 egg
2 tablespoons butter
1 pinch savory
Salt and pepper to taste

The sauce:
3 tablespoons flour
3 tablespoons butter
1 cup milk
½ cup grated cheese

Blend together the mashed turnips, egg, butter, savory, salt and pepper. Stir well. Place in a buttered baking dish.

Top with a thick white sauce made with the butter, flour and milk. Sprinkle with the grated cheese and bake in a 400°F. oven for 25 minutes or until the cheese has melted.

CONVENTIONAL TURNIP

1 medium turnip (2½ to 3 lbs.)   4 slices bacon
1 can mushroom or celery soup   ¼ cup parsley, minced

Peel the turnip and dice. Cook and drain.

Fry the bacon, remove from fat and break into small pieces. Add the undiluted soup and parsley. Add to the cooked turnip and warm over low heat for 5 or 6 minutes. Serve.

TURNIP SALAD

5 cups turnips, peeled and grated
1 large red onion, finely chopped
½ cup cider vinegar
1 teaspoon salt
¼ teaspoon pepper

3 tablespoons maple sugar or
   brown sugar
2 tablespoons fresh grated horseradish (optional)

Mix together the vinegar, salt, pepper, maple or brown sugar and grated horseradish.

Pour this mixture over the vegetables. Stir well. Cover and refrigerate 24 hours before serving.

CORNED BEEF CHOWDER

A soup that is a meal. Hungry outdoor men sometimes place a large hardtack biscuit in the bottom of the bowl, pour the hot chowder on top, then at the end eat the biscuit all nicely softened by the hot liquid.

5 thick slices fat salt pork, diced	1 can corned beef
1 large onion, chopped fine	1 can (28 oz.) can tomatoes
1 teaspoon brown sugar	4 large potatoes, peeled and diced
5 cups water, hot	3 parnips, peeled and diced

In a deep soup pot fry the diced salt pork, until crisp and golden. Add the onion and brown sugar and stir until softened and slightly browned. Add the corned beef, tomatoes, potatoes and parsnips. Bring to boil. Cover and simmer over medium heat, until the potatoes are tender. Taste for seasoning.

MOLASSES HAM STEAK

One of England's gifts to Canada — molasses and spices.

1½ lbs. 1-inch ham steaks	10 cloves
¼ cup molasses	¼ teaspoon cinnamon
¼ cup cold water	

Place the ham in a baking dish. Pour the molasses over the ham and let stand 20 minutes.

Pour water around the ham, sprinkle with the cinnamon and stud with the cloves. Cover and bake in a 325°F. oven, 45 to 60 minutes or until the meat is tender.

BEEF HEART STEW

This is very nice hot, and equally when the meat is cold and served in thin slices with reheated sauce, or the sauce can be served over mashed potatoes or boiled cabbage.

1½ - 2 lbs. beef hearts	1 finely chopped onion
3 tablespoons vinegar	½ cup browned flour
4 cups cold water	¼ cup bacon fat
1 teaspoon salt	1 cup milk
½ teaspoon pepper	2 cups water

Soak beef hearts in vinegar and cold water 4 hours. Drain and cut out the hard inside membranes with scissors.

Mix salt, pepper, onion and flour and roll meat in it until well coated. Melt fat. Brown meat all over at medium heat, then add milk and water. Cover and simmer 1½ - 2 hours, or until meat is tender and liquid has become a creamy brown sauce.

You may instead thinly slice the heart after browning and return it to pan with milk and water. It will cook this way in 40-50 minutes but it is not as good cold the next day.

FRESH BOILED BRISKET WITH SULTANA SAUCE

Brought to Newfie by the British settlers.

4 lbs. brisket or 3 lbs. brisket and 2 lbs. cross shank	Sultana sauce:
	1 cup sultana raisins
1 sliced onion	1 cup boiling water
1 sliced carrot	2 tablespoons butter
1 bay leaf	2 tablespoons flour
½ teaspoon thyme	¼ cup red wine, of your choice
1 teaspoon coarse salt	2 tablespoons brown sugar
¼ teaspoon pepper	The juice of ½ lemon
	Grated rind of 1 lemon
	½ teaspoon salt

Set the beef in a saucepan and add the vegetables and seasonings. Pour enough boiling water over to completely cover the meat. Bring to a boil, cover and simmer over low heat for 3 - 4 hours, or until the meat is tender.

When cooked, start making the sauce. Pour the boiling water over the raisins and place over low heat for a few minutes.

Remove from heat, drain and reserve the liquid. Melt the butter in a saucepan, add the flour, mix well and add ¾ cup of the reserved liquid, and the wine. Stir until creamy and smooth. Add the sugar, lemon juice and rind. Mix well and serve with the boiled beef thinly sliced, and boiled potatoes.

SAUSAGE HASH

Old fashioned sage sausage meat is especially good in this hash, which makes a fine Sunday brunch.

1 lb. sausage meat	½ teaspoon salt
1 large onion, diced	Pinch of pepper
4 cooked potatoes, diced	½ cup cream
¼ cup fresh parsley, minced	

Crumble the sausage meat into a cast iron frying pan and fry lightly. Pour off about half the fat, add the onion and cook over medium heat, stirring well. Add the potatoes, parsley, salt and pepper. Turn heat to high and mix thoroughly. Pat into a flat cake and pour the cream over the cake. Turn heat down and cook slowly until a golden crust forms on the bottom and the whole resembles an omelet. Serve hot, cut into wedges with ketchup and cabbage salad.

MEAT AND POTATO CASSEROLE

A true family meal, easily prepared and very tasty. Three pounds of fresh cod can replace the meat.

1½--2 lbs. pork shoulder chops or steaks	¼ teaspoon sage or ½ teaspoon savory
2 tablespoons flour	6 to 8 medium potatoes
1 teaspoon salt	Hot milk
¼ teaspoon pepper	

Trim off the excess fat and melt it in an enamel cast iron casserole. Pound the chops or steaks to flatten them slightly. Roll them in a mixture of the flour, salt, pepper, sage or savory until well coated, then brown in the melted fat.

Peel and halve the potatoes and place them around the meat. Pour enough hot milk on top to cover the potatoes. Bake for 50-60 minutes at 350°F.

BUBBLE AND SQUEAK

One Newfoundland woman told me that every cook prepares this family dish "following her nose". These are my own quantities.

4 diced salt pork slices	3 - 4 cups coarsely shredded cabbage
1 diced large onion	¼ teaspoon pepper
4 sliced carrots	Hot water
1 cubed small turnip	
4 - 5 peeled and thickly sliced potatoes	

Fry salt pork in a stewing pot. Every Newfoundland housewife has a "bake-pot" for this, a black cast iron pot. When pork is golden brown, add onion and stir until soft. Add remaining ingredients, mixing well. Cover and simmer over low heat 8 - 10 minutes, then stir and add hot water until it comes up 1 inch on the sides of the pot. (The amount of water is important — the mixture should be moist but not wet when the potatoes are cooked.)

Cover and cook over medium low heat until vegetables are tender. Uncover and cook over high heat until most of the liquid is gone. Add salt to taste.

NEVER-FAIL PANCAKES

Make a meal with pancakes, sausages and molasses.

1 cup all-purpose flour	1 cup plus 2 tablespoons
1 teaspoon salt	buttermilk
1 teaspoon soda	2 tablespoons melted butter
1 egg	

Stir the flour, salt and soda together in a bowl. Drop in unbeaten egg, add buttermilk and butter. Stir only until all flour is moistened — you'll see a lump here and there — then let stand 5 minutes. The batter will look thick, spongy and puffy.

Drop by tablespoonfuls on to a hot greased pan, spreading batter a bit with the back of a spoon. Cook on one side until bubbles appear, turning before the bubbles break and become dry looking. Brown a few seconds on other side.

MOLASSES OATMEAL COOKIES

Molasses and some sort of spice are a favorite combination in New-foundland desserts. Use old-fashioned rolled oats, not the quick instant type.

2½ cups rolled oats	¼ teaspoon cloves
1 cup all-purpose flour	⅓ cup raisins (optional)
½ cup brown or white sugar	⅔ cup melted margarine or
2 teaspoons baking powder	bacon fat
½ teaspoon soda	¾ cup molasses
½ teaspoon salt	1 tablespoon milk
½ teaspoon nutmeg	1 beaten egg
1 teaspoon cinnamon	

Measure the rolled oats into a bowl and sift over them the next 8 ingredients. Add raisins and stir well.

Melt fat and remove from heat. To it, add remaining ingredients and mix well. Add to dry ingredients, blend and drop by spoonfuls on to greased pans. Bake 15 minutes at 350°F.

BLUEBERRY ROLY-POLY

Not an English steamed Roly-Poly, but a Newfie loaf pan type, sort of steamed in the middle, crusty brown all around. All types of fruits can be used. The frozen type, thawed and drained are satisfactory. Make a sauce with the juice or use 2 cups of grated unpeeled apples mixed with 1 cup brown sugar and 1 tablespoon of lemon juice.

2 cups all purpose flour	¾ cup milk
3 teaspoons baking powder	2 cups fresh blueberries
½ teaspoon salt	½ to ¾ cup sugar
1 tablespoon sugar	1 tablespoon bottled lemon juice
4 tablespoons margarine	

Sift together the flour, baking powder, salt and sugar. Cut in the margarine and add just enough of the milk to make a soft biscuit dough. Turn on a lightly floured board. Knead lightly for a few seconds and roll to a rectangle about 9x12 inches. Spread with the following mixture: Blend together the blueberries or another fruit of your choice, the sugar and lemon juice.

Then roll the dough like a jelly roll, sealing ends and edges well. Place in a greased 9x5″ loaf pan. Bake in a 400°F. oven 35 to 40 minutes or until deep brown on top. Serve with cream or vanilla sauce.

SUPERB PLUM PUDDING

Another gift from the British settlers.

½ cup grated unpeeled apples	1½ teaspoons ginger
¼ lb. chopped beef suet	¼ teaspoon nutmeg
¼ cup chopped walnuts	½ teaspoon allspice
2 tablespoons diced candied orange peel	¼ teaspoon salt
	1 cup sugar
2 tablespoons diced candied lemon peel	⅓ cup apricot jam
	2 cups fine dry breadcrumbs
⅔ cup diced candied citron peel	4 eggs
1½ cups seedless raisins	2 tablespoons milk
1 cup currants	⅓ cup brandy or rum
1 tablespoon cinnamon	⅓ cup white wine or orange juice

In a large bowl, combine all the ingredients except the last 4 and mix thoroughly. Beat the eggs, then add to them the remaining ingredients. Add to the fruit mixture and mix thoroughly with your hands — a spoon cannot blend this thick mass properly.

Oil and sugar a 1-quart mold or two 1-pint molds. Fill ⅔ full, cover tightly and steam — the quart for 5½ hours, the pints for 4. Serve with Hard Sauce or Vanilla Sauce.

Hard Sauce:

½ cup unsalted butter	1 egg yolk
1½ cups sifted icing sugar (measure after sifting)	2 tablespoons rum or brandy

Cream the butter until very light. Gradually add the sifted icing sugar. When it is very smooth, add the egg yolk and the rum or brandy. Beat well, pour into a dish and refrigerate overnight.

VANILLA SAUCE

½ cup sugar	2 tablespoons butter
Pinch salt	1 tablespoon vanilla
1 tablespoon cornstarch	Pinch nutmeg
1 cup water or apple juice	

Mix the sugar, salt and cornstarch. Add the water or apple juice. Stirring constantly, cook over medium heat, until thick and clear. Add the butter, vanilla and nutmeg. Serve warm.

MANITOBA

When you think of western hospitality, of warm companionship and hearty meals, you have to think of Manitoba, which this year celebrated its Centennial. Manitobans, and expatriates returning to the province for the festivities, will reserve a special place in their celebrations for the wide range of uniquely Manitoba fare — dishes created from the many nationalities that pioneered and gave substance to the gateway to Western Canada.

Among the frontier favorites were pemmican, a dried venison or bison meat that the Indians sometimes mixed with wild cherries and fresh suet; the settlers' sourdough bread that has remained a favorite of all Canadians; and wild rice, or Indian wild rice as it was sometimes called, which, though a luxury today, was then family fare.

The big, cold water of Lake Winnipeg gives us the world famous Winnipeg Goldeye, even a perfect caviar, known to few. I have many a time had the pleasure of finding some and enjoying it greatly. It is superb.

St. Boniface gives Manitoba its French and Indian touch with many colorful dishes. Brandon chosen by the founding fathers of C.P.R. as a new townsite, with time became known as Wheat City and the Mennonites from Steinback and many other parts, created a very interesting type of cooking which soon became part of the Canadian table. Vegetables come from the Red River district and wild birds and big game, beef and honey are plentiful too. For me the very best Canadian honey is the western type. For years I have bought natural honey from the Red River district. These are just a few of Manitoba's table treasures enjoyed by the rest of Canada.

THE NATIVE STORY

The pemmican that used to be prepared with bison or buffalo meat, stirred with wild berries, can still be prepared and enjoyed as you will find in the recipe that follows. Pickled Beaver Tail is still enjoyed by trappers and guides, and the wild rice of the Indian has become gourmet fare "worth its weight in gold". Corn hominy is the same as the "blé-d'Inde lessivé" of Québec, and rose hips (to be gathered from the wild rose bushes after a first autumn frost has touched them) should be used as tea or made into jam, jelly or syrup. 3 rose hips equal 1 orange in Vitamin C. Our ancestors may not have compared this statistic, but instinctively knew of its health value. Dandelion greens, lamb's quarter or wild mustard were signs of spring and tonic. In my house, we still boil lamb's quarter with salt pork and eat the first young dandelions as a salad.

PEMMICAN (CHIPPEWA)

I found this way of making this early Canadian food of the Prairies in the *Prairie Pantry* cook book. I had some venison smoked at a local smoke house, but dried beef, when you can find a good one, also works very well.

1 lb. dried beef or smoked venison	**½ lb. fresh beef suet, chopped fine**
¾ lb. dried crushed choke-cherries	**½ cup light brown or natural sugar**

Pass all through meat grinder, except the sugar. Add the sugar. Mix thoroughly. Pack in a bowl and keep covered and refrigerated. Serve with sourdough bread.

*I dry my own chokecherries in a 200°F. oven. They are usually easy to find in Health Food stores. Dried currants can replace them, or fresh lingonberries when available.

INDIAN WILD RICE CASSEROLE

Perfect to serve as is for luncheon or as a vegetable with venison or game birds.

1½ cups wild rice*	**6 slices bacon, diced**
2½ cups cold water	**1 cup grated carrots**
2½ teaspoons salt	**½ cup light cream or milk**
1 large onion, diced	**1 egg**
½ lb. mushrooms, sliced	

Place the wild rice, water and salt in a large saucepan, bring to a fast rolling boil. Boil for 10 minutes. Turn off the heat, cover and let stand 30 minutes or until all the water has been absorbed.

Brown the bacon, then add the onion and mushrooms, stir until lightly browned, and the carrots and mix well. Then add the rice and blend the whole thoroughly. Beat the cream and egg together and add to rice mixture.

Place in a casserole. Cover and bake 30 minutes in a 325°F. oven. Remove cover, stir with a fork and bake covered for another 15 to 20 minutes. Serve.

*Wild rice can be replaced by an equal quantity of brown rice or packaged wild rice dinner. Then cook according to directions on package.

BOILED CORN PUDDING

A fish head stock is equally as good as a chicken broth. A surprising recipe I learned from a Manitoba Indian. We eat it as a lunch with green salad or coleslaw or as a vegetable with roast pork or goose.

4 cups chicken or fish broth
2 tablespoons butter
1 cup oatmeal
½ cup all-purpose flour
2 teaspoons baking powder

1 tablespoon sugar
1 teaspoon salt
1 can corn niblets or lye corn
1 egg
Milk

Bring the chicken or fish broth to boil with the butter. Stir together the cornmeal, flour, baking powder, sugar and salt.

Stir together the undrained corn niblets or lye corn, egg and milk. Add all at once to the flour mixture. Mix well. Pour by spoonfuls into the boiling broth. Lower the heat. Cover and simmer 15 to 18 minutes. Uncover and serve the thick pudding to replace potatoes.

BUTTERMILK BANNOCK

Indians all over Canada still make bannock and good they are. After all they are the ancestors of our baking powder biscuits.

3½ cups all-purpose flour
½ cup wheat germ
1¾ teaspoons soda
½ teaspoon cream of tartar
1 teaspoon salt

¼ cup melted butter
2 tablespoons corn syrup or
   treacle or molasses
1½ cups buttermilk

Mix in a bowl the flour, wheat germ, soda, cream of tartar and salt. Combine melted butter, syrup and buttermilk. Pour over the dry ingredients and mix with a fork. It may be necessary to add a little more buttermilk, to make a soft dough. Turn dough on a lightly floured board and knead gently for a few seconds. Shape in 2 thick round cakes about 7 inches in diameter. Place on buttered cooky sheet. Bacon fat gives a nice flavor. Mark into wedges with a sharp knife. Bake in a preheated oven—375°F. 20 to 35 minutes or until golden brown. Brush top with melted butter or bacon fat as soon as out of the oven. Break in wedges and serve.

PIONEER'S BANNOCK

Especially good eaten hot. Spread with bacon fat or half bacon fat, half butter creamed together.

3 cups all-purpose flour
2 teaspoons baking powder
¼ teaspoon salt

2 to 4 tablespoons lard
1½ to 2 cups cold water

Mix in a bowl the flour, baking powder and salt. Cut in the lard and add as much water as needed to make a soft dough. Knead a few minutes. Flatten it out in a well greased cast-iron 9-inch frying pan. Bake in a preheated 375°F. oven, 20 to 35 minutes or until golden brown. Break up pieces to serve instead of cutting with a knife.

ROSE HIP JAM

2 lbs. fresh rose hips   ½ lb. sugar (approximately)
1¼ cups water

Gather rose hips, remove blossom ends, stems and leaves, wash quickly. Place in a saucepan with the water and bring to the boil. Boil 15 to 20 minutes or until tender. Mash with a fork or a wooden mallet. Weigh the pulp and add ½ pound sugar per pound of pulp. Bring to the boil, while stirring, then boil 10 minutes. Pour into hot sterilized jars, cool slightly and seal.

RED RIVER HOMEMADE BREAD

Part of the lukewarm water drained from boiled potatoes can be used in this perfect recipe sent to me from a dear friend living in Manitoba. The ginger is her grandmother's trick, and it helps to give the bread a perfect texture.

4 cups lukewarm water   12 cups sifted all-purpose flour
⅓ cup natural or white sugar   ¾ cup melted lard
½ teaspoon ground ginger   4 teaspoons salt
2 envelopes active dry yeast

Pour the warm water in a large bowl. Add the sugar and stir until dissolved. Add the yeast and let stand 15 minutes or until the water is foamy.

Add the flour to the yeast mixture, adding just what is needed to make a soft dough, then add the melted lard and the salt. Stir well, adding more flour, if necessary, kneading until you have a soft, spongy dough. Place in greased dish, cover and let rise until double in bulk. Punch down, let rise again for 1 hour. Punch down. Cut into 3 equal portions, knead lightly and place in well greased bread pan, cover and let rise again. Bake in a preheated 350°F. oven. Unmold as soon as cooked and cool on cake rack.

HOMESTEADER PANCAKES

These light, fluffy pancakes are made with a sourdough base. The same base can be used for bread. Serve the pancakes with molasses warmed up with a piece of butter.

Starter dough: 2 cups all-purpose flour
  1 envelope active dry yeast   1- 2 eggs
  2 cups warm water   1 teaspoon soda
  2 cups all-purpose flour   1 teaspoon salt
Pancakes: 1 tablespoon sugar
½ cup starter dough   2 tablespoons fat, melted
  2 cups warm water

For the starter, thoroughly mix yeast and water. Let stand 10 minutes, stir and add flour. Beat until well mixed, cover and let stand overnight in a warm place.

For pancakes, next morning place ½ cup of starter in a mixing bowl. Add water and beat in flour. Cover and let stand again in a warm place overnight. In the morning, add eggs, soda, salt and sugar. Stir to blend, beat in melted fat, and cook as for any pancake.

For sourdough bread: Prepare the starter dough, but let stand 4 days in a warm place. Stir, then reserve 1 cup refrigerated in a covered glass jar (this will be your starter for the next time). Stir into remaining starter 2 cups of flour, 1 teaspoon of baking powder and 1 cup of warm water. Stir until well mixed, then add enough wholewheat or white flour to make a soft dough. Knead and let rise covered in a warm place. Punch down, shape and place in a greased 9x5-inch loaf pan. Let rise again and bake in a 400°F. oven 35-40 minutes, or until brown and crusty.

STICKY BUNS

Bake these traditional western delights in a round 9-inch cake dish. Tuck 6 buns around the outside and one in the middle. Sticky buns, unmolded, and set on a round plate, are nice served at tea time or with coffee. A true western sticky bun must have enough syrup to soak up half an inch of the bread.

1½ cups milk	2 eggs
¼ cup warm water	¼ cup soft butter
1 envelope active dry yeast	½ cup brown sugar
5 cups all-purpose flour	2 teaspoons cinnamon
1½ teaspoons salt	½ cup chopped walnuts
1 tablespoon sugar	½ cup raisins or currants
½ cup shortening	1 cup maple or corn syrup
¾ cup sugar	

Scald the milk, cool to lukewarm. Dissolve yeast in warm water, let it stand 10 minutes and stir into the milk. Beat in 2 cups of the flour, the salt and the 1 tablespoon of sugar. Beat until smooth. Set aside in a warm place to raise this sponge.

Cream shortening with the ¾ cup of sugar. Add eggs, one at a time, beating each in thoroughly.

When the sponge is bubbly, gradually beat in the sponge mixture. Stir in the remaining flour or enough to make a soft dough. Cover and let rise until double in bulk.

Divide dough in half and roll each portion to ¼ inch thickness. Spread with soft butter. Sprinkle mixture of brown sugar and cinnamon. Scatter nuts and raisins on top. Dribble with part of the syrup. Roll tightly as for a jelly roll. Cut into 1½-inch lengths. Stand buns in two deep 9-inch pans. Cover, let rise until double. Bake at 350°F. about 45 minutes or until brown. Unmold as soon as cooked.

BOILED RAISIN CAKE

Often referred to as Pioneers' Boiled Cake, this is a delicious, low-cost type of fruit cake with excellent keeping qualities.

1 cup dark brown sugar	½ teaspoon salt
½ cup pure lard	1 teaspoon baking powder
1 cup seedless raisins	1½ cups all-purpose flour
1 cup hot water	2 teaspoons allspice
1 teaspoon soda	1 teaspoon cloves
1 tablespoon water	1 teaspoon cinnamon
1- 2 eggs, beaten	

Bring the sugar, lard, raisins and hot water to a boil while stirring, then boil over medium heat 5 minutes. Pour into a bowl and let cool.

Stir soda into 1 tablespoon of water. Add to raisin mixture with egg (2 will give a richer cake), salt, baking powder, and mix well. Add flour sifted with spices, beating until well mixed.

Bake in a well greased 9 x 5-inch loaf pan at 325°F. for 1 hour, or until well done. Let cool 10 minutes, then unmold on a cake rack. When cold, keep wrapped in foil in a cool place.

OATMEAL MUFFINS

A 10-year-old girl made these for me when I was judging a honey contest in Winnipeg. They were so good that I asked her for the recipe. Serve them hot with whipped butter and Manitoba honey.

1½ cups sour milk or buttermilk	1 egg, beaten
1 cup old-fashioned oats	1 cup all-purpose flour
4 tablespoons melted butter	1 teaspoon baking powder
½ cup honey or light brown sugar	½ teaspoon soda
Pinch of mace	¼ teaspoon salt

Pour the milk over the oats and let stand 30 minutes (don't use instant or quick cooking oats—they make a tasteless muffin).

Mix butter, honey or sugar, mace and egg in a bowl, then add oatmeal and mix again. Sift remaining ingredients together, add and stir enough to blend—the less stirring, the better tthe muffins.

Grease 1½ to 2-inch muffin cups, fill ⅔ full with batter and bake in a 400°F. oven 12-15 minutes.

WINNIPEG GOLDEYE

Goldeye, a sweet white fish smoked to a beautiful golden color, is equally delicious hot or cold. I found this way of heating it, published in the *Prairie Pantry* cook book. It brings out all the delicate flavor without letting the fish become oily. Serve with lemon wedges and boiled potatoes cooked in their skins.

Winnipeg goldeye　　　　　　　**Pepper**
Fresh lemon juice

Place the fish, wrapped individually in aluminum foil, in a cold oven, then set control at 450°F. and leave 15 minutes. Remove fish, open paper, sprinkle each with 1 tablespoon of lemon juice and sprinkle with pepper. Each fish serves 2.

PICKLING FOR CORNED BEEF

Surprisingly easy. Use a 3 to 4-pound boned beef brisket, not too fat.

2 **tablespoons salt**	2 **tablespoons brown sugar**
3 **crushed red peppers**	1 **clove garlic (chopped)**
1 **teaspoon saltpeter**	**Water to make paste**
2 **heaping teaspoons pickling spice**	

Place meat in glass dish. Pour mixture over, refrigerate for 10 days, turning every other day.

A Memorable St. Boniface Picnic

Although this was served outside at what was called "A French pioneer barn raising" it can easily be duplicated with oven broilers.

ST. BONIFACE PICNIC BROILERS

6 **broilers**	½ **teaspoon marjoram**
½ **cup salad oil**	¼ **teaspoon pepper**
Juice of 2 lemons	12 **to 14 potatoes**
½ **teaspoon salt**	

The day before the picnic have the broilers dressed and cut in halves. (Keep the giblets for the stew). Brush each half broiler with a mixture of oil, lemon juice, salt, marjoram, and pepper. Lay halves in wax paper lined roaster or large dish—one on the other, and cover with wax paper. Refrigerate overnight. Before packaging for picnic brush again with oil mixture.

When the fire is a gray mass of coals, place chicken, bone side first, on oiled broiler. Brown 15 minutes, turn and cook until skin is brown and crisp. Then place pieces in roaster, cover and allow to remain in a just-warm spot on the grill, 15 to 20 minutes. Just before serving brush the birds with the remaining oil mixture.

The potatoes were wrapped in foil and baked in the gray coals for 35 to 40 minutes.

GIBLET STEW

This was cooked at home, placed in a fireproof baking dish and warmed up on the grill when ready to serve.

2 tablespoons chicken fat	1 teaspoon salt
1 cup diced celery	¼ teaspoon pepper
1 large onion, diced	¼ teaspoon thyme
8 cups water	1 bay leaf
Giblets, neck, etc., of 6 broilers	1 cup uncooked rice

Melt the chicken fat, add the celery and onion, cook over low heat until soft. Add the giblets, salt, pepper, thyme and bay leaf. Cover and simmer 1 hour or until meat is tender—then cut gizzards, hearts in pieces, leave liver whole, pick meat from neck.

Then bring to a rolling boil. Add the rice, reduce heat and simmer 25 minutes, stirring once or twice, or until the rice absorbs the liquid without being dry. Salt and pepper to taste. Cool. Cover and refrigerate until ready to warm up.

A TASTE OF HONEY

There is probably no other food that can boast the romance and history of honey. From the first light of civilization, this golden sweet liquid has been held in high regard by man as a food, medicine, trading commodity, and as a social and spiritual force.

It is hard to imagine the work that goes into its production. The worker bee of a hive must literally work herself to death during her six-week life span. It takes 556 worker bees flying one and one-third the distance around the world, to produce one pound of honey! And, the honeybee is essential because of her ability to pollinate crops. The value of this service to farmers outweighs the dollar value of the entire honey production.

Most of us are familiar with honey in its liquid state, clear and shimmering. But it can be found in other forms too. Look for these:

LIQUID HONEY — is extracted from the comb and strained. Freshly extracted honey may crystallize within a few weeks. When heat-treated to remain liquid, it should keep for several months at room temperature, and is best kept tightly covered.

CREAMED HONEY — is made by seeding liquid honey with finely granulated honey and storing it under controlled conditions until completely granulated. Since it has a smooth, fine texture and spreads easily, it is becoming increasingly popular.

COMB HONEY — is natural honey sealed in wax that is made by the bees in the hive. It may be sold in sections in wooden frames or it may be cut in sections and each piece wrapped separately.

CHUNK HONEY — is labeled as such. It is sold in a container and consists of pieces of comb honey as well as liquid.

Pasteurized honey may be either liquid or creamed honey that has been heated or "pasteurized" to destroy the yeasts that might cause the honey to ferment. Pasteurization does not affect the quality of the honey and it will keep almost indefinitely. It is labeled "pasteurized."

Honey is sold in various size containers from 8 ounces to 8 pounds. It is a more economical buy in large containers.

COLOR AND FLAVOR

Honey varies in color, flavor and aroma depending on the kind of flowers from which the bees have gathered the nectar. As a rule, the lighter the honey, the milder the flavor. Clover honey is white and mild, while buckwheat honey is dark and strong. Honey may be a blend of several flavors. The color classes are: White, Golden, Amber and Dark. The color is stated on the label.

STORING

Honey is best stored at room temperature in a dry place. High temperatures may cause honey to darken. Creamed honey will change in texture when stored in a hot room and in this case is best refrigerated. Honey when well sealed may be stored almost indefinitely in the freezer without any changes occurring in flavor or texture.

USE IN COOKING AND BAKING

Honey may be used in place of sugar in many recipes but the amount of liquid must be reduced. One cup of honey may replace one cup of sugar but the liquid should be cut by one quarter. In a plain cake recipe, honey may be substituted for one half the sugar. Some baked foods made with honey may brown more quickly than those made with sugar and the oven temperature should be slightly lowered.

Darker honeys give a distinctive flavor to muffins, breads and bars.

To liquefy honey, place container over warm water.

A cup of honey weighs 12 ounces.

A pound of honey measures 1⅓ cups.

Here are a few suggestions in the use of honey:

HONEY CINNAMON BUTTER — Cream ¼ cup butter and blend in ¼ cup honey and ½ teaspoon cinnamon. Spread on hot toast.

HONEY BUTTER SAUCE — Heat until blended, ¾ cup honey and 3 tablespoons butter. Cool and add 1 teaspoon lemon juice and ¼ teaspoon vanilla. Serve with pancakes or waffles.

HONEY NUT SAUCE — Dissolve 1 tablespoon of instant coffee in 2 tablespoons boiling water. Combine with 1 cup liquid honey and ¼ cup toasted almonds. Serve over ice cream.

HONEY BRAN MUFFINS

1½ cups sifted all-purpose flour	1 egg, beaten
1 cup cooking bran	⅓ cup liquid honey
1 tablespoon baking powder	⅔ cup milk
½ teaspoon salt	¼ cup butter, melted
1 teaspoon cinnamon	

Mix dry ingredients. Combine egg, honey, milk and melted butter. Make a depression in dry ingredients. Pour in liquids and stir quickly until just mixed but still lumpy. Fill well greased muffin tins two thirds full. Bake at 400°F. until browned (20 to 25 minutes).

HONEY FUDGE SQUARES

½ cup butter
2 1-ounce squares unsweetened chocolate
2 eggs
½ cup liquid honey
½ cup sugar

1 teaspoon vanilla
1 cup sifted all-purpose flour
½ teaspoon salt
½ teaspoon baking powder
½ cup chopped walnuts

Melt butter and chocolate in top of double boiler; cool slightly. Beat eggs until fluffy. Gradually beat in honey, sugar, vanilla and chocolate mixture. Stir in sifted dry ingredients and nuts. Pour into a greased 9-inch square pan and bake 20 to 25 minutes at 350°F. Cool. Spread with chocolate icing or melted semisweet chocolate and cut in squares.

HONEY CRUNCH

Similar to apple crisp, only the combination of honey and fresh lemon juice makes it something quite special. The first time I ate it in St. Boniface it was covered with thick farm cream. With it our hostess served black coffee with a stick of cinnamon in it.

6 - 8 medium apples
Juice of 1 lemon
8 whole cloves
¼ teaspoon cinnamon
½ cup honey (buckwheat when available)

1 cup brown sugar
3 tablespoons butter
¼ cup flour
½ cup salted peanuts or plain walnuts

Peel and core apples, cut into thin slices. Arrange in generously buttered baking dish. Pour lemon juice on top, sprinkle with cloves and cinnamon. Then drizzle over all 2 to 3 tablespoons of the honey. Bake uncovered in a preheated 350°F. oven for 30 minutes.

Meanwhile cream together the brown sugar, butter and flour. Add remaining honey. Stir in the peanuts or walnuts. Spread over hot apples. Place dish in broiler 6 inches from source of heat, broil until topping melts and browns. Cool 20 minutes. Serve with cream or ice cream.

WESTERN MENNONITE SWEETS AND PICKLING

HIGHBUSH CRANBERRY JELLY

Wash fruit. Put in preserving kettle and add just enough water to cover. Bring to boil over high heat then reduce temperature to simmer and cook until fruit is soft. Turn into jelly bag and let drip overnight. In the morning measure juice. Bring juice to a boil and boil for 3 minutes. Add 1 cup of sugar for each cup of juice. Stir until sugar is dissolved. Bring to boiling point and boil at full rolling boil until the jelly stage is reached. Start testing for jelly about 2 minutes after the sugar has been added. These berries are very rich in pectin and jell quickly. If using a candy thermometer, 220°F. is the jelly stage. Pour into sterilized jelly glasses then seal with melted paraffin. When jelly is cold add a second layer of paraffin.

PINCHERRY JELLY

Wash and pick over the cherries and cover with water. Simmer gently until the fruit begins to lose its color and the juice is extracted. Turn into jelly bag and drain well. Measure this juice and allow 1 cup of sugar to each cup of the juice, but return the juice to the stove for 5 minutes of hard boiling before adding sugar.

Add the sugar and stir until it is dissolved. Then boil as hard as possible for 3 minutes and test for jelly. It comes very rapidly so start testing after 3 minutes boiling and test frequently until the mixture jells. Pour at once into hot sterilized jars and seal with paraffin wax.

CHOKECHERRY-APPLE JELLY

Wash, stem chokecherries; crush. Measure and add an equal amount of stemmed apples, cut into eighths. Add enough cold water to come just below top layer of prepared fruit. Simmer, covered, until fruit is soft and mushy, crushing it during the cooking. Pour into moistened jelly bag and let drain overnight or until dripping ceases.

Boil juice, uncovered, for 3 minutes. Remove from heat and test for pectin. Add sugar accordingly; about 1 cup of sugar for each cup of juice.

BOHNENIKRA

18 cups cut wax beans	1 cup sugar
6 cups onions	2 tins tomatoes
1 cup vinegar	1 bottle ketchup
1½ cups vegetable oil	

Precook beans and slightly fry onions. Cook all ingredients together, but not too long. Put in sealers and seal.

SASKATCHEWAN

Geographically Saskatchewan is the heart of Canada, and such names as Saskatoon, Regina, Medicine Hat, Moose Jaw, Prince Albert and Gravelbourg, certainly stir many table memories in my head.

Some of my relatives who long ago moved to Saskatchewan used to send my mother recipes from the Homemaker's Club founded in 1905, the first and oldest Canadian Women's group that still functions today. They wrote the *Saskatchewan Homemaker's Kitchens* for the Golden Jubilee in 1955, and a very interesting book it is. *The Rural Home,* written by Winfred Taylor is a very interesting portrayal of the good life as it used to be. One can feel love for Canada all through it. I believe this is the true grit that has made our Canadian woman what she is.

THE OLD AND THE NEW

BUTTER BALLS CHICKEN SOUP

The butter balls, very tiny dumplings, are called rivels in the West and dropsley in Ontario. This combination makes a perfect light supper. I sometimes replace the chicken soup in this recipe with a can of consommé and an equal amount of water.

3 lbs. chicken	2 tablespoons chopped fresh
½ cup chopped celery leaves	parsley
1 bay leaf	2 tablespoons butter
10 peppercorns	2 eggs
1 teaspoon salt	5 - 6 tablespoons flour
5 cups hot water	¼ teaspoon salt
1 cup diced celery	

Cut chicken into portions, place in a saucepan with celery leaves, bay leaf, peppercorns, the one teaspoon of salt and the water. Bring to a boil, cover and simmer over low heat for about one hour, or until chicken is tender. Strain, then return broth to saucepan. Cut chicken into small pieces, add to broth with celery and parsley, then simmer.

To make the butter balls, cream butter, add eggs and beat. Gradually add flour and the ¼ teaspoon of salt. Beat hard until whole is like a very soft batter. Drop by ¼ or ½ teaspoonfuls into broth, cover and let stand 5 minutes over low heat.

CABBAGE SOUP

The way the Saskatchewan French Canadians make their vegetable soup is in a sense nearer to French cuisine than the Québec style.

3 tablespoons butter or fat	½ teaspoon pepper
2 medium carrots, grated	½ teaspoon sugar
3 onions, sliced thin	4 cups water or consommé
4 to 6 cups cabbage, chopped fine	2 cups milk
A few celery leaves, minced	Slices of bread, browned in butter
1 teaspoon salt	Grated cheddar cheese

Melt the butter or fat in a saucepan, add the carrots, onions, cabbage, celery leaves, salt, pepper and sugar. Mix well, cover and simmer for 25 minutes over very low heat. Add the water or consommé, bring to a boil and simmer for 15 minutes. Add the milk, heat and taste for seasoning. When ready to serve, place a slice of bread, browned in butter, in each plate, sprinkle with cheese and pour over the soup.

COUNTRY BEAN SOUP

If you can't get a ham bone, ask your butcher for ham or bacon rind, or use 1 or 2 thin ham steaks, diced or 3 - 4 sliced frankfurters.

1 lb. dried navy beans	3 carrots, thinly sliced
3 quarts cold water	1 tablespoon salt
1 ham bone or substitute (above)	½ teaspoon pepper
	1 teaspoon sugar or molasses
1 cup celery, chopped	1 cup tomato juice
1 large onion, diced	

Wash the beans and place them in a large saucepan. Cover with the cold water and let stand overnight to soak.

The next morning bring the whole to a fast rolling boil over high heat. Add the ham bone or substitute, cover and simmer over low heat for two hours. Add the remaining ingredients and simmer, covered for one more hour, or until the beans are tender.

PAINLESS CORN SOUP

A young bride from Saskatoon gave me this recipe. Her grandmother taught her how to make it, but she always used green corn that she creamed. Our bride said she finds the "painless way" just as good.

3 cups water	3 tablespoons butter
1 can cream style corn	2 teaspoons flour
¼ teaspoon sage	1 teaspoon salt
1 onion, thinly sliced	¼ teaspoon pepper
2 cups milk	

Combine water, corn and sage in a saucepan and simmer 20 minutes. Strain and press through a sieve (I use my blender). Scald the onion in the milk, over low heat.

Melt 1 tablespoon of the butter, blend in the flour, salt and pepper. Add to the corn mixture. To taste, remove or leave onion in the milk. I prefer to leave it. Bring to boil over medium heat, stirring most of the time.

When creamy, serve, adding ½ teaspoon butter to each plate. A teaspoon of rich cream can also be added.

CORN FRIED CHICKEN

I have never seen chicken cooked quite this way in the East. It was served at a women's group luncheon, and I was assured it was typically Saskatchewan. Whatever it is, it is good.

1 3-lb. chicken	¼ teaspoon pepper
1 cup milk	1 cup cornmeal
¼ teaspoon turmeric	¼ cup bacon fat or butter
½ teaspoon salt	1 cup light cream
¼ teaspoon sage	

Cut the chicken into individual pieces. Blend the milk with the turmeric, salt, pepper and sage. Roll the chicken in this milk, then in cornmeal, until well coated.

Melt the bacon fat or butter in a large cast-iron frying pan. Fry the pieces of chicken in it, over medium heat, until light brown on both sides.

Then pour the cream over all. Cover and simmer over low heat for one hour. The cornmeal thickens the sauce and makes a beautiful gravy. It was served with small onions slowly cooked in butter until golden, then set in a nest of green peas.

TURKEY LOAF

A Swift Current special — very interesting to use when bits and pieces of leftover turkey are available.

2 cups cooked turkey	1 small onion, chopped fine
½ cup cooked carrots	The juice of ½ a lemon
1 cup well drained No. 4	½ teaspoon savory
green peas	1 teaspoon salt
½ cup diced celery	¼ teaspoon pepper
1 cup fresh white breadcrumbs	1 cup diced crustless bread
½ cup milk or cream	¼ cup melted butter
2 egg yolks, well beaten	

Put the chicken, carrots and peas through the food chopper. Place in a bowl and add all the remaining ingredients.

Butter an 8 x 4-inch loaf pan generously. Put mixture in it.

Mix the bread cubes and melted butter and spread on top of loaf. Bake in a preheated 350°F. oven 35 to 45 minutes. Serve with a light white sauce flavored with parsley.

MOOSE JAW ROAST BEEF ROLL

If you have any leftover roast beef, try to use it up this way. Whenever you make hot biscuits use the topping recipe — they are delicious.

2 to 3 cups ground leftover	1 - 3 tablespoons melted beef suet
roast beef or pork	Salt and pepper to taste
1 medium size onion, chopped fine	

Grind the beef through the chopper. Melt the beef suet, add the onion, and fry until golden brown, over high heat. Add to beef, fat and all. Salt and pepper to taste. Prepare the biscuits.

Topping: Home on the Range Hot Biscuits

2 cups all-purpose flour	½ teaspoon cream of tartar
½ teaspoon salt	½ cup shortening
3 teaspoons baking powder	⅔ cup buttermilk or sour milk
1 teaspoon soda	

Sift together in a bowl the flour, salt, baking powder, soda and cream of tartar. Cut in the shortening. Stir the buttermilk or sour milk in with a fork.

Turn on lightly floured board and knead gently ½ minute. Roll dough in rectangular shape ¼-inch thick. Spread with meat mixture. Roll as for jelly roll. Cut in 8 to 10 pieces. Set in well greased muffin pan or well apart in greased square casserole. Pour on top any of the leftover roast beef gravy, heated without boiling.

Bake in preheated 400°F. oven 25 to 40 minutes, depending on pan used or until biscuits are golden brown. Serve hot or warm.

BUCKWHEAT KASHA CASSEROLE

The following is one of the interesting dishes the Ukrainians brought to Canada. Serve it with the creamed mushrooms for a very interesting buffet dish.

1 box medium buckwheat Kasha
2 - 3 tablespoons butter
Salt, pepper to taste
1 - 2 cups cottage cheese

2 eggs
3 - 4 green onions, chopped
(optional)

Cook the box of buckwheat kasha according to directions on the box. When done, add the butter, salt and pepper.

Place half in a deep casserole. Mix together the cottage cheese, eggs and green onions. Place over the kasha. Top with the rest of the kasha.

Bake, uncovered, in a 350°F. oven for 20 to 25 minutes.

CREAMED MUSHROOMS

Onions browned in a heavy metal pan without any fat is an intriguing way to deal with them. It retains all their fine flavor with none of the harshness.

1 onion, chopped fine
½ lb. fresh mushrooms, sliced
⅓ cup cold water
2 tablespoons butter

2 tablespoons flour
½ cup sour cream
Salt and pepper to taste

Place the onion in a heavy metal frying pan without any fat. Cook over medium heat, until lightly browned. Add the mushrooms, mix well and stir together for a few minutes, add the water, simmer 10 minutes.

In the meantime, brown the butter in a saucepan. Add the flour and brown together. Add the liquid from the mushrooms and cook, while stirring, until creamy and smooth. Pour over the mushrooms. Blend well together and add the sour cream. Heat, but do not boil. Taste for seasoning and serve.

CHOP SUEY

The advent of the C.P.R. line in the Western prairies has brought to Canada the fathers of instant foods, the Chinese. Ever since, across the country chop suey and other Chinese dishes have become part of the Canadian picture.

3 tablespoons salad oil
2 teaspoons salt
½ teaspoon pepper
1 lb. cubed pork or veal
shoulder or chicken breast
3 tablespoons soy sauce
3 cups celery, in 1-inch pieces

2 large onions, each in 6 pieces
1 tablespoon molasses
2 cups boiling water
2 cups bean sprouts
3 tablespoons cornstarch
¼ cup cold water
3 cups cooked rice

Heat the oil, salt and pepper in a large frying pan. Sear the pork over high heat for 2 - 3 minutes. Turn the heat to low and cook uncovered for 5 - 8 minutes.

Add the soy sauce, mix well, then add the celery and onions. Cook for 3 minutes, then mix the molasses and boiling water and pour over the mixture. Cover and cook over low heat for 10 - 20 minutes, then add the bean sprouts and cook for another 3 minutes.

Blend the cornstarch with the cold water. Add to the chop suey and continue cooking for 3 - 4 minutes, stirring constantly, until the sauce thickens and becomes transparent. Serve with the rice.

STEWED OR BAKED WINTER RHUBARB

Rhubarb is a versatile fruit which was brought West by the first settlers. Cut off the tender green leaves, don't peel the stalks, and wash in cold water. Then you are ready to stew or bake your hothouse winter rhubarb.

2 cups rhubarb, in 1-inch pieces   **½ cup sugar**
¼ cup cold water

To stew: Place rhubarb and cold water in a saucepan and cover. Cook over low heat, barely simmering, about 20 - 25 minutes, or until rhubarb is tender.

Remove from heat, pour sugar over it, then ease it gently through the juice (it will dissolve without stirring). Cover and refrigerate until cold. It will taste sweeter then, but sweetening can be adjusted to suit your taste.

To bake: Place ½ cup sugar in a baking dish. Add 2 cups cut-up rhubarb. Stir with a fork and let stand until some liquid is formed at bottom of pan. Do not add any water.

Cover and bake at 350°F. until rhubarb is bubbling and tender. Let it cool, then refrigerate.

ONION-PARSLEY MUFFINS

These hot muffins combine beautifully with salad or cold cuts.

2 cups all-purpose flour   **¼ cup salad oil**
1 tablespoon sugar   **1 cup milk**
3 teaspoons baking powder   **4 green onions, chopped**
1½ teaspoons salt   **¼ cup finely chopped parsley**

Sift together the flour, sugar, baking powder and salt. Combine the salad oil, milk, green onions and parsley. Add the dry ingredients all at once and mix lightly — just enough to blend. Spoon into greased muffin pans, filling them two thirds full. Bake 20 to 25 minutes in a 400°F. oven.

HONEY CARROT CUSTARD

As a rule, few can guess what this intriguing dessert is made of. The color is beautiful and, if you would like a sauce with it, use a tart lemon sauce.

4 eggs
½ cup honey
¼ teaspoon salt
3 cups hot milk

¾ cup finely grated raw carrots
2 tablespoons sherry
Grated peel of 1 orange
¼ teaspoon cinnamon

Beat the eggs with honey and salt until frothy and light, then stir in milk. Add carrots, sherry, orange peel, and blend well.

Pour mixture into individual buttered custard cups and sprinkle each with a dash of cinnamon. Set cups in baking pan, then add water to pan until it is halfway up the cups. Bake at 325°F. for 45 - 60 minutes, or until custard is firm.

NEVER FAIL MEDIVNYK
(Ukrainian Honey Cake)

This cake will keep one month, well wrapped in transparent paper. Keep it in a cool place. It improves with age.

1 cup Saskatchewan or Manitoba honey
3 cups all-purpose flour
1 teaspoon soda
1 teaspoon baking powder
1 teaspoon cinnamon
¼ teaspoon salt
½ cup strong cool coffee

Grated rind and juice of 1 orange
1 teaspoon vanilla
2 tablespoons butter
1 cup sugar
4 eggs, separated
1 cup chopped walnuts

Bring the honey to a boil, then cool it. Sift the flour with the soda, baking powder, cinnamon and salt, twice.

Combine the coffee with the grated rind, orange juice and vanilla.

Cream the butter with the sugar. Add the honey. Beat the egg yolks and add to the honey.

Add the flour mixture alternately with the coffee mixture. Stir in the nuts.

Beat the egg whites until stiff and fold into the batter.

Pour into a generously greased bread mold. Bake in a 325°F. oven 50 to 60 minutes or until done when tested.

Unmold and cool on cake rack.

BERRY COBBLER

Use Saskatoon berries, strawberries or blueberries.

1 quart fresh berries
½ cup sugar
  A few drops rosewater
1 cup cornmeal
¼ cup sugar
1 teaspoon baking powder
1 teaspoon salt

½ cup sour milk or buttermilk
2 tablespoons melted butter
¼ cup Saskatchewan or Manitoba honey
1 tablespoon melted butter
The juice of ½ a lemon

162

Clean the berries, place them in a 2-quart baking dish, sprinkle with sugar and rosewater.

Mix together the cornmeal, sugar, baking powder and salt. Quickly stir in the buttermilk and the melted butter. Mix gently.

Drop this batter by tablespoons on top of the sweetened berries forming a design of rounds.

Mix together the honey butter and lemon juice. Pour over the berries and biscuits. Bake in a 375°F. oven 40 to 45 minutes. Serve tepid with rich cream.

FARMERS ALMANAC BARS

This recipe is a must in every prairie kitchen.

½ cup unsalted butter or margarine	12 - 16 oz. chocolate chips
1 cup Graham cracker crumbs	1 can condensed milk
1 cup coconut	½ to 1 cup chopped nuts

Melt the butter. Add the Graham crumbs and mix thoroughly. Pat into a jelly roll pan (14 x 11 inches). Sprinkle with coconut, then chocolate chips. Dribble the condensed milk on top. Top the whole thing with the chopped nuts.

Bake 25 minutes in a 350°F. oven. Cool thoroughly and cut into squares. Will keep from 8 to 10 days.

HONEY BUTTER

Serve with Home on the Range Hot Biscuits. (You will find the recipe as the topping under Moose Jaw Roast Beef Roll.) To make hot biscuits, instead of rolling dough in rectangular shape, pat to desired thickness and cut with floured cutter. Bake at 425°F. 10 to 12 minutes.

Mix an equal quantity of soft butter and Western honey, until creamy and smooth. Add the grated rind of one lemon. Keep it refrigerated.

SASKATOON APPLESAUCE

Wash and cut in four, 6 to 8 apples, place in saucepan with ½ cup water and 1½ to 2 cups Saskatoon jam or jelly. Cover. Simmer until tender. Pass through food mill or sieve. Serve cold with ice cream or whipped cream.

SASKATOON AND RHUBARB JAM

To make this one and the jam or jelly, you must first of all find the Saskatoon berries, if you do not live in the West.

4 lbs. of juicy saskatoons	3¾ lbs. sugar
1 lb. rhubarb	

Mash the saskatoons well after you have put them into the preserving kettle. Add rhubarb, then sugar and stir well. Bring to a boil and cook until thick. Pour into sterilized jars and seal while hot.

SASKATOON JAM

Pick over saskatoons and then cover with just enough water to cover berries. Cook covered for 15 minutes or until soft. Put through coarse sieve or colander and measure. To every 4 cups of juice and pulp add 4 cups sugar and ½ cup orange juice or juice of two lemons. Cook slowly until fairly thick, about 15 minutes and seal with wax. Makes a nice spread.

SASKATOON JELLY

3½ cups saskatoon juice   7½ cups sugar
½ cup lemon juice   1 bottle commercial pectin

Take about 4 lbs. berries. Place in kettle and crush. Add ½ cup water. Heat until juice starts to flow. Simmer gently 20 minutes. Squeeze out juice and measure into kettle. Add sugar and lemon juice, bring to a boil over a hot fire, stirring constantly. Add 1 bottle of pectin, stirring. Bring to full rolling boil for ½ minute, remove from fire and skim. Pour quickly.

ICE WATER CAKE

A very interesting cake which can even be described as thrifty because 5 egg whites are required, and it is often a problem for many women to know what to do with them. It was sent to me by a Saskatoon home-maker. Make sure the water is ice cold.

1½ cups water   1 cup ice water
½ cup butter   2¼ cups flour
5 egg whites   2 level teaspoons baking powder
1 teaspoon vanilla   1 teaspoon salt
½ teaspoon almond extract

Cream butter and sugar, sift the dry ingredients and add to first mixture alternately with the ice water. Beat well. Beat the egg whites and fold into the cake batter. Bake 45 minutes at 350°F.

THE WILD AND THE TAME

Do you like to have "a bird in the hand" or are you a fish fancier? Man the hunter, who knows a good spot when he sees one, surely has Saskatchewan in his book.

As a centennial project a very interesting book was published called the *Saskatchewan Sportsman's Gourmet Guide* dealing with fish, game birds, large game and wild fruit recipes tested by its author Mrs. Goplen. Each fish, bird, game or fruit has a diagram showing where in the province the item is most readily available. With this clever, well prepared book and another wonderful one *Canadian Game Cookery* by Frances Macelquham, no one hunting in Canada should have any problem cooking his catch.

My radio friends Wal 'n Den in Saskatoon once presented me with a superb Canada goose for which Saskatoon and its surroundings are famous.

I followed the recipe in the *Gourmet Guide:* "Roast Goose with Potato Dressing." When it was ready to serve I poured a quarter cup of hot rye whisky on top and flamed it. Although this was not in the recipe, it was fabulous!

Here are three interesting recipes from the *Gourmet Guide:*

SMOKED GOLDEYE

A superb recipe which I enjoyed all summer with brook trout caught by my grandson.

Prepare the fish—scale, remove viscera. Be very careful to have fish clean and wash thoroughly. Do not remove head, tail or fins unless space is crowded on your barbecue. If fish is frozen, thaw in refrigerator.

4 1 - pound Goldeye or trout   1 gallon water
1¼ cups coarse salt

Place salt and water in plastic pail and stir until dissolved. Put in fish, cover and allow to soak in brine for 10 hours. Remove from brine and rinse in cold water.

Also soak overnight 1 pound of hickory chips or hardwood sawdust (available from larger meat markets) in 2 quarts of water.

To smoke the fish, use a charcoal fire in a barbecue grill with a hood or cover. Raise grill to highest position. Bricks standing on end around the edge of the barbecue will raise the grill the proper distance from the fire. Grease grill well.

Start a charcoal fire in the back of the barbecue under the hood and allow it to burn to an even heat. Cover with one third of wet chips. Place fish on grill. Cover and smoke for about 2 hours. Add wet chips or briquettes as needed to keep the fire smoking. Temperature of the grill should be about 110°F. Turn fish carefully every half hour during smoking. When fish are ready to eat they should be lightly browned and easily halved. Any leftover fish must be well wrapped and refrigerated. Smoked fish may be reheated by placing in the oven for a few minutes.

If you do not have a barbecue with a hood remove the bottom of a 5 gallon pail with a chisel. Punch several holes near the bottom of the pail for draught. Place this pail over your charcoal and chips. Place grill on top of pail, put on fish, then cover (an old canner works well). Follow procedure as above. NOTE: The longer a fish has been frozen the less time it takes to brine. If fish is too salty, shorten the brining time.

ROAST GROUSE WITH APRICOT DRESSING

A well cooked bird with moist meat and crisp skin.

2 grouse	3 cups soft bread cubes
¼ cup butter or margarine	½ teaspoon salt
¼ cup onion, chopped	⅛ teaspoon pepper
1 cup apple, chopped	2 tablespoons bacon fat
1 cup dried apricots, chopped	¼ cup dry bread crumbs
or	1 cup water
1 cup dried prunes, chopped	

Sprinkle grouse inside and out with 1 teaspoon each of ginger and lemon juice. For game birds over three pounds in weight use 1½ teaspoons each of ginger and lemon juice. Place in a plastic bag and refrigerate for at least two hours, preferably overnight. Rinse thoroughly in cold water, drain and dry.

Melt fat, cook onions until tender, add apple, apricots or prunes, bread cubes, salt and pepper. Spoon lightly into cavity of bird. Close opening with skewers and string. Rub bird with bacon fat, roll in crumbs. Place on rack in lightweight roaster. Add water. Cover and cook at 350°F. for 2½ hours.

SWEET TREAT CHOKECHERRY JELLY

This different method of obtaining juice gives a jelly with an interesting flavor.

10 cups chokecherries, washed   5 cups hot water

Grind chokecherries with a food chopper, using a coarse blade. Place in a bowl, add water and mix well. Let stand 12 hours. Drain through moistened jelly bag.

3 cups chokecherry juice   1 bottle commercial pectin
6 cups sugar

Place juice in saucepan, add sugar. Mix well. Cook over high heat until boiling, stirring constantly. Stir in pectin at once. Then bring to full rolling boil, boil hard for 1 minute. Remove from heat, skim off foam. Pour into hot, sterilized jars. Cool slightly, then seal with paraffin.

THE GOLDEN TASTE OF CORN

How difficult it is to talk of Canadian foods without mentioning the corn that is grown and eaten from coast to coast. Our liking for corn goes back to early Canadian history when our forefathers were so often saved from starvation by the corn they bought, or stole, from the Indians.

Corn was the staple food of the frontier towns because it grew faster than other grains, and yielded a more than fair harvest. Pioneers all over Canada learned from the Indian women how to make lye corn or hominy—Quebeckers adding it to pea soup and Ontarians to a cream sauce made with bacon fat. To this day these dishes are still made and they're still good to eat. Even the cobs had their uses; they were turned into corn pipes and toys for the young, and the corn, stone-ground into meal or flour, became an ingredient for the famous Johnny cake.

Although corn is a Canadian heritage, I feel we do not do enough for it. Fresh corn is such a treat and it can be served in so many ways.

Ideally, corn on the cob should be picked, partly husked and cooked, all within 30 minutes, but this is not always possible. There is an important rule to remember: the less time corn cooks, the better it will taste. So often it suffers from overcooking.

Another caprice of corn is its preference for sugar rather than salt. Unless you cook your own garden-grown corn immediately after it is picked, sugar is needed to improve the flavor of corn that has been gathered many hours previously and may have lost some of its freshness.

CORN OYSTERS

The old-fashioned name for corn fritters. They are light, tasty and easy to make. My family eats a double portion.

2 cups corn cut from the cobs	¼ teaspoon baking powder
2 egg yolks, beaten	¼ cup all-purpose flour
½ teaspoon salt	3 egg whites, stiffly beaten
¼ teaspoon pepper	

Add the beaten egg yolks to the corn. Add salt and pepper, baking powder. Mix well. Add the flour and stir until thoroughly blended. Gently fold in the beaten egg whites. Melt 1 inch hot lard (or salad oil) in a large frying pan. Drop in mixture in oyster-sized blobs; brown on both sides. Serve when ready.

GREEN CORN PUDDING

Green corn is what the old folks called fresh corn. The pudding is a real company dish, as they used to say, and how right they were.

2 - 3 cups raw corn cut from the cobs	1 teaspoon sugar
4 eggs	½ teaspoon sage (fresh, when available)
2 cups light cream	1½ teaspoons salt
1 tablespoon butter, melted	¼ teaspoon pepper

Beat the eggs with the cream, just enough to blend. Add the corn, butter, sugar, sage, salt and pepper. Pour mixture into a buttered 2-quart baking dish. Place dish in a pan of water and bake 1 hour in a 350°F. oven, or until knife plunged into centre comes out clean.

BOILED CORN ON THE COB

In my youth, in Quebec, we had great fun every autumn at "l'Epluch-ette de Blè d'Inde"—where a party was devoted to the serving of corn. Dozens of cobs were cooked, usually boiled in a large black iron cauldron. How good it was!

Remove the husks, except the last 2 or 3 layers and the silks from each ear of corn. Trim stem and tip with a sharp knife. Bring a large pot of water to a boil with 3 tablespoons sugar and 1 cup milk for each 12 ears of corn. Drop corn into the boiling liquid. Boil 3 to 5 minutes. Remove from water and set on a hot platter covered with a linen napkin and of course, lots of soft butter, salt, and freshly-ground pepper to go with it.

ROASTED CORN

The milk and sugar treatment give it a full flavor and a beautiful golden color.

12 ears of corn	¼ **cup sugar**
2 cups milk	

Remove all the husks and silks from the corn. Trim stems and tips. Stir the milk and sugar in a shallow dripping pan and place the corn in it. Roll it around in the milk. Leave there until ready to roast.

To roast on a barbecue, place, unwrapped, on a grill high over the glowing coals. Roast 10 minutes, turning often.

To roast in the oven, preheat oven to 375°F. Set corn on grill over a dripping pan. Roast 20 minutes, turning a few times.

FRESH CREAMED CORN

To all those who enjoy canned creamed corn during the winter, I recommend this dish. It's good with steaks or baked ham. You will need two ears of corn for each ½ cup corn required. Husk corn and remove the silk. Cut the uncooked kernels from the corn by standing the ear up and cutting along with a sharp knife. Place the corn in melted butter (1 teaspoon per ½ cup) in a saucepan; when possible, use unsalted butter. Cover, and cook over very low heat, stirring a few times, until the corn no longer tastes starchy. Season with salt and pepper and add 2 tablespoons light or rich cream to each cup of corn. If you prefer a thicker sauce add one tablespoon of cornstarch to the cream before adding to the corn. Simmer 5 minutes, stirring all the time.

CORN-STUFFED GREEN PEPPERS

A natural union, as both are at their best in the early autumn. This light, custardy corn filling is the best I know for green pepper.

2½ cups corn cut from the cobs
6 green peppers of equal size
4 eggs
⅔ cup heavy cream
¼ teaspoon savory

¼ teaspoon each salt and pepper
    Pinch of nutmeg
1 cup fresh bread cubes (no
    crusts)
3 tablespoons butter

Cut a slice off the top of each pepper. Remove seeds and membrane carefully (My mother always pared away the thin outer layer of the pepper with a sharp knife. I use a potato peeler. This is not necessary, but it makes for a delicate stuffed pepper that never has any bitterness.)

Place prepared peppers upright in a shallow buttered baking dish.

To make the filling, beat eggs and cream slightly in a bowl and add the rest of the ingredients. Blend well and use to fill each pepper. Bake 40 minutes in a preheated 325°F. oven. Sprinkle top with paprika and serve in a nest of cooked and buttered or plain rice.

CORN YORKSHIRE PUDDING

Unite the old world with the new. Make your Yorkshire pudding with fresh corn, when it is in season. Canned corn kernels are not as good because they are too heavy for the pudding.

1½ cups corn cut from the cobs
¼ lb. fresh beef suet or
    1 cup roast beef drippings
    (the fat part)

1 cup all-purpose flour
1 teaspoon salt
2 eggs
1 cup milk

Cut suet into small pieces and fry crisp and brown in a cast-iron frying pan, or heat the beef drippings. Place in a 400°F. oven while preparing the batter.

Sift together the flour and salt. Beat the eggs until frothy then stir in the milk and flour, beat with a rotary beater or wire whip until smooth. Stir in the corn and pour into hot frying pan. Bake 25 minutes, or until the pudding is puffy all over and golden brown. Serve as soon as ready. Without roast beef, serve with a green salad or sliced tomatoes.

SUCCOTASH

The famous Indian pudding made with lye corn and fresh corn combined in a white sauce flavored with lots of fresh parsley.

2 cups corn cut from the cobs
1 can lye or hominy corn
2 tablespoons butter
1 teaspoon salt
1 teaspoon sugar
    Pinch of sage

¼ cup water
¼ cup milk or cream
2 teaspoons cornstarch

Put the corn, lye corn or hominy, butter, salt, pepper, sugar, sage and water in a saucepan. Cook, uncovered, over medium heat, 8 to 10 minutes. By then, the water should be partly evaporated and the corn tender. Gradually add the milk, mixed with the cornstarch. Cook until creamy.

WESTERN CORN PIE

This is a true family corn pie, tasty and nourishing — a meal in one dish. Serve it with hot, tasty, spicy tomato sauce or ketchup.

2 cups corn cut from the cobs	¾ teaspoon salt
1 lb. ground beef	4 fresh tomatoes, peeled and
1 large onion, chopped	diced
1 tablespoon salad oil or butter	½ package corn muffin mix or
2 tablespoons chili powder	½ recipe Johnny cake
(optional)	

Brown meat and onion in salad oil (or butter), just long enough for the meat to lose its rawness. Add the chili (or curry powder), salt and tomatoes. Cover and simmer over low heat for 15 minutes. Add the cut corn. Blend well. Taste for seasoning. Pour mixture into a greased 1½-qt. casserole. Top with corn muffin mix (or Johnny cake), spreading it all over with a knife dipped in cold water. Bake in a 425°F. oven for 20 to 30 minutes or until batter is cooked.

RAISED CORN ROLLS

4½-5½ cups unsifted all-purpose flour	2 cups very hot tap water (as hot as the hand can stand)
2 tablespoons sugar	1 egg white (at room
2 tablespoons salt	temperature)
1 package active dry yeast	Cornmeal
3 tablespoons softened margarine	

In a large bowl thoroughly mix 1 cup flour, sugar, salt and undissolved active dry yeast. Add softened margarine. Gradually add very hot tap water to dry ingredients and beat 2 minutes at medium speed of electric mixer, or vigorously with mixing spoon, scraping bowl occasionally. Add egg white and ¾ cup flour. Beat at medium speed one minute, or vigorously with a mixing spoon, scraping bowl occasionally. With mixing spoon, stir in enough additional flour to make a soft dough. Turn out onto lightly floured board; knead until smooth and elastic, about 8 to 10 minutes. Place in greased bowl, turning to grease top. Cover; let rise in a warm place, free from drafts, until doubled in bulk about 45 minutes.

Punch dough down; turn out onto lightly floured board. Cover; let rest 10 minutes. Divide in half. Form each half into a 9-inch roll. Cut into nine 1-inch pieces. Form into smooth balls. Place about 3 inches apart on greased baking sheets sprinkled with corn meal. Cover, let rise in a warm place, free from drafts, until doubled in bulk, about 45 minutes. Sprinkle cornmeal on rolls. Bake in a very hot oven (450°F.) about 15 minutes, or until done. Remove from baking sheets and cool on wire racks.

ALBERTA

Beef and "Red Eye", ranch barbecues, the dashing wide brim of cowboys' hats, the French touch in Edmonton, the Euterites in Lethbridge, in the prairies wheat pools, sheep in the mountains, cattle ranches, perfect steak, pioneer's spirit, the F.W.U.A. women who keep the pioneer traditions alive, the beauty of Banff and Jasper, all give Alberta her interesting personality.

THE WEST AND THE WAY

BEEF AND "RED EYE"

I remember my mixed feelings the first time I was served a superb slice of roast prime rib surrounded with big baked beans in Calgary. I wondered how I could possibly eat them together. One bite of each made me understand the why of this luscious Western fare.

2 lbs. large navy beans or red kidney beans	1 teaspoon dry mustard
1 cup tomato ketchup	2 cups canned tomatoes
1 large onion, finely chopped	1 lb. fatty salt pork, in 1" cubes
1 teaspoon pepper	½ cup white sugar
	3 teaspoons salt

Wash the beans, cover generously with cold water in a bowl and soak overnight. The next morning, pour beans and water into a saucepan, adding more cold water so they'll be well covered. Bring to a boil, then simmer over medium heat 30 minutes.

Add remaining ingredients, bring back to a boil, cover and simmer over low heat 2 hours. Uncover and cook over medium heat 1 - 1½ hours, or until beans are tender and sauce is thick, then taste for seasoning.

These beans freeze very well and can be kept 3-4 months. Place uncovered and still frozen into a 375°F. oven until hot.

BEEF BRISKET BAKED BEANS

The brisket may be plain or salted, or you may substitute 2 pork shanks or 4 pig's feet.

1 lb. dried navy beans, precooked	2 teaspoons salt
1½ lbs. brisket of beef	2 tablespoons brown sugar
2 teaspoons prepared mustard	½ cup molasses

Preheat oven to 325°F.

Place the beans and their liquid in a pot and bury the brisket in the middle. Mix the mustard, salt, brown sugar and molasses. Pour over the beans and bake for 4-5 hours.

HOT PEPPER STEAK

The western "he-man" cracks his heaping tablespoon of black peppercorns very coarsely so that his steak has "branding fire" (however, you need use only 1 teaspoon of peppercorns.)

172

Choose a good porterhouse or sirloin steak about 1¾ to 2 inches thick. Trim excess fat and score remaining fat. Half an hour before cooking the steak, press 1 tablespoon coarsely cracked pepper into the meat with the heel of your hand. The pepper must be freshly cracked.

Pan broil by rubbing cast-iron frying pan with a piece of beef suet. When the pan is very hot, place the steak in it and cook 5 to 10 minutes on each side, turning only once. When the steak is turned, lower the heat slightly.

Just before removing steak to a hot platter, pour ⅓ cup brandy or whisky over it. Flame. Pour pan juices over meat. Salt and serve.

RANCH IN THE PRAIRIE STEW

The following recipe was made to serve fifteen hungry people who had spent the day rounding up cattle. With it were served huge baskets of hot biscuits and butter whipped with half its quantity of molasses spiked with cinnamon and ginger.

5 lbs. stewing beef, cubed (round or shoulder)	**3 lbs. medium size onions, left whole**
1 cup diced beef suet	**4 bay leaves**
4 - 6 lbs. potatoes, peeled and diced	**1 tablespoon salt**
	½ teaspoon pepper
2 lbs. carrots, scraped and diced	

Melt suet in large iron kettle or saucepan or Dutch oven until only small pieces of fat remain, add meat and stir over high heat until browned. Add 10 cups hot water, cover and simmer for 2 hours or until meat is tender. Add the remaining ingredients and simmer another 45 minutes. Taste for seasoning and serve.

WAGON WHEEL DINNER

As this dish travelled around Canada it changed both name and ingredients. But the true Wagon Wheel Dinner originated in Alberta and was made with whatever was on hand. Today bottled and convenience foods have streamlined the recipe.

1 lb. ground beef or lamb or pork   1 large onion, minced
½ cup rolled oats   1 teaspoon dry mustard
1 clove garlic, crushed   1 teaspoon Worcestershire sauce
1 teaspoon salt   3 tablespoons ketchup
¼ teaspoon pepper   1 can whole kernel corn
⅔ cup milk   2 tablespoons butter

Stir together meat, oats, garlic, salt, pepper, milk, onion. Place in a bacon greased 8-inch cake pan.

Combine mustard, Worcestershire sauce and ketchup, spread over meat mixture. Bake in a preheated 375°F. oven for 30 minutes. Drain corn, boil liquid until reduced by half, add corn and butter, stir, spread over meat and bake another 20 minutes.

WESTERN CORNED BEEF AND CABBAGE

A 4-lb. piece of corned beef will make enough for 8 servings, and what is left can be used for hash. Double the amount of potatoes, add a few beets, and there will be enough hash for four.

4 lbs. corned beef brisket   1 celery stalk with leaves
3 sliced onions   1 quartered carrot
4 whole cloves   1 head green cabbage
6 peppercorns or ½ teaspoon   Pinch of caraway seeds
  pepper   (optional)
1 bay leaf
1 garlic clove or ¼ teaspoon
  powdered garlic

Check the label on the meat—a mild cured brisket, doesn't have to be soaked. Otherwise, soak it unwrapped overnight in cold water.

Place the meat in a large saucepan (or if you prefer it wrapped, use cheesecloth). Cover with cold water and all the ingredients except the last two.

Bring to a boil, cover and simmer over low heat for 4-5 hours, or until fork-tender. Don't boil the meat to hurry the cooking, this will only coarsen the texture. It's better to simmer it an extra hour.

Clean the cabbage and cut it into quarters or sixths. About 30 minutes before the meat is done, skim the excess fat from the top of its liquid. Arrange the cabbage on the meat, sprinkle it with the caraway seeds, cover and simmer.

If you wish, make the following Irish mustard sauce, which will be somewhat clear:

In a small saucepan, place ½ cup of cider vinegar, 1 tablespoon of butter, 1 slightly beaten egg, 1 tablespoon of brown sugar, 2 tablespoons of prepared mustard (strong English or horseradish mustard are best), and 1 tablespoon of paprika. Beat over low heat until smooth and slightly creamy.

EGGS AND CORNED BEEF PUDDING

This is what I call a man's dish. It makes an impressive company brunch or lunch dish, and features two of our favorite Canadian foods, cheddar cheese and corned beef.

5 slices bread, cut in cubes	2 tablespoons flour
3 egg yolks, beaten	¾ cup milk
1 cup milk	¾ cup light cream
½ teaspoon prepared mustard	1 bouillon cube
1 pinch salt	3 spring onions, minced
½ pound Canadian cheddar	2 hard-cooked eggs, minced
cheese, grated	1 teaspoon curry powder
3 egg whites, beaten stiff	1 cup canned corned beef,
2 tablespoons butter	shredded

Place the bread cubes in a deep buttered casserole. Mix together the beaten egg yolks, the cup of milk, salt, mustard and grated cheese. Fold in the beaten egg whites. Pour over the bread cubes. Bake in a 375°F. oven for 45 minutes or until golden brown and puffed. In the meantime, make a sauce with the butter, flour, milk and cream. When smooth and creamy add the bouillon cube, spring onions, minced hard-cooked eggs, curry and corned beef. Simmer together 15 to 20 minutes, stirring often. Taste for seasoning and serve this sauce over spoonfuls of the crusty, fragrant Canadian cheese pudding.

CORNED BEEF HASH

1½ cups chopped cooked or	2 tablespoons butter
canned corned beef	¼ cup light cream or milk
4 - 6 cooked potatoes	1 tablespoon soft butter
1 large onion, chopped	2 onions thinly sliced
¼ teaspoon freshly ground pepper	1 teaspoon sugar

Chop coarsely the corned beef and the potatoes into separate bowls. Mix together, add the chopped onion and the pepper. Melt the 2 tablespoons butter in a heavy iron frying pan, add the cream or milk. When hot, spread the hash evenly in the pan. Dot the top with soft butter. Cover with the two sliced onions broken into rings. Sprinkle the onions with the sugar. Cover the pan and cook over low heat 30 - 40 minutes.

To serve, sprinkle the sugar over the onions and place the cooked hash under the broiler for 2 - 3 seconds to caramelize the onions. Serve.

PIG AND CORN IN THE PAN

A typically Western dish and very good winter fare, this can be cooled, wrapped and frozen, then warmed up at 400°F.

6 rib pork chops, ½ or 1-inch	½ teaspoon marjoram
thick	2 cans corn kernels, 12 oz. each
1 tablespoon salad oil	Salt and pepper, to taste
¼ cup water	6 tablespoons chili sauce
1½ teaspoons salt	6 thick dill pickle slices
¼ teaspoon pepper	(optional)
¼ teaspoon thyme or	

In a frying pan, brown the chops slowly in the salad oil, then add the water, salt, pepper, and thyme or marjoram. Cover and simmer over low heat for 45 minutes.

Remove the chops to a heated platter and add the corn to the pan juices. Add salt and pepper, then put the chops back over the corn and top each with 1 tablespoon of chili sauce and a pickle slice. Cover the pan and simmer for 10 minutes.

PICKLED PIG TONGUES

2 pig tongues	2 teaspoons salt
Hot water to cover	2 bay leaves
3 peppercorns	½ cup vinegar
6 whole cloves	¼ cup sugar

Cover the pig tongues with hot water. Simmer for 1 hour. Add the pepper, cloves, salt, bay leaves, vinegar and sugar. Cover and simmer until the tongues are tender.

Cool in the broth. Skin and clean. Leave whole or cut in pieces. Place in sterilized jars.

Skim the fat from the broth. Strain and bring to a boil. Pour boiling broth over the tongues. Seal. Keep refrigerated.

BEEF PANCAKE

2 onions, finely chopped	3 tablespoons meat fat
¼ cup parsley, chopped	2 cups milk
2 - 3 cups boiled leftover or roast	3 eggs, well beaten
beef, chopped	½ cup flour

Mix together all the ingredients in given order and pour into a buttered baking dish. Bake in a 375°F. oven 25 minutes. Serve with a tomato sauce. This dish resembles a golden pancake easily unmolded. Sliced thin and served with a green salad, this pancake makes an excellent cold dish.

SOUR CREAM CABBAGE

On a large sheep ranch I was served this cabbage for lunch along with a mess of sausages. My hosts referred to the cabbage as Chuff-Chuff cabbage.

¼ cup butter or bacon fat	½ teaspoon pepper
4 - 6 cups chopped cabbage	1 tablespoon sugar
1 teaspoon salt	½ cup sour cream

Melt the fat in a large frying pan. Add the cabbage and cook over low heat for 15 minutes, stirring every now and then. Add salt, pepper, sugar and sour cream, stir until the ingredients are well blended in the cabbage but do not let it boil. Serve very hot as soon as it is ready.

BUTTERMILK PANCAKES

Sausages, bacon, eggs and molasses are true friends of buttermilk pancakes.

1 cup all-purpose flour	1 egg, beaten
½ teaspoon soda	¾ - 1 cup buttermilk
¼ teaspoon salt	2 tablespoons melted butter
1 teaspoon sugar	Soft butter or fat

Sift flour, soda, salt and sugar together. Add egg, buttermilk and stir with a large spoon until mixed. Stir in melted butter.

Control the pancakes' thickness with the buttermilk—try a little one and add a little more liquid to the mixture if you wish it thinner.

Grease a pan with soft butter or fat and cook the pancake as usual. If you use an electric frying pan or grill, set it at 400°F.

WHEAT BERRY BREAD

The wheat berries, or whole kernels, make this bread something special.

4 cups wheat berries (kernels)	½ cup salad oil
Potato water	½ cup molasses
2 envelopes dry yeast	2 tablespoons salt
½ cup lukewarm water	½ cup wheat germ
3 cups cooled, scalded milk	6 to 7 cups whole wheat flour

Soak the wheat berries in potato water to cover for 48 hours. (Potato water is water in which potatoes have been boiled). Drain and grind them in a food chopper using the finest blade. Soak the dry yeast in lukewarm water for 10 minutes. Stir well and add to the cooled, scalded milk. Add the salad oil, molasses and salt. Mix wheat germ with whole wheat flour. Add the ground wheat berries to the milk mixture. Blend well and gradualy add the whole wheat flour, mixing thoroughly with your hands. Let the dough rest for 10 minutes. Oil your hands and a board or countertop and knead the bread for 10 minutes. Put the dough in a bowl, cover and let rise in a warm place for 1 hour or until double in bulk. Punch down and divide into three loaves. Put loaves into oiled bread pans, let rise again until double in bulk and bake in a 325°F. oven for 1¼ hours.

APPLE SPONGE PUDDING

This pudding is more of a sponge cake over an upside down mixture. An Alberta Mennonite sent me the recipe and said it was three generations old. Baking powder is a modern change, and the lemon peel is my addition.

5 - 6 medium apples	½ cup cold water
¼ cup butter	1 teaspoon vanilla
2 cups brown sugar	1 cup all-purpose flour
1 teaspoon lemon juice	½ teaspoon salt
Grated peel of ½ a lemon	1 teaspoon baking powder
2 egg yolks	2 egg whites
1 cup sugar	

Pare, core and slice apples. Melt butter in a deep, 9-inch round cake pan, add brown sugar and stir until well mixed. Top with apples and sprinkle with lemon juice and peel.

Beat egg yolks and sugar until light and pale yellow. Mix water and vanilla. Stir flour with salt and baking powder and add to egg mixture alternately with vanilla mixture.

Beat egg whites until stiff, fold into batter and pour over apples. Bake at 350°F. for 45 - 50 minutes. Serve hot or tepid, and it is best not to unmold the pudding.

WHEAT PUDDING

This is a quickly made, flavorful pudding. I make it when I have some cold wheat porridge on hand.

3 eggs, beaten	4 tablespoons honey
3 cups milk	1 tablespoon grated orange rind
1 cup seedless raisins	¼ teaspoon mace
2 cups cooked wheat grains or porridge	Pinch of salt

In a large bowl, mix all the ingredients. Pour this mixture into a well buttered casserole and bake, uncovered, 1 hour at 325°F. Serve hot or cold topped with cream or sliced fresh fruit, lightly sweetened with honey.

AS THE MAN MOVES INTO THE KITCHEN

Men cook mainly for pleasure because they like to eat and are not obliged to do it. Their stint in the kitchen being relatively short lived, they feel freer to make the most of what they cook. They like to try new creations, however wild they are.

I have a good collection of recipes given to me by Alberta men at different parties I have been to. All had been barbecued or cooked in their kitchens: Keith's Drunken Meat Balls, Jack M's Barbecued Lamb Shank, Richard C's Steak in the Rye, Laurence B's Eggs in Onion, Clifford R's Pioneer Omelet, Williams' Farmer Pancakes. They are very different and very good!

KEITH'S DRUNKEN MEAT BALLS

He said: "I always enjoy their wallop!"

1½ to 2 lbs. chopped beef	1 tablespoon ketchup
1 egg beaten	¼ cup water
1 teaspoon salt	1 slice white bread, diced
¼ teaspoon freshly ground pepper	

Place all the ingredients in a bowl and blend until well mixed. Shape into small balls, the size of a whole walnut. Refrigerate 20 minutes to 1 hour.

178

2 tablespoons bacon fat
1 medium size onion, chopped
  fine
1 clove garlic, crushed
¼ teaspoon salt
2 dashes Angostura bitters

1 teaspoon dry mustard
1 teaspoon flour
1 cup undiluted consommé
½ cup rye or scotch
¼ cup Italian sweet vermouth
¼ teaspoon marjoram

Heat the bacon fat in a cast-iron frying pan, fry the meat balls in it, shaking the pan over medium high heat, until they are well browned all over. Take out of the pan. To the remaining fat, add the onion and garlic, stir until soft. Then add all the other ingredients and bring to boil. Cook uncovered 30 minutes or until mixture thickens slightly and is reduced by one third. Add the meat balls to the sauce. Simmer 5 minutes. My friend is convinced they improve by being cooled and refrigerated overnight, then warmed up. With these, he served mashed potatoes and fresh corn that we rolled in the "drunken" gravy rather than using butter.

JACK'S BARBECUED LAMB SHANKS

My friend Jack preferred beer to rye! He called it the "new dimension flavor".

2 cloves garlic
4 - 6 lamb shanks
3 tablespoons melted lamb fat
  or bacon fat
3 tablespoons flour
½ teaspoon salt

½ teaspoon freshly ground pepper
½ teaspoon savory
½ cup beer
2 bay leaves
¼ cup fresh lemon juice
Grated peel of ½ a lemon

Put slivers of the garlic into the lamb shanks, make incisions with a pointed knife. Melt the pieces of lamb fat or heat the bacon fat in a Dutch oven. Blend the flour, salt, pepper and savory. Roll shanks into it and brown all over in the hot fat. Then add all the other ingredients. Cover and simmer for 2 hours or until meat is tender. The more it simmers, the more gravy forms. Serve as he did with boiled rice loaded, as he said, with butter, parsley and sliced fried mushrooms.

LAWRENCE'S EGGS IN ONION

The combination of nutmeg, tarragon and cider vinegar does the trick.

6 hard cooked eggs
¼ cup butter
4 large onions, chopped
1 tablespoon flour
1 cup milk

Salt and pepper to taste
⅛ teaspoon nutmeg
2 teaspoons cider vinegar
4 slices rye bread

Peel the eggs and slice thickly. Set aside. Melt the butter, add the onions and cook over low heat, stirring often, until soft and transparent, but not brown. Stir in the flour, add the milk, salt, pepper, nutmeg and vinegar. Stir and cook over medium heat for 15 minutes. Then add the eggs and simmer 5 minutes over very low heat.

Fry the slices of rye bread in melted butter, over low heat. To serve place a slice in a hot plate and pour some sauce on top.

CLIFFORD'S PIONEER OMELET

In the summer he serves this with a bowl of minced chives. In the winter he uses tops of green onions, chopped fine.

2 tablespoons butter
2 teaspoons salad oil
2 potatoes, peeled and diced
½ cup grated cheddar cheese

4 - 6 slices bacon, cut in four
4 eggs
Salt and pepper to taste

Heat the butter and salad oil. Add the potatoes. Cook over medium high heat, stirring often, until they are golden brown. Add the bacon. Stir until bacon starts to brown. Add the cheese. Mix and pour on top the eggs, seasoned to taste and beaten with a fork. Cook, pushing the eggs toward the middle as they cook. Serve as soon as ready, with a bowl of chives and homemade chili sauce.

RICHARD'S STEAK IN THE RYE

If you have the Calgary spirit, try this 1½-inch thick boneless sirloin steak cooked over hot coals or on the stove.

½ teaspoon coarse or sea salt
1 teaspoon coarsely ground pepper
A boneless 1½-inch sirloin (about 2 lbs.)

3 tablespoons melted butter
1 tablespoon salad oil
¼ cup consommé
2 tablespoons rich cream
¼ cup rye whisky

Mix the salt and pepper and rub into both sides of steak, patting it in.

Blend the melted butter and oil, roll steak into it, until most of it is absorbed. Do this if you intend to barbecue or broil the steak. Broil as you usually do the steak.

To pan fry, use a large cast-iron frying pan. Heat the oil and butter until quite hot. Quickly brown the steak on both sides over high heat for 3 minutes, then lower the heat to finish cooking as you like it.

Remove steak to a hot platter. Add to the pan the cream, consommé and rye. Simmer over low heat, 4 to 5 minutes, and pour over the steak. When the steak is barbecued — warm up the ingredients in a pan and pour over the steak. Serve with "a mess" of French fries and sliced tomatoes.

WILLIAMS' FARMER PANCAKES

The wheat germ and the honey give these pancakes a special personality.

1½ cups all-purpose flour
½ cup wheat germ
1 teaspoon soda
½ teaspoon salt

1 tablespoon honey
1 tablespoon butter
1¾ - 2 cups sour milk or buttermilk
2 eggs

Stir together the flour, wheat germ, soda and salt. Heat together the honey and butter. Make a hollow in the flour mixture, put in the honey, butter, 1¾ cups of the sour milk and egg yolks. Beat until well mixed, adding enough sour milk to make a light batter. Beat the egg whites and fold into mixture. Bake the same way as any other pancakes. Serve with fried sausages, bacon and molasses.

BRITISH COLUMBIA

Here is a man's world! Appetites are hearty, food is plenty, fruit is the biggest, berries the juiciest. Rich is the soil and lush the valley, swift the rivers and fast the salmon in their tearing hurry to spawning grounds. There's superb Murchie's tea; and Roger's big, luscious Victorian chocolates and hard bonbons; and Andrea's wines, . . . the best of all Canadian wines. There's Armstrong unique cheese too, and jellied candies from Okanagan fruits.

Gwen Lewis' delightful book — *Buckskin Cookery* takes us on a nostalgic trip in the yesterday of this land of giant timber, and abundant water. The pioneer section and the hunting section are all about cooking on the trail, hunting deer, moose, bear, home tanning, trapping, bannock, berries, homestead hints, witch doctors, and Indians. Muriel Wilson's *Colonist Cookbook of Victoria* is also amusing, witty, down to earth, and filled with good recipes; as are the countless leaflets on all food subjects, published by *Edith Adam's Cottage,* a Vancouver home maker service. Each has provided tremendous research assistance for this book, as has *The Galley Slaves Guide,* compiled by the Ladies' Sailing Group, West Vancouver Yacht Club, for cooks with limited facilities. In their helpful hints and staples store guide they recommend tea — try "Murchie's No. 10 blend". Delicious!

There are in British Columbia regional foods, of course, but fresh salmon and seafood are the greatest delicacy. That is where I learned how to cook it with respect and enjoy it to the full.

FROM SALMON TO CAKE

ENGLISH POACHED SALMON

A most attractive way of serving salmon for a buffet supper or garden party.

4 - 6 lbs. fresh salmon	**½ teaspoon basil**
2 cups milk	**¼ teaspoon dill seeds**
2 cups water	**1 cup mayonnaise**
1 tablespoon salt	**2 hard-boiled eggs**
2 bay leaves	**1 peeled lemon, thinly sliced**
¼ cup parsley, coarsely chopped	**2 carrots, finely shredded**

Wrap salmon in cheesecloth. Bring the milk, water, salt, bay leaves, parsley, basil and dill seeds to a fast boil. Boil 5 minutes. Add salmon and simmer, covered, over medium low heat, for 20 to 35 minutes.

Let fish cool in its water. Then remove from water, but do not unwrap. Cover and refrigerate until ready to serve.

To serve, unwrap, remove the skin, place on a silver platter, garnish by spreading mayonnaise and making a long line of overlapping lemon slices on top. Grate the eggs and sprinkle them over the whole fish. Place the finely shredded carrots all around to form a red crown.

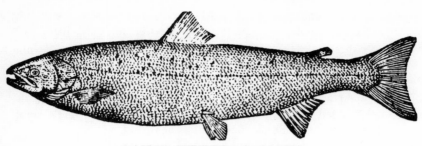

BAKED STUFFED SALMON

This is the king of all salmon dishes, and should be done with a large salmon. Serve with new potatoes and fresh green peas in cream sauce. A treat that comes once a year.

8 - 12 lbs. salmon	**¼ cup butter or salad oil**
1 tablespoon salt	**4 cups whole wheat or rye**
3 tablespoons lemon juice	**bread, diced**
1 cup celery, chopped	**¼ teaspoon thyme or sage**
1 cup celery leaves, minced	**Salt, pepper to taste**
2 medium onions, thinly sliced	**2 eggs, lightly beaten**

Mix the salt and lemon juice together. Rub cleaned fish inside and out with this mixture until it is all used. (It is best to use the fingers to do this.)

For the stuffing: Sauté over medium low heat the celery, celery leaves and onions in the butter or salad oil until the onions are soft, transparent and lightly browned here and there. Pour over the diced bread placed in a bowl. Blend well, add the seasoning herbs and eggs. Stir until the whole is well mixed. Stuff the fish with it. Sew with coarse thread or tie securely.

Place the fish on a well oiled baking sheet (it can also be rubbed with a thick coating of bacon fat). Bake in a preheated 400°F. oven 10 minutes per pound (weight after stuffing) or

Serve with a Hollandaise sauce, a rich white sauce flavored with dill, a tomato sauce, or simply with a bowl of equal amounts of butter and lemon juice heated together.

MOLDED SALMON

Not the usual jellied mold — creamy, gentle, beautifully flavored.

1 tablespoon unflavored gelatine	**Grated rind of ½ a lemon**
2 tablespoons cold water	**2 tablespoons butter**
2 egg yolks, slightly beaten	**¾ cup milk**
¼ cup fresh lemon juice	**2 cups cooked salmon, flaked**
1 teaspoon salt	**¼ cup minced parsley**
1 teaspoon curry powder	

Sprinkle gelatine over cold water, let stand 5 minutes.

Combine egg yolks, lemon juice, salt, curry powder, butter in top of double boiler. Add the milk gradually, while beating. Cook over hot water for 6 to 8 minutes or until thickened, stirring constantly. Add gelatine and stir until dissolved. Add salmon and parsley. Pour into a well oiled fish mold or 1-quart mold. Refrigerate until firm, then keep covered until ready to serve. Serve on a nest of lettuce.

VERY SPECIAL SALMON PATTIES
These were served at a luncheon party given on a fishing boat. I told the chef I had never had such salmon patties, so he gave me the recipe, and added "but the fish must be freshly caught". He's right! But even with canned salmon these patties are good.

2 cups salmon, flaked	**½ teaspoon salt**
4 eggs	**¼ teaspoon pepper**
2 tablespoons rich cream	**2 tablespoons cold water***
½ cup fresh breadcrumbs, cut fine	

Combine the salmon, 2 of the eggs slightly beaten, cream, breadcrumbs, salt, pepper. Stir with the hands until thoroughly blended. Then shape into 12 flat cakes — they are not big as they would be difficult to cook. Refrigerate for one hour. Beat the remaining eggs with the cold water. Dip cold patties into the eggs and roll into fine dry breadcrumbs. Sauté in butter, over medium low heat, until well browned on both sides, turning only once. Serve them as the chef did — with a cup of chutney stirred with 3 tablespoons Scotch whisky — or with a white sauce garnished with diced celery and parsley.
* My chef used 2 tablespoons whisky instead of water.

CAPILANO CRAB SALAD
Here is a memorable salad which I had at an equally memorable luncheon offered by the British Columbia Department of Fisheries. Fresh crab — just caught!

½ cup sour cream	**¼ teaspoon salt**
¼ cup finely minced celery	**Shredded lettuce**
2 tablespoons chopped black olives	**2 large tomatoes, peeled and halved**
2 green onions, chopped fine	**12 ounces crabmeat, just pulled out of the shell***
1 tablespoon chopped parsley	
Grated rind ½ a lemon	**1 hard cooked egg**
2 tablespoons chili sauce	

Combine sour cream, celery, black olives, green onions, parsley, lemon rind, chili sauce and salt. Beat well and refrigerate a few hours to blend the flavors. Arrange a bed of lettuce on four salad plates — put tomato half on each. Pile crabmeat on each tomato. Spoon sour cream dressing on top. Sprinkle grated egg on the whole.
* Two 6½ - 7-ounce cans of crabmeat may replace the fresh.

TAKE A CAN OF SALMON AND . . .
— Make good everyday light croquettes. Mix 2 cups mashed canned or fresh salmon with parsley and fresh lemon juice to taste. Add

1 cup very thick white sauce, (a tablespoon flour, 4 tablespoons fat, 1 cup milk or cream) flavored with 1 teaspoon curry and 1 tablespoon chutney or chili sauce. Add salt and pepper to taste. Chill the mixture. Shape into cones, roll in fine crumbs and brown over medium heat in vegetable oil.

— Make a never-fail soufflé. Make 3 cups mashed potatoes with your favorite instant brand. Add 2 cups flaked salmon, 2 egg yolks, minced onion to taste, a good handful of finely minced celery leaves, salt and pepper to taste. Fold in two beaten egg whites. Pour into a greased casserole and bake 30 to 40 minutes in a 350°F. oven or until you have a beautiful golden puff.

— Make a quick and tasty light supper. To a cup of very hot medium white sauce, add 2 diced hard cooked eggs, ¼ cup minced chives or green onions. Pour over a 1-lb. can of cold salmon unmolded on a platter.

— Make an easy salmon loaf. Unmold a 1-lb. can of salmon on an ovenproof platter. Pour the juice of a lemon over the top. Cover and heat 10 minutes in a 350°F. oven. Serve with egg sauce or a cucumber salad.

BUTTERBURGERS
Muriel Wilson's way — quite good!

1 lb. lean ground beef	1 teaspoon MSG
½ cup cottage cheese	1 tablespoon chopped green
1 egg	onion
¾ teaspoon dry mustard	5 tablespoons melted butter
3 tablespoons melted butter	1 teaspoon Worcestershire
1 teaspoon salt	sauce

In a bowl mix the cottage cheese, egg, seasonings and green onion. Add the 3 tablespoons melted butter. Beat to mix. Add the ground beef and mix well. Make into 4 patties. Melt the 5 tablespoons butter in a hot frying pan. Cook the "burgers" to your liking, turning only once. Cut 4 hamburger buns in half. Dip cut sides into pan drippings and place under broiler until lightly toasted. Place meat between bun halves and garnish with pickle fans. These have a good beefy flavor enhanced by the goodness of butter. When you want flavor . . . use butter.

SAUSAGE IN YORKSHIRE PUDDING
Another Muriel special!

1 egg	½ teaspoon salt
½ cup flour	1 lb. pork sausage
½ cup milk	

Partially cook the sausage in the pan which is to be used for baking. Pour off part of the fat. Beat the egg well, add the flour and salt gradually, then add the milk. Mix this an hour before using. Have a fair amount of fat in the pan with the sausages and have it piping hot before pouring in the batter. Bake in a 450°F. oven for ½ hour or until it is well raised and brown.

HER OWN ECCIES TARTS

One of the English traditionals we all enjoy eating.

Short-cut puff paste:
1½ cups all-purpose flour
    Dash salt

½ lb. butter (scant)
Sour cream to mix, a little
    more than ½ cup

Cut in butter until it resembles coarse meal. Add sour cream a little at a time mixing with a fork until all is moistened. Gather dough together with the fingers so that it cleans the bowl. The dough must be refrigerated a few hours or overnight. I like to make three or four flat cakes of it which I wrap in foil. The smaller pieces are easier to roll out than one large piece. Roll on a floured board and cut in 5-inch circles. Place a spoonful of filling in each circle. Dampen edges. Bring dough up around sides and pinch together in centre. Turn upside down and roll lightly with rolling pin. Make 2 or 3 gashes in top with a knife. Brush with egg white and sprinkle with sugar. Bake on ungreased baking sheet in a preheated 425°F. oven for 10 to 15 minutes.

Filling:
1 tablespoon butter
1 tablespoon lemon juice
½ cup brown sugar
¼ teaspoon each nutmeg and
    allspice

½ cup currants (scalded to
    soften)
½ cup glace fruit

Simmer 5 minutes. Cool.

MOLDED PORK AND VEAL

2 lbs. lean pork shoulder
2 lbs. veal shank
6 cups hot water
2 tablespoons salt
15 peppercorns
10 whole allspice
2 bay leaves

4 cloves
1 onion
1 large carrot
2 tablespoons cider vinegar
Salt and pepper, to taste
1 envelope unflavored gelatine
¾ cup cold water

Place the meat in a saucepan, pour the hot water on top and bring to a boil. Remove scum, then add salt, peppercorns, allspice, and bay leaves. Stick cloves into onion and add to meat with carrot. Bring back to a boil, cover and simmer 2 hours, or until meat is tender.

Remove meat from broth and, when cool enough to handle, remove all bones and return to stock. Boil 30 minutes uncovered over high heat.

Let cool a bit, cut meat into small pieces or pass it through a food chopper. Strain stock, add meat, vinegar, salt and pepper, then simmer 5 minutes. Soak gelatine in cold water 5 minutes. Add to hot broth and stir until dissolved.

Pour into an oiled fancy shaped mold and refrigerate until set, then cover and keep refrigerated until ready to serve. It will keep a week.

BARBECUED SHOULDER OF LAMB

I tasted this well flavored barbecued shoulder of lamb, my favorite cut, while visiting an interesting lamb flock in Saltspring Island.

1 boned and rolled 3 to 4-lb. shoulder of young lamb	Salt and pepper to taste
Juice of 1 lemon	1 cup ketchup
¼ cup salad oil	1 cup apple juice
¼ teaspoon thyme	2 tablespoons brown sugar
1 medium onion, chopped coarsely	4 tablespoons lemon juice
2 tablespoons butter	3 tablespoons Worcestershire sauce
	2 tablespoons cider vinegar

Mix together the lemon juice, salad oil and thyme. Roll the shoulder in it. Refrigerate 12 hours. Force the sharp end of an iron rod through the center of the rolled shoulder and place over a good bed of gray coals. Turn every half hour, brushing each time with the following sauce. Barbecue for 2 to 3 hours or until tender.

Sauce: Brown the onion in the butter until golden brown, season with the salt and pepper to taste. Add the remaining ingredients. Cover and simmer 30 minutes.

COUNTRY MINCED LAMB DINNER

Minced lamb has a delicate flavor. This dinner shows all its qualities.

2 lbs. minced lamb	1 cup whole kernel corn
½ teaspoon basil	6 boiled potatoes
6 - 8 slices bacon	2 tablespoons grated mild cheddar
6 large tomatoes	

Season ground lamb with salt, pepper and basil. Shape into 6 to 8 patties. Wrap around with a slice of bacon. Sprinkle top with paprika.

Place on broiling rack. Broil until well browned, turn and brown other side. About 8 minutes on each side.

When patties are turned, place on rack the whole tomatoes, hollowed out and filled with corn, dotted with butter — and the potatoes rolled in the grated cheese.

By the time the patties are done the tomatoes and potatoes will be hot and slightly browned.

WEST COAST TOMATOES

At a remarkable barbecue party on the west coast, I was served superb huge, thick tomato slices topped with lemon tartar sauce. Now I use this recipe all year round it is so good.

6 - 8 tomatoes
1 lemon
1 cup mayonnaise (homemade if possible)
¼ cup minced green onions
¼ cup minced green olives
¼ cup minced parsley
1 tablespoon sugar
Chives and tarragon, to taste (optional)

Peel the lemon and remove all white parts and seeds, then cut up pulp as finely as possible — use a very sharp knife to prevent crushing the fruit. Add it to mayonnaise along with onions, olives, parsley and stir well.

Wash tomatoes, slice thickly and set on a flat dish. Sprinkle with sugar, top with sauce, sprinkle with chives and tarragon and refrigerate.

SOUR CREAM CUCUMBER SAUCE

This is a classic accompaniment for cold, boiled salmon.

3 medium cucumbers, peeled and sliced
Salt
¼ cup sour cream
2 tablespoons lemon juice
1 tablespoon onion, minced
¼ teaspoon sugar
Pinch of pepper

Peel the cucumbers and slice them as thinly as possible. Sprinkle with salt and mix well. Refrigerate for 1 hour, drain carefully and cover with ice cubes. Refrigerate until ready to serve. Just before serving, mix the sour cream, lemon juice, minced onion, sugar and pepper. Add the cucumber slices and mix well together. Serve chilled on bed of lettuce leaves, sprinkled with parsley.

CANADIAN TIPSY CAKE

Our Canadian tipsy cake is a variation on the famous, and scrumptious, English trifle.

1 large sponge cake, two to four days old
Sweet sherry
Plum or black currant jam
Strawberry jam
Toasted, slivered almonds or walnuts
¼ cup brandy
1 teaspoon almond essence
2 cups table cream
4 whole eggs
⅓ cup sugar
Red and green candied cherries

Slice the cake into six layers. Place one layer in a large glass serving dish. Sprinkle lightly with sweet sherry and butter with plum or black currant jam. Put another layer of cake on top, sprinkle with sherry and butter with strawberry jam. Repeat this, alternating jams until the six layers have been put together. Sprinkle the top layer with toasted, slivered almonds, or walnuts. Blend the brandy with the almond essence and pour over the top.

Make a light, rich custard by scalding the cream over low heat. Beat the eggs with the sugar and add ½ cup of the scalded cream. Mix well and pour into the remaining cream. Cook until creamy, beating all the time. Don't let it boil. Cool 10 minutes and pour over the tipsy cake. Decorate the top with stars of red and green candied cherries. Chill overnight and serve cold.

FRUIT BOUNTY

FRESH FRUITS OF BRITISH COLUMBIA

For lovers of juicy, orchard-fresh fruits, British Columbia's Okanagan Valley has everything to offer: cherries, apricots, peaches, pears, prunes and apples. If you want to see the Okanagan orchards in blossom time or when the fruits are ripe, it is well worth the trip. Here are the dates:

Blossom Times

Apricots	April 7 - 30
Cherries	April 15 - May 10
Peaches	April 15 - May 10
Prunes	April 20 - May 16
Pears	April 20 - May 16
Apples	April 25 - May 20

Fruit Ripening Dates

Cherries	June 10 - July 10
Apricots	July 1 - July 10
Peaches	July 30 - August 30
Prunes	September 5 - September 15
Pears - Bartletts	September 15 -
Apples	October 5 -

FRESH APRICOT TOPPING

This shiny apricot topping is delicious on your best plain white cake or sponge cake. It has a tart, genuinely apricot flavor with a beautiful golden color.

Cut up about eight fresh apricots and place in a saucepan with one tablespoon water. Cook until mushy and fairly thick. Measure ¾ cup pulp and add ½ cup light brown sugar, 3 tablespoons butter and a pinch of salt. Return to saucepan, cook 3 minutes. Remove from heat, add ¾ cup coconut. Spread over cooled cake while topping is still warm. Makes enough for 9 x 13-inch cake.

SPICED PICKLED APRICOTS

6 lbs. firm apricots	⅛ teaspoon celery seed
1 tablespoon whole cloves	1 tablespoon mustard seed
1 tablespoon whole allspice	6 cups sugar
1 2-inch cinnamon stick	2 cups cider vinegar

Tie spices, except mustard seed, in a bag. Combine sugar, vinegar, spice bag and mustard seed. Bring to a boil. To this add 10 apricots at a time and cook until tender (about 3 minutes). Remove fruit and place in hot, sterilized pint jars. When fruit is finished, use remaining syrup to cover it. Seal jars at once.

SUNDAE SHORT PIE

1 cup biscuit mix
¼ cup soft butter
3 tablespoons boiling water

1 pint vanilla ice cream
½ to ¾ lb. fresh cherries, pitted and halved

Place biscuit mix and butter in 9-inch pie plate. Add boiling water. Stir with fork until dough forms ball and cleans pan. With fingers and heel of hand, pat evenly in pan, bringing dough up to edge. Flute edges if desired. Bake for 8 to 10 minutes or until golden. Cool. Fill with ice cream. Cover with a generous layer of halved cherries.

FREEZING APRICOTS

Choose fully ripe, tender, smooth, rich-flavored fruit with yellow-orange skin. Handle rapidly and carefully. Wash, sort as to size, removing any damaged or over-ripe fruit. Halve and remove pits. Peel if you prefer, but it is not necessary. To peel, scald whole apricots 15 - 20 seconds in boiling water. Cool quickly in ice water. Pack in moisture-proof freezer containers in cold 40% syrup (3¼ cups sugar, 4 cups water and 1 teaspoon ascorbic acid), or with 1 - 2 teaspoons ascorbic acid and 1 lb. sugar to 4 to 5 pounds of fruit.

SHERRY CREME PEAR HALVES

6 Anjou Pears
½ cup sugar
1 cup water
2 tablespoons sherry
4 egg yolks

1 cup sifted icing sugar
⅛ teaspoon salt
¼ cup sherry
1 cup whipping cream

Beat egg yolks with icing sugar and salt in top of double boiler until smooth. Add ¼ cup sherry. Cook over hot (not boiling) water for about 8 to 10 minutes, stirring constantly. Remove from heat and cool. Whip cream until it holds peaks. When sauce is completely cold, fold in whipped cream.

Boil sugar and water for one minute. Add two tablespoons sherry. Poach peeled and cored pear halves until tender but still whole. Chill. Serve two halves in a sherbet glass. Top with mounds of cream mixture. Garnish with preserved ginger finely sliced.

PRIZE APRICOT JAM

8 cups quartered apricots
4½ cups sugar
¾ cup light brown sugar

1 orange
1 cup crushed pineapple
⅛ teaspoon salt

Wash, pit and quarter about 3 lbs. of apricots. Measure 8 cups. Place apricots, sugars, coarsely shredded rind and juice of orange, pineapple and salt in heavy kettle. Bring quickly to boil, stirring until sugar is dissolved. Cook rapidly, stirring often, until two thick drops of syrup will run together off side of cold metal spoon (about 30 to 35 minutes.) Ladle into sterilized jars. When cool, cover with layer of melted paraffin. Top with clean lids.

PICKLED PEARS

For this favorite recipe, you'll get best results with Bartletts that are still slightly under-ripe.

2 quarts pears (6 to 8 cups)	**1 piece ginger root**
3 cups granulated sugar	**1 stick cinnamon**
1 cup water	**1 teaspoon whole allspice**
2 cups vinegar	**1 teaspoon whole cloves**

Use only firm, slightly under-ripe pears. Pare and leave small fruit whole. Halve or quarter and core large pears. Combine sugar, vinegar and water in a large kettle. Add spices tied in a cheesecloth bag; boil 10 minutes. Add pears, putting them one layer deep in the kettle, and cook 3 to 6 minutes or until barely tender but not soft. Let pears stand overnight to absorb the syrup. Next morning, carefully lift pears out of syrup and pack in hot, clean jars. Bring syrup to a boil, pour over pears and seal at once.

STRAWBERRY MILK SHERBET

A delightful sherbet, this should only be made with fresh strawberries. For a special occasion, serve it topped with crushed baked meringue.

1 envelope (1 tablespoon) unflavored gelatine	**1½ teaspoons vanilla or rose water**
¼ cup cold water	**2 cups milk or light cream**
2 well-beaten egg yolks	**2 cups crushed fresh strawberries**
¾ cup sugar	**2 egg whites**
¼ tsp. salt	**¼ cup sugar**

Soak the gelatine in the water for 5 minutes. Dissolve over hot water, or by placing the bowl in a pan of hot water. Beat together the egg yolks, sugar, salt, vanilla or rose water, milk or cream, and crushed strawberries (measure the berries after they are crushed). When well mixed, beat in the dissolved gelatine, mix thoroughly, then freeze in ice cube trays.

When frozen, break into chunks; place in a chilled bowl. Beat with an electric or hand beater until smooth and fluffy. Beat the egg whites until stiff, gradually add the ¼ cup of sugar and beat until thick. Fold this egg white meringue into the beaten strawberry mixture. Return quickly to trays and freeze until firm.

PLUM JUICE

I usually serve this just as it is, but you may also use it to make sherbet or to stew other fruits. Make small quantities at a time.

2 lbs. or 4 cups B.C. blue plums, pitted	**½ cup apple juice**
	1 cup sugar

Cut the plums into coarse pieces and place them in a saucepan with the apple juice. Bring to a boil and simmer over low heat for 20 minutes. Pour into a bag of cotton cloth, or several thicknesses of cheesecloth. Place the bag over a bowl, pour the fruit into the bag and let it drip 3 - 4 hours.

Measure the juice (you should have 2 cups), and bring to a full rolling boil. Add the sugar and boil rapidly for 5 minutes. Pour into a hot sterilized bottle, cork and store in a dark place. Makes 1 pint.

DEEP PLUM PIE

When the first B.C. plums arrive on the market, I make this pie. If I'm in a hurry, I replace the pastry circles with a big round ball of vanilla ice cream set over the slightly warm plum mixture.

12 - 16 halved and pitted blue plums
½ cup brown sugar
½ cup white sugar
¼ teaspoon ground cloves or
½ teaspoon cardamom
Pinch of salt

2 tablespoons quick-cooking tapioca
2 tablespoons lemon juice
1 tablespoon butter
Pastry for 1-crust pie

Fill a 9x9x2-inch baking dish about ¾ full with the plums placed cut side down. Combine the sugar, cloves or cardamom, salt and tapioca and sprinkle over the fruit. Shake the dish slightly so that the sugar will sift down through the fruit. Sprinkle with the lemon juice and dot with the butter. Bake at 375°F. for 20 minutes.

Roll the pastry and cut nine 3-inch circles from it. Remove the pie from the oven and place the circles of pastry over the fruit in a slightly overlapping design. Return the pie to the oven and bake for an additional 20 minutes or until the fruit is tender and the pastry brown. Serve warm or cold.

N. W. TERRITORIES

The people of the north, as those who live in the Northwest Territories are so often referred to, are very well known as Eskimo Art is known and admired across the world. After the Eskimo art the next most famous produce is the Arctic char. A whole one with head on can weigh as much as 12 lbs. It is caught by the Eskimo in the cold northern waters. The supply, fresh or canned, is not plentiful, but it is delicious and tender, very much like salmon.

Reindeer, hare, seal and the famous canned muktuk (the inside skin and fat of the whale), mipku (dried and smoked black whale meat), the rich pemmican (dried moose or deer meat, ground fine, mixed with melted moose fat, and eaten cold)—is all good Canadian fare to the people of the north although not readily available to everyone, nor indeed acceptable to most of our delicate palates.

As a centenntial project the Northern Administration Branch Department of Indian Affairs and Northern Development published an extremely interesting book—*The Northern Cookbook,* edited by Eleanor A. Ellis. It is sold at Government bookshops across Canada.

The following quotation in the book, by Gordon Robertson, Clerk of the Privy Council, certainly proves the importance of having such a book at the disposal of any Canadian interested in our foods:

'A nation must have a picture of itself as somehow unique. There has to be an ethos and a spirit that hold the people together with a sense, not only of sharing something in common, but of having a something that no other nation quite has. There must be a mystique and a romance that enable the national household to survive the strain of life.

We think the recipes that follow reflect the mystique and romance of our north. They have been created by some of Canada's most brilliant chefs, using indigenous foods, certainly 'a something that no other nation quite has'. By sharing these unique recipes with you, perhaps we can make a small contribution towards building up the ethos and spirit of our national household."

In the Arctic gourmet chapter there are many excellent recipes for char. Here is my own creation, which is very good as a spread or for cocktails.

GAME FOR THE GOURMET

POTTED CHAR

1½ - 2 lbs. char
1 cup clam juice or white wine
1 cup water
Juice of half a lemon or 1 tablespoon bottled lemon

1 small onion, chopped
1 carrot, diced
1 tablespoon parsley, chopped
½ to 1 cup melted butter

Clean fish. Place in saucepan with the clam juice or white wine, the water, lemon juice, onion, carrot, and parsley. Simmer 20 minutes. Cool in bouillon. Remove skin and bones, break into pieces. Place in earthenware pot. Pour melted butter on top. Cover and bake in 350°F. oven, for 30 minutes. Cool, cover and refrigerate until ready to serve.

Potted char will keep two to four weeks refrigerated.

BAKED STUFFED ARCTIC CHAR

Salt	**Desired stuffing**
Melted fat or oil	**Arctic char, pan-dressed**

Wash and dry fish. Sprinkle on inside with salt.

Stuff loosely with desired stuffing (¾ cup for each pound of stuffed fish, or 1 cup per pound of stuffed fish if backbone is removed).

Fasten opening with small skewers or sew with large needle.

Place stuffed fish on greased baking pan.

Brush with melted fat or oil.

Measure char at thickest part. Bake in hot oven 450°F. Cook 10 minutes for each inch of thickness.

Basic Bread Stuffing:	**½ teaspoon seasoning**
⅓ cup chopped onion	**Pinch of ginger, savory, thyme,**
⅓ cup diced celery	**sage or dried mint**
3 tablespoons butter	**3 cups dried breadcrumbs**

Cook onion and celery in fat until tender.

Add cooked vegetables and seasoning to breadcrumbs. Toss lightly.

MOOSE

Moose meat is delicate when young, but tough and chewy when the moose is full-grown. It then requires marinating to tenderize it. Cook it the same as reindeer.

Moose or reindeer are cut in the same manner; and the following are the different cuts and how to cook each one:

The neck (cut to the shoulder blade and the leg shanks): Cook in stew or mince and serve in loaf or meat balls or use for pâté. Excellent sausages are also made from the minced meat.

The shoulder blade: Roast, braised or cut in 1 or 2-inch-cubes to stew.

The ribs: The whole rib usually weighs 15 to 22 pounds. It is divided in two parts. The rib near the shoulder is roasted.

The rib containing the tenderloin is the tenderest part. At its best, cut into steaks and cutlets. Pan-fry or broil quickly avoiding overcooking which toughens the meat.

The saddle: It is similar to the tender part of the beef rump. Spit or oven-roast at 400°F., 15 minutes per pound.

The bottom of the saddle: Same at the beef round. It is better cooked as steak or cube steak. Moose and reindeer freeze well. Wrap in a double moisture-proof paper. Mark and freeze. Will keep 3 to 4 months. Thaw before cooking.

To can moose or deer, it must be sterilized in a pressure cooker at 10-pounds pressure, the same length of time as beef and pork.

To flavor the meat, use salt, freshly ground pepper, sugar, tomatoes, onions, garlic, celery, rosemary, marjoram, lemon rind and juice.

To the gravy add currant jelly, vermouth, port wine or brandy.

The top fat on the moose gives a strong flavor to the meat. If objectionable, remove all traces of natural fat. Use fat salt pork or bacon to replace it.

The heart can be stuffed with bread, onion and celery and braised the same as beef heart.

The tongue must be soaked 1 hour in cold water. Then drain and cover with fresh cold water and add 1 teaspoon ground or fresh ginger, 1 unpeeled lemon cut in four, 1 teaspoon dry mustard and salt to taste. Simmer 2 to 3 hours or until the tongue is tender. Remove the skin and cool in its cooking water.

The kidneys can be prepared the same as beef kidneys.

The best vegetables and accompaniments to serve with venison are red cabbage salad, chestnuts or puréed squash, red wine, beets, tomatoes broiled or in a sauce, brown rice or wild rice, mushrooms, Hollandaise sauce, currant jelly, spiced crabapples, chutney, horseradish.

REINDEER

A general rule when cooking reindeer is to follow beef recipes, but never the recipes for veal or pork. It is important when roasting reindeer to retain all the inner red juices. The following paste will do it. Mix together 3 tablespoons melted fat with 1 tablespoon dry mustard (never use prepared mustard for this). Spread over the raw part of the meat only, before roasting.

Roasted reindeer is more tender and flavorful when roasted rare or medium. Roast 5 minutes at 450°F. Reduce the heat to 400°F. and roast 15 minutes per pound, basting every 15 minutes. Reindeer fat when roasted is soft and flavorless. It is advisable to remove all visible fat before roasting and replace it with salt pork or bacon or diced beef suet.

Reindeer steak: Cook same as beef steak.

BRAISED REINDEER

4 to 6 pounds reindeer shoulder
   or shoulder ribs, boned
¼ pound fat salt pork
¼ cup flour
1 cup flour
1 teaspoon salt
   Pepper to taste

½ teaspoon marjoram
½ cup salt pork, melted
½ cup orange and apple juice
   or red wine
1 tablespoon vinegar
2 apples, unpeeled, grated

Wipe the reindeer with a cloth dipped in vinegar.

Cut the ¼ pound fat salt pork into strips and place them on top of the meat. Roll and tie. Blend together the flour, salt, pepper and marjoram. Sprinkle over the reindeer.

Brown the roast in the melted ½ cup salt pork. Add the orange and apple juice, vinegar and the apples.

Cover. Cook over medium heat 2 hours, turning occasionally. Strain the gravy and serve.

REINDEER STEW

1½ to 2 pounds reindeer meat
2 tablespoons salad oil
1 tablespoon butter
1 large onion, minced
1 tablespoon flour
1 clove garlic
¼ teaspoon salt
⅓ cup white wine

1 tablespoon tomato paste
1 cup water or consommé
⅛ teaspoon pepper
   A pinch of rosemary
   A pinch of thyme
1 bay leaf
¼ cup chopped parsely

Cut the meat in 1 to 1½-inch cubes. Chop the onion. Mince and crush the garlic with the salt using the flat of a knife.

Heat the oil in a heavy metal saucepan, add the butter. When it is bubbling, add the meat and brown quickly over high heat. Remove from the fat and set aside. Remove the saucepan from the heat.

Add the onions to the fat remaining in the pan. Stir over low heat until coated with the fat. Add the flour and stir until a good brown color. Remove from the heat.

Add the garlic, wine, tomato paste, water or consommé, pepper, rosemary, thyme and bay leaf. Stir over medium heat, until boiling. Add the meat and the parsley. Cover and simmer 1 to 1½ hours or until the meat is tender. Serve with mashed potatoes or boiled rice, garnished with parsley.

HARE WITH BACON

3 to 4-lb. hare	3 slices salt pork
½ cup flour	9 - 10 slices bacon
½ teaspoon salt	2 large onions, sliced
¼ teaspoon pepper	¾ cup water
½ teaspoon curry	1 tablespoon parsley, minced

Cut the hare into individual pieces. Mix together the flour, salt, pepper and curry. Roll the pieces in the mixture. Set aside the remaining flour.

Melt 3 slices of salt pork in a cast-iron saucepan. Add the onions and brown. Remove with a skimmer.

Wrap each piece of floured hare in a slice of bacon. Brown in the fat remaining in the saucepan. Remove the pieces as they are browned. Replace the onions in the bottom of the saucepan and cover with the hare and also ¾ cup water.

Add the hare liver and kidney, chopped with a knife. Cover and simmer 1½ to 2 hours over low heat or until the hare is tender.

To make the gravy, remove the hare from the saucepan and place it on a warm platter. Thicken the sauce with the remaining flour blended in 1 cup cold water. Bring to a boil, stirring, until the gravy thickens. Add the parsley and serve.

HARE COOKED IN BEER

1 large hare	¼ teaspoon allspice
1 pint ale	¼ teaspoon nutmeg
1 clove garlic, minced	½ cup bacon fat
1 teaspoon salt	½ cup all-purpose flour
¼ teaspoon pepper	½ teaspoon salt
1 bay leaf	1 teaspoon paprika
4 onions, sliced thin	6 potatoes
1 carrot, peeled and grated	

Cut the hare into pieces. Wash in some beer.

Place in a large bowl, the beer, garlic, salt, pepper, bay leaf, onions, carrot, allspice and nutmeg. Place the hare in this mixture. Mix well together, cover and marinate for 24 hours in the refrigerator.

Heat the bacon fat. Place in a bag the flour, salt and paprika. Remove the pieces of hare from the marinating mixture and wipe with absorbent paper. Put in the bag with the flour, shake well to coat with flour.

Brown in the hot bacon fat over medium heat. Add the marinating mixture with its vegetables. Cover and simmer for 1½ hours or until the hare is tender.

Peel the potatoes and slice ¼-inch thick. Place on top of the hare ½-hour before the end of the cooking period. Cover and simmer until the hare and the potatoes are cooked.

YUKON

The Yukon is a land rich in natural beauty and bounty, filled with more big game, more fish, than any other part of Canada. Its natural beauty has few rivals. It seems to stand alone.

As the years pass too many of us think that White Horse, Dawson or the gold rush are the whole story. This is not so. Because of its climate and ruggedness, the Yukon is a strong man's world—as are the foods they eat: game birds, caribou, venison, some mountain sheep and goat, bear, hare, beaver and beautiful fish from the icy waters, wild fruits and vegetables, lingonberries, highbush and lowbush cranberries, —all served with sourdough bread and pancakes. This is wilderness fare. Where life has reached the cities however, the fare in many ways is like that of the rest of Canada.

In the *Centennial Food Guide,* written by Pierre and Janet Berton, you can find a menu from the Regina Café of Dawson City for Dominion Day, 1898. This is a delightful mixture of French and English cuisine, which shows that some sophistication has been there a long time.

THE EDIBLE WILD

MAX GUSSIE'S WILD GOOSE

Max Gussie's Wild Goose is a perfect guide for birds, and how to cook them. The following is adapted from his recipe which he sent me.

Bleed bird by sticking a sharp knife down the throat to sever the main artery, and hang bird head down until bleeding stops. Remove crop and entrails as soon as possible, though feathers may be left on without spoiling the flavor. If not cleaned when caught, birds should be dressed as soon as they arrive in camp. To leave birds undrawn results in poorly flavored meat.

To roast your goose, cut and core as many unpeeled fresh apples as needed to make 5 cups or use 3 cups dried apples soaked 1 hour in cold water to cover.

Take a large brown paper bag. Make several holes in the bottom of the bag to allow grease to drain out.

Fill the cleaned bird with apples. Salt and pepper inside and out. Make a thick bed of apples in bottom of bag and sit goose in it. Close bag. Place in a large pan—at home bake 3 hours in a 275°F. oven; at camp cook 2 hours over grey coals. The bird will brown nicely without basting because of the holes in the bag.

IF YOU MUST DUCK

This is the name given by the father of a friend living in the wilds of the Yukon. My friend is in Saskatoon. He refers to the "black coot duck" which he calls fish duck because of its fishy flavor. I must admit it is the only way I could ever down a Coot duck—he advises cooking it only when the meat supply is low.

Skin out the breasts of 2 or 3 coots. Place in pot and soak in salt water and vinegar for 3 to 5 hours. (8 cups water, 2 teaspoons salt, ½ cup vinegar). Dry and roll into flour. Brown in cast-iron pan in lots of bacon fat on fairly fast fire. Add a whole mess of chopped onions (4 to 5), salt and pepper and 1 teaspoon allspice. Stir to mix. Cover and simmer until bird is tender, anywhere from 2 to 4 hours. If available —add a good nip of something strong and eat.

VENISON CASSEROLE

Take a leg or shoulder roast of venison. Season with salt and pepper, rub with ginger or curry. Brush with a generous coating of bacon fat. Roast in 350°F. oven, 30 minutes per pound. When done, remove from pan to a hot dish. Keep hot. Add 4 cups water to fat and residues in the pan. Bring to a boil. Add 8 or 16 ounces of spaghetti. Stir and return to oven for 25 minutes, stirring 3 or 4 times, scraping bottom of pan. Place around the roast and serve.

SLUMGULLION

Take any minced meat from game. Season and shape into patties. Brown in fat then stew for 1 hour with 1 large can of tomatoes, a spoonful of sugar or molasses, salt, pepper and cooked noodles added in the last 20 minutes. The whole is well simmered and eaten with a spoon.

HOOLIGAN

Here is another interesting casserole made with smelts.

Clean and wash 18 smelts. Place a layer in a casserole greased with bacon fat. Sprinkle with 1 onion and 1 clove garlic, chopped fine. Salt and pepper to taste. Cover with ¼-inch layer of cracker crumbs. Continue layers until casserole is full. Pour 1 cup milk over it all. Bake in a 350°F. oven for 1 hour. Serve hot.

LOWBUSH OR HIGHBUSH CRANBERRY PIE

2 cups lowbush or highbush
    cranberries (cooked into a sauce)
3 egg yolks
1 tablespoon cornstarch

2 tablespoons butter
1 tablespoon vanilla
Canned peaches
9" pie shell, baked

Boil cranberry sauce 1 minute. Mix egg yolks, constarch and salt (add beaten yolks to dry ingredients, stirring constantly), then add hot berry sauce very slowly, continuing to stir vigorously. Return to heat, keep on stirring, and cook until thick. Remove from heat and add butter, vanilla and a small pinch of salt. Cool. Slice peaches, then pour a layer of cranberry mixture into pie shell, cover with peaches, and cover them with remaining sauce immediately. Top with your favorite meringue and bake 15 minutes in slow oven (325°F.) until meringue is lightly browned.

SOURDOUGH STARTER AND SPONGE

Sourdough starter: Mix 1 cup flour, 1 cup water, ½ to 1 package (or cake) of yeast in a pint jar. Let stand in a warm place overnight.

Sponge: Empty starter into a bowl. Fill the pint jar with warm water (2 cups), empty it into the bowl, add 2 cups flour and beat to a smooth batter. Let bowl stand in a warm place overnight. Batter should be thin enough to pour. If too thick, add a little warm water.

In the morning, take out ¼ to ½ cup of the sponge, put in clean pint jar, and place in refrigerator or cool place for the next sponge.

A sourdough starter will be good for many years if kept in a cool place and used every week. Never add anything to the starter except flour and water.

To carry the starter, or keep it longer than a week, thicken it with flour to form a ball and keep it in the flour or in a covered container. To activate it, thin it out with water.

SOURDOUGH BROWN BREAD

1 cup sourdough sponge
1 teaspoon salt
2 tablespoons molasses

2 tablespoons fat
2 cups coarse graham flour

To the sourdough sponge add the salt, molasses and fat. Mix well. Add the 2 cups graham flour, or enough to make a stiff dough. Knead lightly. Place in warm greased loaf tin, let stand ½ hour, then bake at 375°F. until lightly browned—about 40 minutes. This is a coarse, heavy bread with a good flavor.

SOURDOUGH PANCAKES

To the sponge (which should be about 3 cups after a portion has been put aside for starter) add unbeaten eggs (or ¼ cup dried egg powder mixed with ⅓ cup water). Sprinkle over the top 1 tablespoon sugar, 1 teaspoon soda, 1 teaspoon salt, 1 tablespoon oil or melted fat. Beat with a fork until foamy. If very thick, add a small amount of water or milk. Bake on a hot griddle.

FLOUR MIXTURE FOR CAMPERS

Use this any time you need flour—it is superb for rolling fish and meat for browning. It can replace any type of flour called for in a recipe.

10 pounds white flour   **4 pounds soy flour**
10 pounds whole wheat flour   **4 pounds wheat germ**
** 5 pounds yellow cornmeal**

Mix thoroughly in a large container, then pack in heavy pliofilm bags. This mixture can be used for all flour requirements in camp, and is wholesome and nourishing.

INDEX

INDEX (Continued)

INDEX (Continued)